THE EAL TEACHING BOOK

Promoting Success for Multilingual Learners

REVISED 2ND EDITION

JEAN CONTEH

Los Angeles | London | New Delhi
Singapore | Washington DC

Learning Matters
An imprint of SAGE Publications Ltd
1 Oliver's Yard
55 City Road
London EC1Y 1SP

SAGE Publications Inc.
2455 Teller Road
Thousand Oaks, California 91320

SAGE Publications India Pvt Ltd
B 1/I 1 Mohan Cooperative Industrial Area
Mathura Road
New Delhi 110 044

SAGE Asia-Pacific Pte Ltd
3 Church Street
#10–04 Samsung Hub
Singapore 049483

Editor: Amy Thornton
Development editor: Jennifer Clark
Production controller: Chris Marke
Project management: Deer Park Productions, Tavistock
Marketing manager: Catherine Slinn
Cover design: Wendy Scott
Typeset by: C&M Digitals (P) Ltd, Chennai, India
Printed in Great Britain by
CPI Group (UK) Ltd, Croydon, CR0 4YY

MIX
Paper from
responsible sources
FSC
www.fsc.org   FSC® C013604

First published in 2012
Second edition published in 2015

Revised second edition published in September 2015

Library of Congress Control Number: 2015951086

British Library Cataloguing in Publication Data

A catalogue record for this book is available from the British Library

ISBN: 978-1-4739-5749-7
ISBN: 978-1-4739-5751-0 (pbk)

At SAGE we take sustainability seriously. Most of our products are printed in the UK using FSC papers and boards. When we print overseas we ensure sustainable papers are used as measured by the Egmont grading system. We undertake an annual audit to monitor our sustainability.

Contents

About the author and series editor   ix

Acknowledgements   x

Introduction   1

**Part 1 Understanding multilingual and EAL learners –
theories of learning and language**   7

1 Introducing multilingual and EAL learners   9

1. Defining difference   10
  1.1 Behind the facts and figures   10
  1.2 'Superdiversity' in England   13
2. Who are 'EAL learners'?   15
  2.1 Advanced bilingual learners – Safina   16
  2.2 New to English pupils – Stefan and Jan   17
  2.3 Asylum-seekers and refugees – Joseph   18
  2.4 Isolated learners – Radia   19
  2.5 Sojourners – Hamida   20
  2.6 Roma and Gipsy pupils – case study by Georgina Vince   21
3. Language diversity and learning – some myths and misconceptions   25

2 All about language and learning   29

1. All about language   30
  1.1 What is language?   30
  1.2 Language, culture and identity   33
  1.3 Thinking about teaching languages – the functional approach   35
  1.4 The functional approach and literacy   39
2. Language and learning   41
  2.1 Sociocultural theories of learning and the Zone of Proximal
     Development (ZPD)   41
  2.2 The importance of talk for learning   42
  2.3 The 'funds of knowledge' concept   44

3 What does it mean to be multilingual?   47

1. What does it mean to be multilingual?   48
  1.1 The global context   48
  1.2 Being multilingual in mainstream education in England 49
     One multilingual learner's experience – case study by Zofia Donnelly   52

2. Multilingualism in education   57
    2.1 Policy constructions: assessment, achievement and the 2014 curriculum   57
    2.2 Cummins' theories: CUP, language interdependence, BICS/CALP   62
3. The importance of learning outside school   66
    3.1 Home, family and community learning contexts –
       'funds of knowledge'   66

Principles for planning for multilingual learners   70

Part 2 Promoting learning – practical approaches for multilingual and EAL learners   71

4   Planning across the curriculum for multilingual and EAL learners   73

1. Planning across the curriculum   74
    1.1 Starting points – developing plans   74
    1.2 The Cummins' quadrant   77
    1.3 The importance of joint planning   81
       Planning an RE lesson – case study by Pete Ruse and Linda Sandler   81
2. Organising classes and groups for learning   84
    2.1 Planning for collaborative talk   84
       The Talking Partners Programme – case study by Catherine Porritt   88
    2.2 Including new arrivals in your lessons – buddies and mentors   92
    2.3 Differentiation in planning   93
       Differentiation in planning for one EAL learner in secondary
       school – case study by Ana Korzun   93

5   Strategies and resources for learning across the curriculum   99

1. Linking language learning and content learning   100
    1.1 Focusing on language demands   100
       Teaching science to EAL learners at KS2 – case study by
       Oksana Afitska   103
    1.2 Working with colleagues – skills for EAL specialist teachers   110
       Partnership teaching – case study by Pete Ruse   111
2. Literacy, learning and story   114
    2.1 The importance of 'reading for pleasure'   114
       Reading for pleasure with teenage boys – case study by Ali O'Grady   115
    2.2 Stories for language learning   117
3. Promoting language awareness for all pupils   120
       The Languages Club in a primary school – case study by Anita Conradi   120

6   Assessing multilingual and EAL learners across the curriculum   125

1. Principles for assessing EAL and multilingual learners   126
2. Standardised assessments of attainment   128
    2.1 Issues in national assessment procedures for multilingual and
         EAL learners   128
    2.2 Language need or learning need?   129
3. Assessment for learning   131
    3.1 Profiling and sampling   131
         Assessing multilingual and EAL learners across the curriculum in a
         secondary school – case study by Dianne Excell   134
    3.2 Observing as a tool for assessment   138
    3.3 Pupils' and teachers' views   140
         Talking about teaching and learning science in the EAL context:
         interviewing teachers and learners in primary classrooms –
         case study by Oksana Afitska   140
         Learner voice – case study by Pete Ruse and Linda Sandler   145
    3.4 Consulting with parents   147

7   Promoting independence: using home languages and cultures in learning   158

1. Promoting independent learning   159
    1.1 Principles for independent learning   159
    1.2 Practical strategies to promote independent learning   162
2. Involving families and communities in learning   165
    2.1 The work of supplementary/complementary schools   165
    2.2 Bringing home languages and cultures into school   167
    2.3 Dual language books   171
3. Working with multilingual colleagues   172
    3.1 Using personal funds of knowledge   174
         Spanish in science – case study by Charlotte Wood   174
         Learning place value in Bangla – case study by Shila Begum   177

8   Conclusions: synthesising learning and moving on   181

1. Myths revisited   182
    1.1 Languages should be kept separate in the classroom, or
         learners will become confused (sometimes called 'language
         interference')   182
    1.2 Pupils will 'pick English up' naturally in the classroom; they do not
         need to be explicitly taught (sometimes called 'immersion')   183
    1.3 Language diversity is a 'problem', and it is better if pupils speak
         English all the time in classrooms   183

1.4 It is impossible, or very difficult, to learn a new language beyond a young age (sometimes called 'the critical period')   184

2. Moving forward – some suggestions for further reading and professional development   184

3. Suggestions for further reading   185

Appendix 1 Model answers to the self-assessment questions   187

Appendix 2 Glossary   192

Appendix 3 Principles for planning for multilingual learners   198

Index   199

Author

Jean Conteh is a senior lecturer in the School of Education at the University of Leeds where, among other things, she runs a Master's course for teachers on EAL and Education. She has worked in many countries and has published widely in the field of EAL in primary education, both for teachers and for academic audiences. Her research focuses on ways to promote success for those pupils who are often labelled 'disadvantaged' in our education system, and covers the role of language in teaching and learning in primary classrooms and the expertise and professional roles of bilingual teachers.

Series editor

Alice Hansen is the Director of Children Count Ltd, an education consultancy company that provides continuing professional development for teachers in primary mathematics education and primary schools in curriculum development in England and abroad. Prior to her current role she was a primary school teacher and senior lecturer in primary education before becoming a programme leader of a teacher-training programme. Alice is an active researcher and her research interests include technology-enhanced learning. Her current research focuses on developing effective tasks for children to develop their conceptual understanding of fractions.

Acknowledgements

I wish to thank the following teachers and researchers who contributed case studies from their practice and research to the book:

Oksana Afitska
Shila Begum
Anita Conradi
Zofia Donnelly
Dianne Excell
Ana Korzun
Ali O'Grady
Catherine Porritt
Pete Ruse
Linda Sandler
Georgina Vince
Charlotte Wood

Thanks are due to the following former students who have contributed to this book by providing examples of children's work and classroom activities:

Shannele Cowban
Anna Grant
Sarah Kent
Lian Montgomery

I wish to thank Tracey Burns of the OECD for the use of the cartoon on page 60.

The extract from *The Iron Man* by Ted Hughes is reproduced by kind permission of Faber.

Introduction

This book is a new edition of *Teaching Bilingual and EAL Learners in Primary Schools*, which was published in 2012. This new edition offers fresh guidance for teachers and trainee teachers in teaching pupils who speak other languages besides English in their homes and communities. The title *The EAL Teaching Book: promoting success for multilingual learners* reflects the wider scope and intentions. The use of the term 'multilingual' in the title instead of 'bilingual', as in the previous title, aims to reflect the fact that many pupils experience and have knowledge of several different languages in their daily lives – and, indeed, that we all live in an increasingly multilingual world.

The overarching aim of this book is to show the ways in which 'EAL' needs to be a central aspect of the professional knowledge of all teachers. In such knowledge, theory and practice always need to be closely connected and so the book shows the ways in which the two can be linked in a pedagogy that plays to the strengths and helps to raise the **attainments of** multilingual and EAL learners. Indeed, such a pedagogy will contribute to enhancing the learning of all pupils in mainstream schools, not just those who may have been placed in the category of 'EAL'. In order to achieve this aim of integrating theory and practice, this new edition contains additional material in the form of 14 extended case studies of classroom practice, written by teachers, mostly from mainstream schools with one from a complementary school and one from a university. There is also a new chapter (Chapter 7) about promoting independence through using home languages and cultures in learning.

Just before the publication of the first edition of this book in 2012, the government introduced a new set of professional standards for teachers. These made it very clear that all teachers needed to have training and professional development in order to meet the diverse needs of all the pupils they were expected to teach. This is part of Standard 5, which says that all teachers must:

> *have a clear understanding of the needs of all pupils, including those with special educational needs; those of high ability; those with English as an additional language; those with disabilities; and be able to use and evaluate distinctive teaching approaches to engage and support them.*

In addition, not long after 2012, we had the introduction of the new school curriculum, which has two short statements that lay down some requirements and some principles for teachers in their work with multilingual and EAL learners. The Introduction states:

> *Teachers must also take account of the needs of pupils whose first language is not English. Monitoring of progress should take account of the pupil's age, length of time in this country, previous educational experience and ability in other languages.*
>
> *The ability of pupils for whom English is an additional language to take part in the national curriculum may be in advance of their communication skills in English. Teachers should plan teaching opportunities to help pupils develop their English and should aim to provide the support pupils need to take part in all subjects.*

(DfE, 2013: 8)

Though brief, these statements are important and they align with the key aims and messages of this book. They recognise the need to understand what pupils bring to their learning in mainstream schools, as this is the basis on which they will build their new learning and their identities as speakers and writers of English – a key element of the sociocultural theories of learning that are explained in Chapter 2. Secondly, they emphasise the two crucial points that, for many multilingual and EAL pupils, learning English needs to go on simultaneously with learning all the subjects of the curriculum and that many will have greater knowledge of some subjects than they can express in English. These have implications for the whole cycle of planning, teaching and assessing multilingual and EAL learners and so underpin the ideas presented in Chapters 4, 5 and 6. They are emphasised even more in Chapter 7, which focuses on language across the curriculum and on using home languages and cultures to promote independence in learning.

This book raises issues and challenges misconceptions about language teaching and learning generally and about EAL learners in particular. Such misconceptions have, in the past, contributed to what could be termed a 'deficit' model of EAL, constructing multilingual pupils as on the margins of mainstream education with problems that needed to be sorted out before they could be included fully. This book argues strongly for a positive perspective on diversity and in particular a view of language diversity as a resource and an opportunity for learning, for all pupils. It is my hope that the book will instil in our next generation of teachers enthusiasm and passion for an aspect of their work which offers in return a great deal of professional reward and satisfaction.

The prime audience for this book is people who have chosen to become teachers, no matter what route they are taking, from the well-established, university and college-based PGCE and degree-level courses to the vast array of school-based training programmes that are being developed round the country. It is also relevant for other audiences, such as tutors in initial teacher education, NQTs and their mentors, teachers and other professionals working with multilingual and EAL learners in schools, and those engaged in continuing professional development (CPD) and possibly working towards higher qualifications. It provides a theory-informed, accessible, comprehensive source of practical guidance for meeting the needs of children categorised as EAL learners in both primary and secondary schools. As such, it is perhaps the first book of its kind, and is very timely. Not only are the numbers of children in our schools who speak and write other languages besides English growing rapidly year by year, but the nature of their prior experiences and thus of their learning needs is becoming more and more diverse.

Structure and organisation of the book

The book is in two parts. The first part comprises Chapters 1–3 and the second Chapters 4–8. In between the two parts there is a set of principles, which are intended to show how theory and practice always need to be integrated in considering the best provision for bilingual and EAL learners, indeed any learners.

Part 1: Understanding multilingual and EAL learners – theories of learning and language

The chapters in the first part of the book provide theoretical and contextual information to frame the more practical ideas that form the second part of the book. Essentially, this part aims to provide:

- a contextualisation of the issues surrounding multilingualism both globally and in England, including a discussion of the development of the idea of EAL and illuminative vignettes of children who would come under its umbrella;
- an overview of key theoretical models and principles and their practical implications, which explain the role of language in learning generally and the development and learning of pupils who can be defined as 'EAL' and 'multilingual'.

Chapter 1: Introducing multilingual and EAL learners begins by providing some facts and figures which explain how our present 'superdiverse' society in England has come about. Following this, it aims to answer the question, 'who are EAL learners?' by offering vignettes of individual pupils, using terminology from policy documentation over the years. This section covers pupils in five categories, showing the need to be aware of the complexities and uncertainties in understanding their strengths and needs. It ends with a case study about Gipsy Roma pupils attending a secondary school. The final section raises some common myths and misconceptions about language diversity and learning, which are addressed at different points in the book and returned to at the end of Chapter 8.

Chapter 2: All about language and learning provides a theoretical overview of language, culture and identity in the field of EAL. It explains what is involved in the 'functional approach' to understanding grammar and texts, showing the value of this for teaching and learning. The second section provides an introduction to sociocultural theories of learning, in which talk is a central element, and it argues for the importance of talk in working with **bilingual** and EAL learners in particular. Finally, the 'funds of knowledge' concept is introduced, which is an important one for understanding the role of home and community in learning.

Chapter 3: What does it mean to be multilingual? addresses relevant theories about multilingualism and their practical implications in making the best provision for multilingual and EAL learners. Beginning with an overview of global contexts, it moves on to consider research related to multilingualism and education, in particular the work and ideas of Jim Cummins. A case study illustrates what it is like to be a multilingual learner in a mainstream school in England. The chapter ends by emphasising the importance for pupils' success in school of understanding the nature of home and community learning experiences that many bilingual and EAL learners bring to school.

Part 1 closes by articulating some 'key principles' for promoting success for EAL learners, which are illuminated with practical examples in Chapters 4–7.

Part 2: Promoting learning – practical approaches for multilingual and EAL learners

Based on the key principles identified in the first part of the book, the second part (Chapters 4–8) focuses on practical classroom issues. It covers the important themes of planning, classroom strategies, resources, assessment, language across the curriculum and making links with home and community contexts.

Chapter 4: Planning across the curriculum for multilingual and EAL learners provides guidance for planning language-focused activities across the curriculum using a framework (the Cummins' quadrant) which makes clear the ways that planning can support the progression of learning from simple, context-embedded tasks to higher, more academic levels. There are sections on planning for collaborative talk, on including new arrivals in your lessons and on planning for using home languages in bilingual children's learning. Two case studies illustrate the important role of talk in learning and differentiated planning for one EAL learner.

Chapter 5: Strategies and resources for promoting learning across the curriculum is a very full chapter which provides a wealth of ideas and suggestions for developing activities that link language learning and content learning, use children's 'funds of knowledge' and exploit the rich resource of stories to promote both literacy and language and content learning. Case studies illustrate the role of talk in primary science, the pleasures of reading with teenage boys, the ways subject and 'EAL' teachers can work together and the benefits of setting up a 'languages club' in a primary school.

Chapter 6: Assessing multilingual and EAL learners across the curriculum begins by raising issues for EAL learners related to the national, standardised models of assessment in place in England and suggesting some principles for assessing EAL and multilingual learners. It stresses the importance of assessment for learning (AFL) and introduces activities which can be used to construct it with pupils to enhance their future learning. Case studies are included on assessing learners across the curriculum in a secondary school, teachers' and pupils' views on science in primary schools and newly arrived pupils' views on their experiences in their first year of schooling in England. The possible confusions between language needs and special needs are addressed and the chapter ends with some practical advice on AFL, observing pupils and consulting with parents.

Chapter 7: Promoting independence: using home languages and cultures in learning discusses the importance of promoting independent learning and practical ways of doing it in multilingual classrooms. Following this, it discusses ways of involving families and communities in learning and briefly introduces the work of supplementary/complementary schools. Then there are sections on bringing home languages and cultures into school, and the use of dual language books in promoting independent learning. The final section, on using personal funds of knowledge, includes two case studies; the first on using Spanish as a means of including one newly arrived multilingual learner in science lessons and the second on learning place value through a counting song in Bangla.

Chapter 8: Conclusions: synthesising learning and moving on revisits the myths identified in Chapter 1 and the principles at the end of Part 1. It invites readers to reflect on their developing professional knowledge and suggests ways of moving on in order to extend and strengthen their professional expertise related to multilingual and EAL learners. It ends with an annotated list of further reading.

The new case studies in this revised edition provide a rich resource of classroom practice over a range of topics and learners. In line with other titles in the *Learning Matters Transforming Primary QTS* series, the book contains the following structural and study support features.

- **Learning outcomes** – a list of objectives is given at the start of each chapter, which are reviewed (with self-assessment questions) at the end of the chapter.

- **Research focus** – each chapter contains relevant research focus sections. In Chapters 4–8, there is extensive cross-reference to the research discussed in Chapters 2 and 3.

- **Activities** are included throughout each chapter, linked to the ideas being discussed.

- **Case studies** are included in each chapter, to illustrate the general points being made and to help relate the ideas directly to classrooms. Across the book as a whole, all curriculum subjects are represented in the case studies.

- An annotated list of **further reading** and a full list of **references** are included at the end of each chapter.

- **A glossary** is included at the end of the book where all terms highlighted in bold in the body of the text are explained.

- **Model answers** to the self-assessment questions are also provided.

References

Department for Education (DfE) (2013) *The National Curriculum in England: Key Stages 1 and 2 Framework Document*. London: DfE.

PART 1
UNDERSTANDING MULTILINGUAL AND EAL LEARNERS – THEORIES OF LEARNING AND LANGUAGE

1 Introducing multilingual and EAL learners

Learning Outcomes

This chapter will help you to achieve the following learning outcomes:

- develop understanding of the importance of recognising and reflecting on your own experiences of language diversity and ethnicity for your professional knowledge as a teacher;
- gain awareness of the history of language and cultural diversity in England;
- develop awareness of the diverse range of experiences and knowledge that multilingual and EAL learners bring to their classrooms.

Introduction

This chapter introduces you to the pupils you will be teaching who come under the umbrella term of 'EAL learners'. It shows the many different ways in which 'EAL' has been defined, and that there is still no agreed definition. It raises questions about how we define and label attributes such as 'ethnicity' and challenges you to consider your own views and perceptions of these issues. It begins by providing some background information about the cultural and language diversity of British society today. Then, it provides a set of vignettes of individual pupils, through which you will gain a sense of the rich diversity of the social and cultural experiences that many multilingual and EAL learners bring to their mainstream classrooms. Following this, there is an extended case study by Georgina Vince, who works in a secondary school attended by growing numbers of Roma and Gipsy pupils. Georgina describes the positive ways in which her school has developed strategies to work with the pupils and their families. Finally, there is a set of common 'myths and misconceptions' about teaching EAL learners which – after reading the chapter – you may have questions about. We will come back to these at the end of the book in Chapter 8.

One of the main aims of this chapter is to help you, as a beginning teacher or even a more experienced one, to understand the importance of recognising and valuing all the knowledge and experience that your multilingual and EAL learners bring with them to school. This is crucial, if you are to help them to become successful learners in the mainstream system. Interspersed through the chapter there are questions and activities to help you to think further about the ideas that you will read about, as well as begin to think practically about their implications for your own practice in different classrooms. There are some suggestions for further reading at the end of the chapter.

These are the main sections and subsections of the chapter.

1. **Defining difference**
   1.1 Behind the facts and figures

   1.2 'Superdiversity' in England

2. **Who are 'EAL learners'?**
   2.1 Advanced bilingual learners – Safina

   2.2 New to English pupils – Stefan and Jan

   2.3 Asylum-seekers and refugees – Joseph

   2.4 Isolated learners – Radia

   2.5 Sojourners – Hamida

   2.6 Roma and Gipsy pupils – case study by Georgina Vince

3. **Language diversity and learning – some myths and misconceptions**

1. Defining difference

1.1 Behind the facts and figures

Research Focus

Since 2009, the Department for Education has collected information about the languages spoken by pupils in schools as part of the annual schools' census data. In 2013 (NALDIC, 2013), the figures showed that about 18.1% of pupils in mainstream primary and 13.6% in secondary schools in England were identified as learners with 'EAL' (English as an additional language). It is not easy to find a figure for the total number of languages currently spoken by pupils in schools in England, but it is thought to be about 350 (BBC, 2007). The proportion of ethnic minority pupils is different from those defined as 'EAL'; currently this is 28.5% for primary schools and 24.2% for secondary schools. The data on ethnicity come from the national census, which is done every ten years. The most recent census was undertaken in 2011, and the categories for ethnicity used are shown in Figure 1.1 below.

The percentages for ethnic minority pupils are much higher than those for language diversity, so it is clear that there are many ethnic minority pupils in schools in England for whom English is *not* an additional language. But it is also clear that many pupils can be defined as *both* EAL and ethnic minority, because they belong to an ethnic minority group and also speak another language besides English. It is important to understand, especially for pupils such as those in this second group, that language knowledge and cultural knowledge are interlinked. This idea is discussed further in Chapter 2, along with the implications for teaching. There are also pupils who would ethnically be part of the 'white' majority but who could actually be defined as 'EAL', because they do not have English as their first language and their families are from Europe or other parts of the world.

A. White
British
English/Welsh/Scottish/Northern Irish/British Irish
Gypsy or Irish traveller
Any other White background

B. Mixed/multiple ethnic groups
White and Black Caribbean
White and Black African
White and Asian
Any other Mixed

C. Asian/Asian British
Indian
Pakistani
Bangladeshi
Chinese
Any other Asian background

D. Black/African/Caribbean/Black British
African
Caribbean
Any other Black/African/Caribbean background

Other ethnic group
Arab
Any other ethnic group

Figure 1.1 Categories of ethnicity in the 2011 National Census

Activity 1.1
Who are you?

In Figure 1.1, you can see the categories of ethnicity used in the 2011 national census, which are different from those in the 2001 census. Look at them and think about the following questions.

1. Did you complete the most recent census? If so, which category did you place yourself in? If not, which category would you place yourself in?
2. Could you place yourself into more than one category?
3. Do you find it difficult to place yourself, and if so, why?
4. Would it be difficult to place anyone you know?
5. Would it be difficult to place any pupils you teach or have worked with?
6. How do you think these categories were arrived at?

Despite the ever-increasing numbers of pupils from different ethnic and language backgrounds in our schools, the vast majority of teachers in England are still from 'white British' or 'English' backgrounds and do not speak other languages besides English. This means that most teachers who have pupils in their classes who speak other languages do not share those languages. This can sometimes feel like quite a challenge, on top of everything else you need to know about and be able to do as a teacher. Vivian Gussin Paley (2000) in her book *White Teacher*, describes her experiences as a 'white majority' teacher in a school with increasing numbers of pupils from diverse backgrounds. She soon realised that, in order to understand their needs and make the best provision for them, she had to understand more about her own identity and how it influenced her attitudes to her pupils. She concludes:

> *Those of us who have been outsiders understand the need to be seen exactly as we are and to be accepted and valued. Our safety lies in schools and societies in which faces with many shapes can feel an equal sense of belonging. Our pupils must grow up knowing and liking those who look and speak in different ways, or they will live as strangers in a hostile land.*

(131–2)

Ethnicity is a very hard concept to define, and because we often talk about 'ethnic minorities' we sometimes think of it as a term only relevant for people who are different from ourselves and can be thought of as belonging to a 'minority' group. Of course, the reality is that we all have ethnicity. We all belong to different ethnic, cultural and social groups. But ethnicity is only one part of what makes us who we are. In thinking about your role as a teacher, perhaps the notion of **identity** is a more useful one than ethnicity, as it helps you think about all the factors that contribute to your individuality, and the personal and social issues that are so important in teaching and learning. As suggested in Chapter 2, it is vital that you understand how your personal identity is an important aspect of your professional identity as a teacher, especially when you are teaching pupils from different language and cultural backgrounds to yourself. You need to understand how important your own ethnicity, language knowledge and other aspects of your personal makeup are to you, and how you night feel if any of them were threatened or undermined. This will help you understand the needs of the pupils you will be teaching. As Gussin Paley argues, this is an essential step to developing positive, trustful relationships with the pupils you teach and with their families.

The following activity will help you to think about your 'ethnicity' as part of your identity, in other words, who you are.

Activity 1.2
How does it feel to be different?

You can do this activity on your own. But it would be better if you could do it as a group discussion task, with some of your fellow trainees, or colleagues in a school setting.

- First, think about how you would define your identity. Is it enough just to think about your 'ethnic background' as defined in the categories of the census? What other aspects of your identity are important to you? Where your family comes from might be an important part of your identity, but what else might count for you?
- Make a list of 6–8 attributes that you would say were important aspects of your identity.
- Can you think of a time when you were made to feel different and that you did not belong? This could have been when you were a child, or as an adult in a work situation or in a social context. What did you feel was different about you? How would the quote from Vivian Gussin Paley reflect your feelings? Write a few sentences about how it felt to feel different and perhaps excluded.

1.2 'Superdiversity' in England

In about 120 AD, soldiers from the Roman Empire built a fort at the mouth of the river Tyne and named it Arbeia (Wikipedia, 2013). You can still see the remains today, in South Shields near Newcastle upon Tyne. Some historians think the Romans who lived in the fort named it after their original homelands in what are now Syria, Libya and Spain. Britain has always been multicultural and multilingual – a small island which has experienced successive waves of immigration and emigration from and to all over the world. The English language reflects this, as it contains words from all the languages of the people that have come to this island and enriched its vocabulary over the centuries.

Over recent years, with the growth of the European Union (EU) as well as more global events, the population of England has changed greatly. The addition to the EU of the A8 'accession countries' in 2004 and more recent changes have meant that people travel within Europe much more than they used to. It has become quite normal for people from Poland, the Czech Republic, Slovakia and other eastern European countries to come to England to work, and then return to their countries of origin or move on elsewhere. This has been described as 'circular migration', and is a worldwide phenomenon. Many British cities now, are what have been called '**superdiverse**' communities. People with vastly different languages, histories, cultural and social backgrounds and religions live side by side. Sometimes, new migrants arrive and join with communities from their countries of origin that have lived in the city for generations.

Vignette

A superdiverse corner shop

This photo of a corner shop in a Yorkshire city shows clearly the effects of 'superdiversity' on everyday life in a typical community.

(Continued)

(Continued)

Figure 1.2 Shop front in a 'superdiverse' city

A Lithuanian heritage family owned the shop from the 1950s until they sold it to a Pakistani heritage family in the 1980s. A few years ago, this family sold the shop to a Polish man. He put up a new sign, covering up the old Lithuanian name. He kept the small '**halal** meat' logos from the Pakistani heritage owners at the edges of the sign to show that he still provides meat for the local Muslim community. He also sells phone cards to customers from all over the world. He placed a bright yellow banner in the shop window (at the bottom right of the picture) to show how he catered for the changing community around the shop: 'Everyone welcome English, Arabic, Kurdish, Polish, Slovakia', it says. There are now many multilingual communities like this in cities all over England, where many of our multilingual and EAL pupils live.

It is important also to remember, as we see below in section 2, that an increasing number of multilingual and EAL now also live in towns or villages where they may previously have been very few other such pupils.

Activity 1.3
Language and cultural diversity in school

If you have a placement in a school where there are pupils learning English as an additional language, or in the school where you work, try to find out the following information.

- How many pupils in school are defined as 'EAL learners'?
- How many different languages are spoken by pupils in the school?
- How does the school find out about and record the languages?
- Does the school have a policy for EAL or language diversity?
- How are EAL issues managed in the school?

If you cannot undertake this activity in your placement school, see if you could arrange a visit to a school where it would be possible to do it.

2. Who are 'EAL learners'?

Sometimes the term 'EAL' is applied only to pupils who are new arrivals in school and who are better thought of as being 'new to English'. 'EAL' is an umbrella term, used for many different groups of pupils who bring a vast range of experience and knowledge of languages, literacies, cultures and schooling to their mainstream classrooms. The title of this book refers to 'multilingual' and EAL learners to make the point that we cannot think of the pupils whose learning we are considering as one, uniform group. Different terms have been used over the years in policies and strategy documents to describe the EAL learners you may meet in your classrooms. Here is a list of them.

- Learners who are second and third generation members of settled ethnic minority communities (*advanced bilingual learners*).
- Learners who are recent arrivals and new to English, some of whom have little or no experience of schooling, and others who are already literate in their first languages (*pupils new to English*).
- Learners whose education has been disrupted because of war and other traumatic experiences (*asylum-seekers and refugees*).
- Learners who are in school settings with little prior experience of bilingual pupils (*isolated learners*).
- Learners whose parents are working and studying and are in England for short periods of time (*sojourners*).

Activity 1.4
Thinking about multilingual and EAL learners

Before you read the vignettes that follow, think about the pupils in your current class, or one you have recently taught. Do you think any of them would fit into any of the groups listed above?

Write a list of the names of the pupils, and identify which group you think each would belong to.

What follow are five vignettes, and one case study by Georgina Vince, who works in a large secondary school in Leeds. They will help you to understand something about the pupils that belong to each of the groups listed above and to develop your understanding about who could be defined as 'EAL learners' and the complexity of the term 'EAL'.

2.1 Advanced bilingual learners – Safina

Safina is 13 years old and in a **Year 9** class in a large, multilingual secondary school in a city very like the one where the photo above was taken. Most of her classmates are from similar backgrounds to herself. She represents the largest group in our list of different categories of EAL learners – advanced bilingual learners. She was born in England, the granddaughter of a man who arrived from the Kashmir area of Pakistan 40 or 50 years ago to work in the woollen mills in the city. Safina is multilingual. English is her dominant language, so 'EAL' is not really a helpful way to describe her. As well as English, she speaks Punjabi and Urdu. She is also **multiliterat**e (Datta, 2007). With her sisters and female cousins, she is learning the Koran in Arabic from a Muslim teacher who visits her home. Her brothers go to the local mosque, which is in a converted cinema close to their house. Her mum is teaching her to read and write Urdu, their national heritage language. All these languages have important, but different, roles to play in her life. While English may be the most important, there is no sign that the other languages are fading away. Indeed, the signs are that they will continue to be important for Safina and her community (see Chapter 3). Punjabi has an important, though unofficial, role in British society; it is the foreign language most commonly spoken by British people, with over half a million speakers. Pupils whose families originate from Bangladesh would have very similar histories, with Bengali and Sylheti as their community languages. Bengali is the second most commonly spoken foreign language by British people (Wikipedia, 2014). Safina is doing well in school so far. She is very talkative and keen to answer questions, but is finding things increasingly difficult as she progresses through secondary school. She struggles to understand the range of subjects she is expected to study and to meet the demands of written assessments.

At the end of Year 2, in the KS1 **Standardised Attainment Tasks (SATs)** Safina attained level 2 in English and level 3 in mathematics, and in the KS2 SATs, she attained level 4 in English and level 5 in maths, which is above the standard expectation. But, the data over the years show that she may struggle to attain such a high level in her GCSEs, when they come around. Her family are very supportive of her education. Her father helps her a lot in mathematics at home, in Punjabi. Her mother and aunts do a lot of sewing, and Safina is very good at this and other practical activities. When she was younger, her grandma told her and her siblings lots of stories from Pakistan, in Punjabi. She loved this and knew many of the stories by heart. In her primary school, where most of the pupils were multilingual, teachers encouraged the pupils to tell the stories in school, which had a big benefit for

Safina's literacy. It helped her to understand story structures and the kinds of language found in stories, which is different from spoken language. Pupils like Safina are exactly those whom Deryn Hall describes as 'living in two languages' (Hall *et al.*, 2001), and who are discussed in Chapter 3.

2.2 New to English pupils – Stefan and Jan

Stefan and Jan are both ten years old, and in the same **Year 5** class in a small Roman Catholic primary school in a big, multilingual city in the north of England. They have both been attending the school for a couple of years, having arrived from Poland at almost the same time with their families. About 40% of the pupils in the school are from Pakistani-heritage backgrounds, and the numbers of pupils from Poland, the Czech Republic and Slovakia are steadily growing – currently it is about 10%, that is two to three pupils per class. Stefan and Jan's class teacher is a bit puzzled by the two boys. When they entered her class from Year 4, she checked the school records, and noticed that, since coming to the school, both new to English, their progress had been very different. They seemed to start off from a relatively similar position in relation to their knowledge of English. Both have become fairly confident and fluent in spoken English over the two years they have been in the school. They can answer questions in class, hold conversations with their teachers and their peers and take part in social activities in school. But, while Stefan has made good progress with reading and writing and is beginning to perform in assessments at similar levels to his peers, Jan is struggling. He has taken part in various intervention activities, but never seems to be able to catch up with Stefan or his other classmates.

The class teacher is considering what can be done to support Jan to help him catch up before he encounters the KS2 SATs in Year 6. She wonders whether yet another intervention activity is the answer. In studying part-time for her MA, she comes across the work of Cummins (see Chapter 3) and other writers on bilingualism and multilingualism. She finds their ideas about the links between languages in pupils' learning very intriguing and decides to find out a little about Stefan and Jan's knowledge of other languages, especially their home language, Polish. To her surprise and interest, she finds out that Stefan is an accomplished reader and writer of Polish, and that he regularly attends the Polish Saturday school in the city, where pupils study Polish to GCSE and A level (see Chapter 7, section 2.1). Jan, on the other hand, can only read and write a little Polish – his early schooling in Poland was disrupted because of his family situation. He went to the Saturday class for a short while, but then dropped out.

As an experiment, the teacher asks Stefan if he can bring some of his Polish books into school and tell the class about some of the things he does in the Saturday school. Stefan's dad comes along too, and tells the class a story in Polish, which Stefan translates into English. The visit is a huge success. Afterwards, to her surprise, the teacher notices how Jan seems much more enthusiastic and motivated. So she decides to give the pupils in her class opportunities, from time to time, to work together in same-language groups where they can discuss things with each other, using their home languages and then report back or write in English (see section 2 of Chapter 4 for more information about planning and organising groupwork and Chapter 7 for discussions of using home languages in school). As time goes on, Jan's reading and writing slowly begin to improve, while his confidence steadily grows.

2.3 Asylum-seekers and refugees – Joseph

Joseph is 15 years old and is moving in to **Year 11**. He came to England as a baby with his mother, Jenneh, who had had to escape from her home town in Sierra Leone, when it was overrun by fighting during the civil war that ended about 12 years ago. His father was a solicitor and his mother an administrator in a large secondary school in the town. At first, Joseph and his mother lived temporarily in bed and breakfast accommodation in London, and after 18 months they moved to a small town in the north west of England where Jenneh had a Sierra Leonean friend. Other friends helped with accommodation and Jenneh found a job in a supermarket. They settled fairly well, although they were the target of racial abuse for a while. But they had lost touch with Joseph's father because of the unsettled situation in Sierra Leone. Jenneh applied for political asylum and, after a long struggle, she gained it.

Though they had been in their new home for two years by the time Joseph began school, their future was still uncertain. Events in Sierra Leone had calmed and Jenneh had made contact with her family, but Joseph's father had died. All the problems she faced were a great strain on Jenneh and she became depressed. The school was a fairly small, Church of England primary school with very few non-white pupils. At first, Joseph was a well-behaved little boy and he made a good impression on his teachers. He was very polite and spoke good English, as Jenneh had been careful to teach him because English is the official language of Sierra Leone. However, the teachers knew nothing about his home country apart from the awful events that had sometimes been shown on television. This made the teachers feel sorry for Joseph, and they did not push him very hard in his work. There were other ethnic minority pupils in the school, but none from Africa. As time went on, Joseph's attendance at school was sometimes irregular as he had to stay at home to look after his mother when she was unable to go to work. His school work suffered and he did not make many friends.

Joseph did not do well in the KS1 SATs at the end of KS1 (Year 2), and was placed in a special needs (SEN) group, where he became very withdrawn. He got further and further behind in his work, and his behaviour also began to suffer as his anxiety about his mother grew. No one at school knew of his home situation. When he reached Year 6, he attained level 3 in both maths and English, which was commendable in many ways, but not a reflection of his true ability and below the national expectation. Most of his classmates in primary school moved on to the local secondary school which was very much part of the community. Joseph did not get a place there, and was instead given a place in a large, inner city secondary school where he knew nobody, and the teachers knew nothing of his background. No one suggested to his mother that they could appeal against this decision. Joseph has had a tough time in secondary school. In Years 7 and 8, he was very isolated and withdrawn, and as he moved into Year 10, he got into a bad set of friends and began truanting from school. The school took a somewhat punitive line on this, which led to Joseph being excluded on a couple of occasions. Now, as he approaches his GCSEs, his school record is very patchy and the signs do not look very good for his success.

2.4 Isolated learners – Radia

Radia is in **Year** 4 in a primary school in a village near to a small city in the south west of England. The family have been living in England for five years altogether. She has been attending the school for two years, after moving to the village with her family when her father began a job at the local university, where he had recently completed his PhD. When the family first arrived in England from their home country, Algeria, they lived in the city, near the university. Radia attended a large, busy, multilingual primary school where she had some friends whose parents were also students. She did very well and was happy. When the job offer came, Radia's parents decided to move to the village in order to have a bigger house and garden and – they hoped – better schooling for their three children, of whom Radia is the eldest.

All is not going as well as they hoped. Radia's mother is finding it lonely living in the village with no Algerian friends nearby. Although her neighbours are very pleasant, none of them visit her as regularly as she would like, and she often spends days alone with her young child. She takes the two older pupils to school every day and would like to be able to talk to their teachers more than she does. But she never seems to be able to engage them in conversation. Radia has not settled very well into school. She misses the friends she made in her old school, and has not really made any new friends in the village school. She is the only 'EAL' pupil in her class, and one of only eight or ten in the whole school, all of whom are from well-educated, middle-class backgrounds, some from Islamic countries in the Middle East and others from China. Their parents are either students or former students, like Radia's, or professionals working for companies in the city.

The school has taken steps to find out how to support their new pupils. One teacher has been given responsibility for their induction, and went on a training course, which was part of the *New arrivals excellence programme* (DfE, 2011). But she did not find anything very relevant for the pupils coming to the village school. They all seem to be very fluent in English so language does not seem to be an issue for them. One of the strategies recommended on the course was to form good relationships with the pupils' parents, and she would like to be able to do this. But when she meets them as they bring their pupils to school and come to collect them, she finds it difficult to think of ways to generate conversations with them. She has not had much prior experience of people from different cultural backgrounds. She raises this in a staff meeting, and this leads to a long discussion. One of the outcomes is a decision to organise a social event to give parents an opportunity to meet their pupils' teachers and see something of the work they do in class. This proves a great success, and greatly helps the processes of communication in the school.

2.5 Sojourners – Hamida

Hamida is five years old and in **Year 1** in a large, mainly white school in a prosperous city in the south of England. She arrived in the city with her family from Saudi Arabia at the start of the school year. Her father is doing a PhD at the university, and her mother also has plans to study, once childcare arrangements are made for Hamida and her two younger brothers. Hamida speaks Arabic and is learning to read and write it in a Saturday class run by the wife of another Saudi Arabian student. Her parents are very keen for her to maintain her skills in Arabic, as they will be returning home in three or four years' time. They are also very eager for her to learn to speak English – indeed, this was one of the main reasons why they decided to bring her to England with them, rather than leaving her at home with relatives, as other students have done with their children. They want her to learn 'proper' English so that she speaks as far as possible with a **Received Pronunciation (RP)** accent, which will afford her high status in Saudi Arabia. They also, quite naturally, want her to retain her Muslim identity, and hope that the school are aware of, and sensitive to, Islamic rules and practices.

The class that Hamida has joined comprises mostly 'white British' pupils, though there is one other multilingual child, whose parents are students, like Hamida's. He is from Indonesia and – like Hamida – his family is Muslim. Both pupils are new to the school, and so have not been through the Foundation Stage in the English system. The class teacher is very positive and enthusiastic about having them as her pupils, but is having to work hard to find relevant background information and resources such as stories and information books from their home countries. She is a little wary of the anticipated requirements related to the pupils' Muslim identities but willing to find out and to be flexible in her teaching. She is very keen to establish good relationships with the pupils' families as she sees this as a support for her in meeting the needs of their pupils.

Activity 1.5
Understanding diversity

Each of the six pupils in the vignettes have particular experiences and knowledge that can be seen as strengths as they benefit their learning in mainstream school, and particular gaps in their experience that may create issues for their progress and their **achievements**. Make a chart like the one below and, in discussion with other trainees or colleagues in your placement school, list what you think could be seen as each child's strengths and needs, from the vignettes. There are some suggested answers at the end of the chapter.

Child	Strengths	Needs
Safina		
Stefan		
Jan		
Joseph		
Radia		
Hamida		

2.6 Roma and Gipsy pupils – case study by Georgina Vince

When I first started working in my current school six years ago, we had 12 Roma students in the school, which was considered a challenge at the time. Since then, the number has increased dramatically so that we now have more than ten times as many and they are one of the largest ethnic groups in school. We have learnt a lot about this group, their backgrounds, the issues they face and how best to work with them and support them. I hope to share some of this experience with you here although I cannot say that we have any magic solutions and I know that there is still much more that we need to do and learn to continue to close the achievement gap and enable students in this group to achieve their potential.

Our school is a secondary school serving a highly diverse multicultural, economically deprived inner-city catchment area. Approximately 65% of our students are EAL and about 50% were born overseas, with students from a huge variety of backgrounds. Large numbers of international new arrivals come each year. Initially, most of our Roma students were new arrivals, but this has changed over time as the community has become more established. So now we have many Roma students who transfer from primary school, and even some who were born here. The majority of our Roma students are from the Czech Republic and Slovakia with smaller numbers from Poland and Romania.

Understanding and celebrating Roma history and culture

When we first started working with the Roma, we knew very little about them. 'Funds of knowledge' research (see Chapter 2, section 2.3) suggests the importance of recognising the culture of different ethnic groups. I think this is especially true for the Roma, who may well have had to hide their culture in the past in their countries of origin. We worked with organisations such as the local Gypsy Roma Traveller Achievement Service in Leeds (see website details at the end of the chapter) and used different resources to learn more. This knowledge was further enhanced by visits to the Czech Republic, which I describe below.

As you may know, it is believed that the Roma originated in India and gradually migrated to and across Europe over 500 years ago. There are now Roma living in most countries of Europe and further afield. We tend to use the word Roma to refer to Eastern European Roma but English Gypsies are believed to have the same origins. Most of our Roma students were completely unaware of this history until we did some assemblies about it with the students. What particularly brought it home to them was the language. Some of the resources we used showed the similarities between the Roma language and languages of India and Pakistan and it made their history seem more real when the Roma students realised how close numbers were in the Roma language to those in Urdu and Punjabi, familiar to our Pakistani-heritage students. This also helped to build bridges between the different groups of students in our school.

Following this initial assembly, we continued to have regular activities to teach students about Roma history, particularly during Gypsy Roma Traveller History Month in June (see website details at the end of the chapter). We have also brought issues around the treatment of the Roma in the Holocaust and discrimination into history and PSE curriculums. However, the most significant difference was made in recognising and celebrating Roma culture. We first found out about the musical abilities of some of our Roma students by chance as they turned up in the music rooms and started playing. Many of the boys especially were found to be highly skilled musicians, playing regularly at home and in the community – largely self-taught and playing by ear. We initially used music as a way to get them to feel happier at school and encourage attendance, before trying to encourage them to perform in public. As we got to know them, we also found out that many of them, especially the girls, did traditional Roma dance, so we set up a group at lunchtimes and bought some skirts. Initially they were reluctant to perform in front of the wider school and it took a lot of support and practice before they took part in a musical and dance performance for the school diversity day. This was a real breakthrough as, prior to this performance, the Roma students had been largely viewed negatively as students who didn't come to school and didn't speak English. Suddenly, people could see how skilled they were. Other students and staff came up and told them how great they had been, which was a huge boost to their confidence and made them feel like a real part of the school.

We followed this up by a Roma festival, organised by local schools and the council and held at our school. Roma students and parents from all over the city came and performed. This was so successful that we are now looking to organise a future festival ourselves. We have also tried to bring their culture into school in other ways, such as including Roma artists in art and music lessons and stories about Roma in English lessons.

One important point to remember is that not all Roma will want to celebrate their culture and may find it patronising to be told to, preferring for example hip-hop dancing, but it is important that their culture is there, as part of wider opportunities.

Understanding the situation of Roma in their home countries

As more and more Roma continued to come to our area, we started to wonder what it was that was causing them to leave their countries of origin. As we got to know our students, we gradually learnt more and this was reinforced by a project in which we took part, which linked

$\rightarrow$

schools in England with schools with large numbers of Roma in the Czech Republic. On visits to the Czech Republic, we found out more and saw how the Roma lived. This helped us understand some of the issues we faced with our Roma students.

Roma and Gypsies have faced huge amounts of discrimination throughout history; I believe that many were kept in slavery in Romania for a long time and this culminated in their treatment in the Holocaust in which nearly all Czech Roma were wiped out. This discrimination still continues to a lesser extent and is the main reason why so many Roma leave. Although some Roma in eastern European countries now live a more integrated life with the non-Roma community, many continue to live separately, often in very deprived conditions. They suffer discrimination in areas such as employment and education. Prior to one of my visits to the Czech Republic, there had been large anti-Roma protests and attacks on Roma in a nearby town. While there, I experienced Roma going to largely segregated schools despite this now being illegal. This is partly due to Roma living in such segregated communities and also due to Czech parents not wanting their children taught along with Roma. Some of these schools were quite negative towards their Roma students while others seemed more positive, but even in these schools there was never the expectation that Roma could achieve, such as going to university. Roma children also tend to be overrepresented in special schools.

This can be a sensitive subject – Czech people may deny it and obviously not all Czech people feel this way. Some Roma children may also be unaware of the true situation in their country. However, it is worth bearing this in mind for example when looking for a Czech interpreter as Roma parents will quickly pick up on any prejudice.

Ascription

One issue that we regularly come up against is the reluctance of families to ascribe as Roma. This is understandable, given the situation they may face in their country if known as Roma and the advantages to hiding their identity. There may also be some misunderstanding as most feel that they are both Roma and Czech and therefore Eastern European. It could be argued that it is not important what it says on the official records as long as you know who your Roma pupils are and can monitor and support them. While this is true to a certain extent, I think it is important that students feel safe to acknowledge who they are and are proud of their identity. They should not feel they have to hide this. Imagine if you always had to keep such an important thing about yourself hidden; it cannot be good for a child growing up. In addition to having Roma culture visible around school, a strategy we have used is to use a Roma student who is happy to identify as Roma in admissions meetings with new students. It is essential that all staff are aware of the issues around ascription and do not undermine work done by asking about it in an insensitive way.

Attendance

One particular problem schools often have with Roma students is attendance. Our Roma attendance has improved greatly over the years with strategies we have put in place and although Roma attendance is still below the school average, it is above Gypsy Roma attendance nationally.

$\rightarrow$

We have found that a mixture of 'carrot and stick' approaches works best. Firstly, it is important that the families understand the system in this country, which is very different to that in the Czech Republic and many other eastern European countries where attendance is not monitored and followed up in the rigorous way it is in this country. This is an area where a Czech-speaking worker who can communicate with the families is invaluable. We first employed a Czech worker two years ago and it has made a huge difference and led to an immediate improvement in attendance. She meets all new Czech and Slovak families and ensures they know the consequences of not coming to school, and what to do if a child is absent. In addition, as families have been in the country longer and have got used to the system, attendance has improved anyway. Employment of a Czech worker has also helped greatly in following up absences and visiting families with attendance issues, whereas before this we had no real way of communicating with our Roma families.

However, I think that more important in improving Roma attendance has been the fact that they now feel part of the school community and happier at school. In addition, as their language has improved, they feel more confident to participate in lessons and see they are making progress. In addition to this, we have organised attendance groups where students who struggle with attendance meet our Czech worker each week and improvements in attendance are rewarded.

Working with families

Some of our feeder primaries have built up good relationships with families as parents bring their children to school each day, but we always struggled to get parents in to school. However, I think we have started to have something of a breakthrough in the last year. This is partly due to the employment of the Czech worker who tries to meet all families before they start at the school, either in admissions meetings for new arrivals or by visiting primary schools and organising meetings for the parents of Year 6 students who will be joining the school. She is also able to ensure that there is good communication with parents through letters and phone calls in Czech telling them about important events in school. We have found that once parents understand what is happening at school they are in most cases keen to support their child and attendance at parents' evenings especially has improved greatly. It is also important to recognise that many of the Roma parents may have had very negative or little experience of school themselves – a number of our parents are not literate. We therefore tried to encourage them to come into school for fun events, such as music shows and the Roma festival, which proved successful. We have also offered them support through such things as ESOL classes and drop-in sessions with our Czech worker for help with benefits and job applications.

Raising aspirations and achievement

Once we had developed our understanding of our Roma students and their attendance had improved, we realised that this was not enough and that we needed to do more in order to raise their achievement. I had noticed the low expectations of Roma students at schools in the Czech Republic and this was reinforced when a number of our students who were predicted

$\rightarrow$

very good GCSEs said that what they wanted to be were hairdressers or mechanics. When we told their parents they had the potential to go to university, they were nearly in tears. We realised that we had to do more to raise students' aspirations, so last year we introduced a student mentoring programme with some of the older Roma students mentoring some of the younger students and we are looking to develop this further this year. We also identify students with potential in the lower years and take them to visit universities. We are now looking to develop this further by getting university students to mentor some of our older students and getting some of our Roma students who have done well and gone on to higher study to come back and speak to the younger students. In addition, we noticed that some of the students who were joining us from primary school were struggling due to their lack of literacy in Czech or Slovak so we are looking at introducing Czech lessons at school and also going into some of our feeder primaries to tackle these literacy issues at an earlier stage. I hope that you have found our experiences useful and have learnt something. If you are interested in learning more, there are some sources of further information/support listed at the end of the chapter.

3. Language diversity and learning – some myths and misconceptions

This brief, final section is intended to raise some questions about the best approaches to teaching pupils with EAL. You may already have experience of teaching English to pupils or adults in other countries, which is normally defined as **English as a Foreign Language (EFL)** teaching, and you may even have done a **Teaching English as a Foreign Language (TEFL)** course. There are parallels between EFL and EAL learners and some ideas from TEFL teaching can be very useful in EAL. But, there are also important differences, as the vignettes and case studies in this chapter show. Some ideas from TEFL teaching may seem obviously appropriate, like common sense. But they may not seem to be so helpful when you understand something of the complexities of the experiences of many multilingual and EAL learners. You will read a lot about theories of language, learning and multilingualism in Chapters 2 and 3, which will develop your understanding of the needs of multilingual and EAL learners. They will also help you to see how these myths and misconceptions can sometimes be unhelpful. So, here are my 'myths and misconceptions' – we will return to them at the end of the book, in Chapter 8.

- Languages should be kept separate in the classroom, or learners will become confused (*this is sometimes called 'language interference'*).

- Pupils will 'pick English up' naturally in the classroom; they do not need to be explicitly taught (*this is sometimes called 'immersion'*).

- Language diversity is a 'problem', and it is better if pupils speak English all the time in classrooms.

- It is impossible, or very difficult, to learn a new language beyond a young age (*this is sometimes called 'the critical period'*).

Learning Outcomes Review

This introductory chapter has provided you with background information about the pupils who are categorised as multilingual and EAL learners, and their families and communities. This should have helped you gain awareness of the history of language and cultural diversity in England, and the diverse range of experiences and knowledge that multilingual and EAL learners bring to their primary classrooms. One of the aims of this is to help you think about the importance of recognising and reflecting on your own views on language diversity and ethnicity for you as a primary teacher.

Self-assessment questions

1. In what ways do you think your own identity might influence your views and perceptions of the pupils you teach? Think about specific situations where this may have happened.
2. Why do you think it is important to understand something about the family backgrounds of the pupils you teach? (You will read more about this in Chapter 3.)
3. Think about the teachers mentioned in each of the vignettes in this chapter. Following what you have read in this chapter, if you had been the teacher for any of the pupils described, would you have responded in the same way, or might you have done something different?
4. Think of a group of multilingual and EAL learners you know. Which of the categories introduced in section 1.2 would your learners fit into? Write a brief vignette of one of your learners, along the lines of those in the section.
5. What distinctive factors influence the learning and achievement of Gypsy and Roma pupils? How do you think stereotypes in the media may affect their success in school?

Suggested answers to
Activity 1.5 – Understanding diversity

Child	Strengths	Needs
Safina	Strong speaking and listening skills Supportive home and community Diverse experiences of learning at home	Sustained support in developing writing skills in English
Stefan	Strong literacy in home language Opportunities to develop expertise and take exams in home language	Continued support in developing writing skills in English
Jan	Teacher who is interested in understanding the problems he is facing Positive attitude in class to recognising pupils' home languages	Personalised provision to develop his skills in English

Joseph	Good level of English language Loving relationship with mother	Understanding (on the part of his teachers) of the broader cultural background of Sierra Leone Personalised provision to help him catch up
Radia	Supportive home and family background Positive attitudes in school towards EAL pupils	Improved communication between home and school
Hamida	Supportive home and family background Positive attitudes in school towards EAL pupils	Greater awareness on the part of the school of cultural and religious factors underpinning Hamida's experiences

Further Reading

Gussin Paley, V. (2000) *White Teacher*, 3rd edn. Cambridge: Harvard University Press.
This a personal account of teaching in a school which becomes increasingly diverse.
Paley reflects on the way that even simple terminology can convey unintended meanings.
She vividly describes what her pupils taught her over the years about herself as a 'white teacher'.

Hayes, D. (2011) Establishing your own teaching identity. In: Hansen, A. (ed.) *Primary Professional Studies* (pp. 118–33). Exeter: Learning Matters.
This chapter encourages readers to think about their own values, motivation and self-identity, and the impact these have on becoming a teacher.

Sources of information about Gypsy Roma pupils:
http://www.natt.org.uk/ – National Association of Teachers of Travellers
http://www.grtleeds.co.uk/ – Leeds Gypsy Roma Traveller Achievement Service
http://grthm.natt.org.uk/ – Gipsy Roma Traveller History Month
http://www.everyculture.com/wc/Norway-to-Russia/Roma.html – information about Roma
http://qualirom.uni-graz.at/home.html – Roma language teaching resources
http://www.romaninet.com/?sec=home – Roma language and culture resources
http://romani.humanities.manchester.ac.uk/# – Manchester University's Roma resources, including excellent language DVD link

References

BBC (2007) *Multilingualism* http://www.bbc.co.uk/voices/yourvoice/multilingualism2.shtml (archived and accessed 17 November 2014).

Datta, M. (2007) *Bilinguality and Biliteracy: Principles and Practice*, 2nd edn. London: Continuum.

Department for Education (DfE) (2011) *The National Strategies: New Arrivals Excellence Programme: CPD Modules*. London: DfE. http://www.naldic.org.uk/Resources/NALDIC/Teaching%20and%20Learning/nswsneapcpdmodule0004108.pdf (accessed 19 September 2014).

Gussin Paley, V. (2000) *White Teacher*, 3rd edn. Cambridge: Harvard University Press.

Hall, D., Griffiths, D., Haslam, L. and Wilkin, Y. (2001) *Assessing the Needs of Bilingual Pupils: Living in Two Languages*, 2nd edn. London: David Fulton.

National Association for Language Development in the Curriculum (NALDIC) (2013) *The Latest Statistics about EAL Learners in our Schools*. Reading: NALDIC. http://www.naldic.org.uk/research-and-information/eal-statistics/eal-pupils (accessed 17 November 2014).

Wikipedia (2013) *Arbeia* http://en.wikipedia.org/wiki/Arbeia (accessed 17 November 2014).

Wikipedia (2014) *Bengali Language* http://en.wikipedia.org/wiki/Bengali_language#Geographical_distribution (accessed 17 November 2014).

2 All about language and learning

Learning Outcomes

This chapter will help you to achieve the following learning outcomes:

- gain awareness and understanding of how language and learning are linked and can be understood theoretically;
- develop understanding of the functional approach to grammar, its importance for teaching and learning, and its implications for literacy;
- understand the important role of talk for learning;
- understand what is meant by the 'funds of knowledge' concept and what it means for understanding the needs of EAL learners in mainstream schools.

Introduction

Together with Chapter 3, this chapter introduces you to the theories related to language, learning and multilingualism that underpin the book. Good teachers understand that theory is not something that is 'applied', but that is actively constructed through all aspects of their own professional experience, part of which it is their understanding of how language works, how children learn and, in relation to EAL learners, how bilingualism and multilingualism can be viewed. They understand also that there is no one particular 'grand' theory that dictates all they should do in the classroom, but that good teaching benefits from a range of theoretical perspectives that complement each other. Good teachers know how to use theory to inform practice in their planning and teaching. Based on their professional knowledge, they know how to critically evaluate official policy and use it in the most effective ways to support their pupils' learning and development. The theories about language and learning outlined in this chapter are relevant for your work with all pupils in primary and secondary settings, and not just those who are defined as multilingual, EAL learners. They will help you to understand the experiences of the multilingual and EAL learners you met in Chapter 1, and those you know and will meet in your own classrooms. They will help you to understand more about the role of language in learning generally. The practical outcomes of these theories flow through the ideas presented in Part 2 of the book and will help you to make informed, strategic decisions about the best ways to help your pupils to succeed.

There are questions and brief activities interspersed throughout the chapter to help you think about how the theories relate to your own experiences as both a teacher and a learner. Following Chapter 3, there is a set of 'key principles' to help you relate the theories to your teaching. Then, the principles are illustrated by practical examples in the chapters in Part 2.

These will help you in planning and evaluating your own teaching strategies and resources for your multilingual and EAL learners.

These are the main sections and subsections of the chapter.

1. **All about language**
   1.1 What is language?

   1.2 Language, culture and identity

   1.3 Thinking about teaching languages – the functional approach

   1.4 The functional approach and literacy

2. **Language and learning**
   2.1 Sociocultural theories of learning and the Zone of Proximal Development (ZPD)

   2.2 The importance of talk for learning

   2.3 The 'funds of knowledge' concept

1. All about language

1.1 What is language?

Language pervades everything we do, at home with our families and in our communities, as well as at school and work. Indeed, according to the Vygotskyan, sociocultural model of language and learning that is discussed in section 2.1 below, language is the medium through which our private thoughts are given life and meaning. We experience language in an infinite range of ways, both within and outside school; orally through our everyday conversations with family, friends and all the other people we engage with, as well as in written modes through traditional forms of print such as books and newspapers and through more modern forms of social media. We use spoken language to engage in face-to-face conversations with the people near us and in **multi-modal** modes of 'conversing' to communicate virtually with others. For all of us, **language diversity** is a normal and natural part of our lived experiences, even if the only language we encounter may be English. If we happen to live in families and communities where different languages are used for different purposes on an everyday basis, language diversity is an even richer aspect of our lives. Many children in England, as in other parts of the world, live in families where English may be the most commonly used language between themselves and their parents and siblings, but other languages are used naturally in interactions with grandparents or other relatives who live nearby or in conversations by phone or social media with relatives in other countries.

Through language, we interact with others in the social groups we belong to, and in this way construct our understandings of the world. This makes the learning of languages in school, whether in literacy, English literature or foreign languages (FL), very different from learning other subjects, in two main ways. Language is not only the medium of communication, it is also the substance of what is being learnt. Learning English in mainstream schools in England is always cross-curricular in that the language itself forms the basis of learning in all the other areas of the curriculum. For all pupils, but especially for EAL learners who need to develop fluency in English because it is a new language to them, language learning takes place in every subject across the curriculum. For many multilingual pupils, language learning does not only take place in mainstream schools, but also in community-based schools (sometimes called **complementary or supplementary schools**), where they learn what is sometimes called their **heritage language**. Even though this language is not taught in their mainstream school, they may be taking a GCSE or 'A' level in it. Many complementary schools make arrangements with the mainstream schools that their pupils attend for them to take exams in languages they have been studying out of school hours. This is the reason why Polish is rapidly becoming one of the most popular languages at GCSE. There is much more about this aspect of being multilingual in Chapter 3, and about complementary schools, their roles in learning and ways that bridges between complementary and mainstream learning can be built in Chapter 7.

As British citizens and members of different social and cultural groups, we all live in a multilingual society. One of the central arguments in Chapter 3 is that the world is becoming more and more multilingual, while at the same time English is spreading in its use and power. It is important to remember that all the pupils you teach, not just those who are categorised as EAL or multilingual, have knowledge and experiences of languages and of varieties of English outside school that are different from those they use and learn in school. Besides all the different languages that we may hear and read around us, we are all continually exposed to different forms and varieties of the English language, and to different languages, in our everyday lives. We may hear and use different **dialects** of English, which have grammar and vocabulary different from **standard English**. We may speak English in different **accents** from the ones most commonly used in school and which are widely regarded as appropriate for educated people to use. All of us, whether we regard ourselves as multilingual, bilingual or monolingual, have our own **repertoires**, or personal resources, of language. This is one feature of what is meant by language diversity. It means that we have a wide range of ways of speaking and writing from which we can choose to interact with others. We use our language repertoires to speak and write in all the different ways we need to in order to get done all the things that we need to do – in other words, to perform different language functions. We make choices from our language repertoires according to a range of factors, which are often called the '5Ws':

- *Who* we are speaking to or writing for (audiences);
- *When* and *Where* (contexts);
- *What* we say or write (topics);
- *Why* we say or write these things (reasons and purposes).

Here is an example of some of the things I can do with my language repertoire: in an ordinary working day, I may wake up to Radio 4, mumble a few words to my husband while eating breakfast, then set off down the road to the station, greeting our neighbour as he walks past with his dog. When I get to work, I head up the stairs to my office, switch on the computer, read and reply to several e-mails and compose a few of my own. After that, perhaps, I have to give a lecture to rows of students in a lecture theatre. This involves a very different way of speaking from the ones I have used so far; an academic form which is more like writing, in many ways. Later on, I may meet a smaller group of students in a classroom for a tutorial. Here, I need to use yet another way of speaking from the others I have used so far, one which is much more tentative and conversational than the lecture, but still academic. As I take part in the discussion, I need to listen carefully to my students' viewpoints and adapt the ways I speak in order to respond to their questions. On the way home from work, I may make a couple of quick calls on my mobile phone – yet another form of speaking, different from all the others I have already mentioned. In all of these interactions and for all of these functions, I choose the ways I speak or write from my repertoire, depending on the '5Ws' indicated above – who, when, where, what and why.

Activity 2.1

Your language repertoire

Make a chart like the one below and list some of the ways you speak and write during a typical day. Answer the '5Ws' questions for each, following the examples given.

Activity	What	Who	When	Where	Why
Speaking	greetings	neighbour	early morning	in the street	to be friendly
Writing	e-mail	student	lunchtime	in the office	to answer a question

The notion of language repertoires is a very useful one in helping to understand how language works and in thinking about how your teaching can be made more focused and effective. It switches our attention from the language itself to the users of the language and the uses to which it is being put. One of its key aspects is the notion of appropriacy, which emphasises the idea that there is always a range of different ways of saying and writing things, and that what we need to do is to choose the one that is most appropriate. This calls into question the idea that there is only one correct way to say or write something, and thus all other ways are wrong. It underpins what is known as the **functional approach** to language and grammar, a model which focuses on the purposes for which we need to use language, rather than just the language itself. If we help pupils to understand the functions – the '5Ws' – of the language in any task they are expected to do, then their thinking will be more focused and their language learning, through the activity, will be more meaningful, purposeful and successful. The functional approach to language is further explained in sections 1.3 and 1.4.

1.2 Language, culture and identity

In addition to being an essential tool for learning, language is an inextricable part of our personal and social lives, of the cultures we live in, and of who we are. It is one of the main ways in which we develop a sense of where we belong, and how we fit in with the social worlds that surround us. In other words, it is part of our **identities**.

Research Focus

There is a great deal of evidence to show that, if pupils have a sense of belonging and of being valued in their classrooms, their attitudes to learning will be much more positive and this will help their achievements to improve. Conteh (2003: 41-57) shows the range of knowledge and experiences that many multilingual and EAL learners bring to their mainstream classrooms, and suggests how they can support their learning in positive ways, if they are recognised and valued. On the other hand, pupils can very quickly gain the sense – even if it is unintended – that their languages are not welcome and must be kept hidden from the teacher. This can have a negative effect on their learning, as the following example shows:

> *Five-year-old Rukshana began school speaking no English. Punjabi was the language of her home. Twenty years later, when she was training to be a teacher, she wrote about the way she felt as a child when, as a new child in the class, the teacher did not allow her to use Punjabi when assessing her knowledge of colours. This is part of what she wrote: 'The teacher left me staring blankly at the other pupils. Every one of them was doing something: playing, reading, working or talking in English, I sat back and felt sorry for myself the teacher was probably thinking 'just another incident with an Asian child who does not know colours', this was a day I felt so many emotions inside me. Feelings that I had never experienced before. I did not want to be myself.*

Multilingual and EAL learners need to feel that their home languages are recognised and valued in the classroom in order to feel that they themselves belong. To do this is often not difficult and it does not involve complex changes to the curriculum. Actions that may seem very small, such as doing the register in different languages or choosing a story with a particular setting or theme can make pupils feel recognised and valued, and that they belong in the classroom. This can open out their potential for learning, as the following vignette shows.

Vignette

Valuing language diversity – making 'safe spaces'

A trainee teacher found out that there was a new child in her class who had recently arrived from an African country. She found out which country it was, went to the library and chose a story to read to the class, which was set in the child's country of origin. It contained words in a language that neither the class teacher nor the trainee knew. She found out from the child's mother that the words were actually greetings in one of the languages that the family spoke. With the trainee's (and her mother's) encouragement and support, the child taught the class how to say the greetings. The rest of the class enjoyed this very much. When the story was over, a little girl came up to the class teacher and the trainee and said, 'Miss, I can speak Arabic, and my dad teaches me every day. Shall I show you how to say hello?' The teacher was surprised, but pleased, and asked her to teach the class, which she did with a beaming smile on her face. The teacher told the trainee afterwards that the child had never done anything like that before. They concluded that she may have felt able to do so because of the 'safe space' (Conteh and Brock, 2010) that had been opened up for her by the story that the trainee had chosen for the new pupil, and the subsequent experience of learning greetings in a new language in the context of an enjoyable whole-class activity.

The links between identity, language and culture are strong. Languages are formed in the cultural settings in which they are situated, their meanings shaped through everyday use. The meanings of English words can change from country to country – light bulbs in Australia are called globes; roundabouts in west Africa are called turntables. Word meanings vary even in different parts of England. There is a story about some road signs put up about 30 years ago at level crossings in Lincolnshire and Norfolk, which read, 'Wait while lights are red'. Some drivers waited until the lights turned red, then tried to race across the track before the train thundered past! It quickly became clear that, in that part of the country, 'while' and 'until' had very similar meanings and the confusing signs were rapidly changed. As teachers, we may sometimes need to think carefully about what our pupils are trying to say, and respond positively to their meanings, even though they may not always be expressed in terms that are familiar to us.

Many pupils from Pakistani-heritage backgrounds, even when they are fluent in English, sometimes talk about their extended family members as 'brother cousins' and 'sister cousins'. When I first heard this, it reminded me of how people in Sierra Leone, where I lived for several years, sometimes talked about their relatives. In a setting where a man might have more than one wife, they would describe the relationships very precisely: 'he's my brother, same mother, same father' and so on. When I asked the Pakistani-heritage pupils I was teaching why they talked about their cousins in this way, they told me that in Punjabi there were eight words for the one English word 'cousin'. So in their language, they could distinguish whether it was mum's sister's son, mum's brother's daughter and so on. I found this fascinating, and it led to several interesting discussions about families, comparing the different ways that we could think and talk about families in different cultures and the words we used to describe them. This is an important way of learning (it certainly was for me), with clear links to personal and social education. It is also an excellent language-learning activity.

It is very important for our self-confidence and identity as learners that we feel we belong and are valued in the communities in which we are learning. Multilingual pupils need to feel that their home languages are recognised and valued in school, even if their teachers do not speak them. These languages are often a significant part of their social lives outside school. Also, if they are in the early stages of learning English, the languages will form a large part of their thought processes and the ways they make sense of the world, as we will see in the discussion on multilingualism in Chapter 3. If you do not share your pupils' languages, you can still do a lot to show that you value them through using multilingual labels in the classroom, stories from their own cultures and dual language texts, of which there are now many available – they can also be produced in the classroom, as shown in Chapter 7. Resources such as these help pupils to transfer their thinking from one language to another and support the development of **additive bilingualism** (Chapter 3, p. 58). Valuing pupils' out-of-school experiences and understandings in this way has been described as developing a **'funds of knowledge'** (Gonzalez *et al.*, 2005) approach to their learning, and is discussed more fully in section 2.3 below.

1.3 Thinking about teaching languages – the functional approach

Like any subject we are expected to teach, we need a way of thinking and talking about the English language in order to understand how it works ourselves and help pupils to learn it. In other words, we need a language to talk about language, and this is part of what **grammar** can offer. Grammars, essentially, are ways of describing languages and there are many different kinds. We sometimes think of grammars as sets of rules to be followed, rather than ways of describing language. We can get very worried about what is 'correct', and anxious about making mistakes. However, when thinking about language and how to teach it, the question of what is or isn't absolutely correct is not always a very helpful one. Some types of grammars are not very helpful in teaching, as they have other purposes; they can quickly become abstract and complex, the terminology difficult to remember and use. The **functional approach** offers a more useful way to think about grammar for teaching. As I said above, a key element in this approach is the idea of repertoire, a focus on the choices we make – often intuitively – in using language to do the things we need to do. We use languages in a wide range of ways to make meaning; we all make choices and we all have repertoires of language to choose from, whether we think of ourselves as multilingual or not. A functional approach to grammar encourages us to think about how we can say and write what we want to in the best ways possible. Using the '5Ws' described above helps to analyse whatever it is we say or write and to consider the choices available.

Within this approach, grammar can be thought of as a set of tools to help us to analyse our language choices in these ways. Thinking differently about language and asking different questions, such as about whether the messages in the text have been conveyed in the most appropriate ways possible for that particular text, is often more productive. And the answers to these questions about appropriacy will be different from text to text – what is appropriate for one text will be inappropriate for another.

Activity 2.2

Saying things in the most appropriate ways: Ted Hughes and *The Iron Man*

Look at the following text, which is from the beginning of *The Iron Man*, one of the best children's stories ever written (in my view!). Identify any features that may be described as 'incorrect' in the traditional way of thinking about grammar. Think about why Ted Hughes (who was poet laureate, so knew a thing or two about language) might have decided to open his story in this way. There are some suggestions to help you check your responses after this activity.

CRRRAAASSSSSSH

Down the cliff the Iron Man came toppling, head over heels.
CRASH!
CRASH!
CRASH!
From rock to rock, snag to snag, tumbling slowly. And as he crashed and crashed and crashed
His iron legs fell off.
His iron arms broke off and the hands broke off the arms. His great iron ears fell off and his eyes fell out. His great iron head fell off.
All the separate pieces tumbled, scattered, crashing, bumping, clanging, down on to the rocky beach far below.
A few rocks tumbled with him.
Then
Silence.
Ted Hughes

These are some of the text features you might have noticed:

1. There are words in capital letters and mis-spelt words at the start – here they help you to imagine the Iron Man tumbling and crashing down the cliff.

2. There are lot of exclamation marks at one point – often they are thought to be 'bad' punctuation if over-used, but here they help with describing the crashing of the Iron Man.

3. The sentence beginning 'From rock to rock...' has no stated subject, so could be considered 'wrong'. But we all know that it is about the Iron Man, and it helps us, again, to imagine him rolling down the hill.

4. The next sentence begins with 'and'! But it is very effective in carrying on the idea of the Iron Man tumbling down the cliff. (And this sentence starts with 'but' – but I think it is the most appropriate way to express what I want to say!).

5. The section of the text beginning with 'His iron legs fell off ...' is rather repetitive, with simple sentences, all with the same structure. But, again, it is effective as we imagine the pieces of the Iron Man falling off, one after the other.

6. There are no descriptive adjectives (so-called 'wow' words) in the whole text, yet it is wonderfully descriptive. The words which do most of the job of describing things in interesting ways are the verbs.

Taking a functional approach means that we look at the ways in which language is used to construct whole **texts** in their **contexts of use**, rather than just at the language itself without any context. The main practical implication of this is that in their learning of language, whether it be of literacy in English, literature in a foreign language or English as an additional language, pupils need to experience listening, speaking, reading and writing as authentic activities through which they can make meanings and do things, not just as sets of skills to be developed or lists of spellings to be learnt. In a functional approach to teaching, teachers explain and model, and learners discuss and analyse the ways in which words are chosen and sentences are structured and brought together to construct whole texts such as stories, letters, reports and so on. All pupils – and particularly multilingual learners – need to encounter examples of **authentic language** in their learning, not just made-up examples of language in exercises, work sheets, tests or traditional grammar books. They need to hear and read, think about, discuss and argue about real texts which writers have written for real purposes and audiences. Grammar can be a useful tool in doing all this. But the grammar will only make sense to them when they can relate it to real texts in this way.

Pupils learn much more effectively about how different texts work and are constructed if they have authentic purposes and audiences for their tasks. Rather than teaching text types in an abstract, mechanical way in literacy lessons, it is far more effective to introduce them through real tasks in different subjects across the curriculum, where they are used to accomplish different functions, e.g. a report in science, a narrative in history and so on. You can see some examples of this in Chapter 4 in the discussion of planning. Understanding of the features of different texts can be reinforced and practised in literacy lessons with meaningful content that is about something that your pupils are learning about in other subjects. There are ideas to help you to do this, in activities across the curriculum, in Chapter 5.

Activity 2.3

Thinking about the functions of texts

All of the following are examples of authentic texts, in particular contexts of use. Decide what kind of texts they are and what contexts they come from (you could use the 5Ws questions to help you to do this). Then, think about what language features (grammar, punctuation, choice of words, etc.) the speakers or writers have used to make their texts meaningful and purposeful. There are some possible answers to these questions below, but you may have other relevant ideas, which you can discuss with your course mates or colleagues.

Texts:

1. 'Cheap day return to Manchester Piccadilly, please.'
2. To make wholemeal rolls, divide the dough into 18 equal portions. Each should weigh about 50g. On an unfloured surface, roll each piece of dough into a ball inside your cupped hand.
3. Parvana was small for her 11 years. As a small girl, she could usually get away with being outside without being questioned. 'I need this girl to help me walk,' her father would tell any talib who asked, pointing to his leg. He had lost the lower part of his leg when the high school he was teaching in was bombed. His insides had been hurt, somehow, too. He was often tired.
4. The Cold War is always portrayed as a global struggle between Communism and capitalism but in the early 1960s the world's Communist superpowers, China and Russia, also fell out. After a few border skirmishes they decided to continue their struggle in the rest of the world. So the Russia–China Cold War spread to Africa where they competed for allies.

Contexts of use and language features

1. This is a spoken text with a very simple purpose: the speaker wants to buy a rail ticket. They do not know the ticket seller personally, so they make their request in a very simple, straightforward way with no greetings or personal language. In some cultural settings, it would be appropriate to preface the request with a simple greeting, but this is not usually necessary in 'British' culture. The speaker ends their request with 'please', which is the way to express politeness in 'British' culture. In other cultural settings politeness is expressed in different ways.

2. This is a written text, a recipe. In some ways it is similar to number 1 in that it is dealing with precise instructions in an impersonal way. So, it needs to be very clear in order to make sure that the reader has all the information they need to carry out the task. It uses imperative verbs (sometimes called 'bossy' verbs in primary schools), and the writer has made sure that all the actions needed to follow the recipe successfully are placed in the correct order, and all measurements are accurate. The writer also uses some 'technical' language, e.g. 'on an unfloured surface', from time to time and also illustrates what needs

to be done by connecting the instructions with everyday examples that can be easily visualised, e.g. 'roll … into a ball inside your cupped hand'.

3. This is a written fiction text, a short extract from Deborah Ellis's book *Parvana's Journey*, a fascinating children's novel about a young girl in Afghanistan during the rule of the Taliban, which Ellis wrote after she had visited refugee camps and found out about the lives of women and children there. The short extract, from the beginning of the book, quickly sets the scene and raises questions in the reader's mind – why might Parvana be questioned if she is found outside? Why was her father's school bombed? Who did it? Who (or what) is a talib? What has happened to the rest of their family? The language is very simple, but we quickly gain an impression of the problems that Parvana faces.

4. This is a written non-fiction text, a short extract from Richard Dowden's book *Africa: Altered States, Ordinary Miracles*. Richard Dowden is a journalist, so his style is straightforward, with the main facts presented at the start of the piece, and reasons and explanations coming later on. He uses a popular kind of 'personification' in the way he presents the 'struggle' between globalism and communism and China and Russia as 'falling out', like two people who have had a quarrel. This is a very vivid way of helping his readers to understand the events he is describing. If he were writing a history textbook rather than a general book for a wide audience, he would probably have used a more formal style, perhaps with longer, more complex sentences.

1.4 The functional approach and literacy

The functional approach to literacy was actually embedded in the curriculum in England in the 1990s when the National Literacy Strategy was introduced, through the extensive work on test types or '**genres**' that it contained. Over recent years, however, the strategy has been overtaken in official policy by the heavy focus on phonics that currently dominates the teaching of literacy. The 'genre' approach to teaching about texts is based on systemic functional grammar principles (Derewianka, 1990), and offers powerful pedagogic possibilities, with its focus on authentic language and on the multimodality of texts. As explained above, it replaces conventional, prescriptive notions of grammar with the idea that grammar is a set of tools with which a speaker or writer achieves their communicative purposes. García (2009) argues that such an approach to literacy **pedagogy** has the potential to recognise and value the diversity of language resources which learners generally, and multilingual learners in particular, bring to their classrooms. Unfortunately, the potential of this for EAL learners was not clearly articulated in the *Literacy Hour* framework that guided the teaching of literacy in the 1990s. This meant that, by and large, mainstream teachers did not develop the knowledge about language, nor the professional confidence to take ownership of the principles underpinning genre-based teaching. There are many excellent pedagogic strategies in the Literacy Strategy, which were developed in multilingual and multicultural contexts. One, which came from New Zealand and was developed by Holdaway and colleagues (1979), included the use of big books and shared reading. This proved very effective in many ways, but it has largely disappeared now from classrooms in

England. It is well worth reviving some of its key approaches, and activities based on these are suggested in Chapter 7.

Debates about the teaching of reading have gone on ever since reading has been taught, and they are not likely to come to an end soon. In England, the debate has – unfortunately – become very political, to the detriment of the ways that reading is discussed and taught. This does not serve well the needs of many pupils in both primary and secondary schools. The current prevailing 'official' model, the so-called 'simple view' of reading originated in the 'Rose Review' (DfES, 2006), was adapted in 2010 and is now embodied in the 2014 curriculum in a slightly different form. The simple view states that reading involves two processes:

- decoding the words;
- comprehending the whole text.

And that decoding needs to be taught before comprehending. Thus the 2014 curriculum prescribes that all pupils should be taught to phonically decode before they engage in reading meaningful texts. While decoding is clearly important, this is no way to develop young learners into independent, confident readers and it goes against all the research which shows that most children learn to read by making meaning with whole texts, not by rote learning disembodied lists of sounds.

We need to remember that there is much more to reading than all of this; literacy is a social and cultural practice, which takes many forms and happens in many different contexts. Indeed, for many multilingual pupils, it is more realistic to talk about 'literacies' in the plural, instead of just 'literacy', as they may have skills in reading in different languages, sometimes in different scripts. In Gregory *et al.*'s (2004) *Many Pathways to Literacy*, different authors present a wide range of examples of the literacy practices of young learners from diverse language and cultural backgrounds. Key theoretical principles can be drawn from this, which help us to recognise the kinds of pedagogy that will most benefit EAL learners in both primary and secondary settings:

- Multilingual learners live in *'simultaneous worlds'* of language use and experience where literacies are performed in different ways for different purposes.
- Literacy learning is *syncretic* – learning to read in one language and script facilitates the learning of others.
- Literacy practices are social, cultural and always connected with issues of power.

In another of her books, Gregory (2008: 123–9) provides food for thought for teachers on ways to consider the teaching of phonics with EAL learners. She presents a case study of Saida, a 9-year-old, newly arrived pupil from Bangladesh, who amazed her teacher by 'reading' correctly from a simple text. However, Saida could not understand the words that she articulated – she was simply using the decoding strategies that she had been taught in Bangladesh. Luckily, her teacher recognised this and quickly realised that what Saida needed was lots of experience of listening to and later talking about meaningful text in English so that her strong decoding skills became part of her repertoire of ways of engaging with the English language in meaningful ways. From Gregory's case study, we can draw some valuable conclusions:

- EAL/multilingual learners are often very good at phonic decoding, though they are unfamiliar with the meanings of many words they can decode (this is borne out by the Year 1 phonics screening check, where EAL learners often do very well at decoding the nonsense words).

- Many new arrivals can decode successfully because of the ways they have been taught to read in their countries of origin.

- Pupils with such early literacy experiences need strategies which are grounded in their early experiences to develop the full range of skills to become good readers.

- Young, multilingual learners need rich experiences of meaningful English text in order to develop their repertoires of words they understand and to gain a 'feel' for what sounds are 'allowed' in a language.

2. Language and learning

2.1 Sociocultural theories of learning and the Zone of Proximal Development (ZPD)

Research Focus

Learning is often theoretically described as 'sociocultural'. This suggests that learning is not simply the transmission of knowledge, but a process of negotiation and co-construction between teachers and learners. Vygotsky, one of the originators of the sociocultural theoretical framework, through his research with pupils with special needs, argued that all learning is social in origin, and that young pupils develop and learn through 'externalised' social inter-actions with their teachers and their peers. As they progress, they develop the capacity to 'internalise' the interactions and to learn more independently. He developed the idea of the **Zone of Proximal Development (ZPD)** to describe in a theoretical way this social mediation between teachers and pupils, suggesting that pupils learn interactively 'through problem solving under adult guidance or in collaboration with more capable peers' (Vygotsky, 1978: 86).

The sociocultural theory of learning has very important implications for all pupils in school, and particularly for multilingual and EAL learners. Sonia Nieto (1999) uses Vygotsky's theories to develop a model to describe the kinds of learning that will best support multilingual learners. She makes the point that it will promote learning for all pupils. Here are the four main elements in her model:

- learning is actively constructed;
- learning grows from and builds on the learner's prior experiences;
- there are cultural differences in the ways that pupils learn;
- learning is socially mediated, and develops in cultural contexts.

One important conclusion we can draw from this is that while learning is something that we all do and so is a common human experience, the specific ways in which pupils learn will vary from individual to individual, depending on the knowledge and experiences they bring to the classroom. This is part of what Nieto means in her use of the word 'context' in the fourth point above. In using that word, she is referring to more than just the learning environment in terms of the physical setting that surrounds the learners. Her concept of context includes all the social, cultural, emotional, affective and cognitive resources, including languages, that both learners and teachers bring to their classrooms. Other researchers besides Nieto argue that it also includes the political and historical influences reflected in the policies, resources and practices that make up the teaching and learning activities. As Nieto points out, this is a very empowering idea, as it means that every child is capable of learning. Most, if not all, pupils can learn successfully, if their teachers understand how to mediate all of the factors that influence their learning.

Bruner used Vygotsky's theories of learning to develop the notion of **scaffolding** for planning and teaching. His ideas are sometimes called 'a theory of instruction'. They are a way of thinking about how to develop teaching strategies to construct the best kinds of contexts to promote learning for individual pupils. To scaffold learning is more than providing 'support' – it is not just about helping pupils to do things, but helping them to do them independently. Beginning with context-embedded activities and gradually moving, with talk and action, towards less context-embedded work means that pupils are never left without support. At the same time, they are encouraged to move forward to the new knowledge, which is the object of the activity. Scaffolding can be developed through a variety of practical resources and multi-sensory experiences, and there are many examples of these in Chapters 4, 5 and 7.

2.2 The importance of talk for learning

Research Focus

There is a great deal of research that shows how collaborative classroom dialogues and discussions support cognitive development in individual learners. In *Constructing Knowledge Together*, Wells and Chang-Wells (1992) provide examples of talk from multilingual classrooms where pupils engage in 'collaborative sense-making' with their peers. Using Vygotsky's key concept of 'internalisation', they reveal how shared talk develops thinking.

This could be seen in the way the pupils could take part in discussions with each other, using much more complex language to consider and express their ideas than they would have been able to do on their own. The examples are similar to the discussions reported by Conteh (2003: 81–7), where pupils in Year 4 are negotiating how to carry out a 'fair test' in science to see which ball will bounce the highest. In the following example, Rehana, Yasmin and Nahida engage in collaborative talk about how to do the test, using language they probably would not be able to use on their own and co-constructing their understanding of what a fair test entails.

JC (teacher):	… to answer the question, 'this is how I will make my test fair'.
Rehana:	fair, I know how to make it fair
JC:	yes
Rehana:	with the ruler, if you hold it like that
JC:	yes
Rehana:	move it with your hand you've got to … and I'll tell you something else, you've got to bounce it from the same height
Yasmin:	do it from the same height
Nahida:	same height
JC:	why is it important to have a fair test?
Nahida:	because like, if the other ball, and they bounce it in a different way, and then … the other balls won't bounce like that, this way.

As Wells and Chang-Wells argue, this kind of discussion is essential to help pupils to develop the thinking skills they need to become fully literate, and so become good readers and writers. Taking part in discussions, in any subject across the curriculum, is also one of the key means through which pupils become confident in using the academic language they need to develop the **cognitive academic language proficiency (CALP)** that is so essential for multilingual and EAL learners, and which is discussed in Chapter 3. In the *Expert Panel Review of the National Curriculum* (DfE, 2011: 52–4), the importance of oral language across the curriculum is very clearly stated:

> *whilst it should find a particular place within the National Curriculum for English, it should also be promoted more widely as an integral feature of all subjects.*

(2011: 53)

Unfortunately, this emphasis has not come through to the 2014 curriculum. Despite the fact that most learning is mediated and accomplished in different ways through talk, we need to remember that the evidence of learning that matters is usually in writing, and pupils are almost always formally assessed through writing. It remains true that literacy is, of course, the main route to academic success in our education system. But it is essential that, as pupils progress through school, talk remains a central element of their learning. Not only do they need to *learn to talk*, pupils also need to be able to *talk to learn*, across the whole curriculum. This has many implications for your planning, which are discussed in Chapter 4.

Activity 2.4
Talk for learning in the classroom

Using the '5Ws' again, make a chart and record all the examples you can think of across one day in your classroom where you think pupils were using talk for learning in any lesson. This will show you the range of ways in which your pupils are developing their talk repertoires.

Activity	What	Who	When	Where	Why
mathematics mental starter	addition and subtraction up to 10	whole-class question and answer	start of lesson	on the carpet	to practise number bonds

2.3 The 'funds of knowledge' concept

I have talked a lot in this chapter about funds of knowledge, and in this final section, I explain briefly where the ideas that underpin the concept came from, and why it is such a powerful theory in understanding the best ways to help multilingual and EAL learners to succeed in school. The funds of knowledge concept was developed in the USA by Luis Moll and his associates (Gonzalez et al., 2005) in their work with Mexican-American families. Their definition of 'funds of knowledge' is as follows:

> *historically developed and accumulated strategies (skills, abilities, ideas, practices) or bodies of knowledge ... which are developed in homes and communities in ways that provide pupils with ... ample opportunities to participate in activities with people they trust.*

> (pp. 91–2)

Funds of knowledge are often developed through extended families and wider communities working together across geographical and political borders in such activities as farming and animal husbandry, building houses, trading goods and so on. Children's roles in these activities, though small, are often vital to the success of the whole enterprise. In their engagement with such activities, children learn a wide range of skills and knowledge. Just as importantly, they also develop a profound sense of belonging and of their own place in their communities. Such learning entails 'maximum identity investment' (Cummins and Early, 2011), an idea which links with the arguments I made in section 1.2 of this chapter to foreground the importance of identity and belonging for success in school. Another important factor that Gonzalez et al. discuss about funds of knowledge is that the children's mainstream teachers usually know nothing at all about the ways that their pupils are learning outside school. But the positive side of this is that, once teachers become aware of them, they can go on to find ways to successfully integrate such knowledge into the mainstream curriculum. There are many examples of this in Gonzalez et al.'s book.

The funds of knowledge concept has clear implications for pedagogy and links with the work of Cummins, discussed in the next chapter. The **common underlying proficiency (CUP)** concept, for example, which you can read about on pages 62–65, suggests that all the input from the different languages that an individual experiences feeds into one common resource for meaning making and expression. Both theoretical concepts of funds of knowledge and CUP surely lead us to see the need for a pedagogy that allows teachers to build on all 'the language and cultural experiences of students, their most important tools for thinking' (Moll, in Gonzalez *et al.*, 2005: 276). All pupils, and particularly EAL and multilingual learners, need safe spaces to use all their language and cultural resources in their learning, and to feel that their identities are valued and respected in the classrooms they inhabit.

Learning Outcomes Review

There are four learning outcomes for this chapter. They each focus on a particular theoretical aspect of language and learning, which is introduced in the chapter. The first is based on sociocultural theories and the notion of the ZPD; the second on functional grammar; the third on theories of learning and the role of talk in learning and literacy; and the fourth on funds of knowledge. Look back over these sections in the chapter, particularly the Research Focuses, and consider the following questions.

Self-assessment questions

1. What are some of the general implications of sociocultural theories of learning and the notion of the ZPD for organising and planning learning activities for primary pupils in general and multilingual and EAL learners in particular?
2. What are some of the differences between functional grammars and more conventional grammars?
3. In what ways do sociocultural theories of learning help us to understand the importance of oral language for learning in multilingual classrooms?
4. Why is it important to develop oral language across the curriculum? Look at the *National Curriculum Review* (DfE, 2011) and follow up some of the references to talk across the curriculum.
5. What kinds of funds of knowledge do you think pupils that you work with might possess?

Further Reading

Cummins, J. (2001) *Negotiating Identities: Education for Empowerment in a Diverse Society*, 2nd edn. Ontario, CA: California Association for Multilingual Education. This is perhaps the most comprehensive of Cummins' books. It explains in detail in a very readable way his ideas about the theories discussed in this chapter, and in the following chapter, and much more.

Gregory, E., Long, S. and Volk, D. (eds) (2004) *Many Pathways to Literacy: Young Children Learning with Siblings, Grandparents, Peers and Communities*. London: Routledge.
This is a collection of papers from across the world, which illustrate the range of ways in which children learn to read and engage with literacy. The introduction provides a clear explanation of the sociocultural approach to learning and its implications for practice.

Thompson, G. (2004) *Introducing Functional Grammar*. London: Arnold.
Not for the fainthearted, but perhaps the most comprehensive and clearest account of functional grammar, for those who wish to gain understanding of its technical aspects. It provides exercises and activities to help develop your capacity to analyse texts using a functional approach.

References

Conteh, J. (2003) *Succeeding in Diversity: Culture, Language and Learning*. Stoke-on-Trent: Trentham Books.

Conteh, J. and Brock, A. (2010) 'Safe spaces'? Sites of bilingualism for young learners in home, school and community, *International Journal of Bilingual Education and Bilingualism*, 14(3): 347–60.

Cummins, J. and Early, M. (eds) (2011) *Identity Texts: The Collaborative Creation of Power in Multilingual Schools*. Stoke-on-Trent: Trentham Books.

Derewianka, B. (1990) *Exploring How Texts Work*. Sydney: Primary English Teaching Association.

Department for Education (DfE) (2011) *The Framework for the National Curriculum: A Report by the Expert Panel for the National Curriculum Review*. London: DfE.

Department for Education and Skills (DfES)(2006) *Independent Review of the Teaching of Early Reading: Final Report* (the Rose Review). London: DfES.

García, O. (2009) *Bilingual Education in the 21st Century: A Global Perspective*. Chichester: Wiley-Blackwell.

Gonzalez, N., Moll, L. and Amanti, C. (eds) (2005) *Funds of Knowledge: Theorizing Practices in Households, Communities and Classrooms*. New York: Routledge.

Gregory, E. (2008) *Learning to Read in a New Language: Making Sense of Words and Worlds*, 2nd edn. London: Sage.

Gregory, E., Long, S. and Volk, D. (eds) (2004) *Many Pathways to Literacy: Young Children Learning With Siblings, Grandparents, Peers and Communities*. London: Routledge.

Holdaway, D. (1979) *The Foundations of Literacy*. Sydney: Ashton Scholastic.

Nieto, S. (1999) *The Light in Their Eyes: Creating Multicultural Learning Communities*. New York: Teachers College Press.

Vygotsky, L. (1978) *Mind in Society*. Cambridge, MA: Harvard University Press.

Wells, G. and Chang-Wells, G.L. (1992) *Constructing Knowledge Together*. Portsmouth, NH: Heinemann.

3 What does it mean to be multilingual?

Learning Outcomes

This chapter will help you to achieve the following learning outcomes:

- develop understanding of what it means to be multilingual from the point of view of multilingual individuals and their families;
- develop awareness of current research and debates about multilingualism in education;
- understand the ways that multilingualism and EAL have been mediated in policy, leading to the 2014 National Curriculum;
- understand why it is important to recognise and value the experiences of learning that children and young people have in their homes and communities.

Introduction

Together with Chapter 2, this chapter introduces you to the theories related to language, learning and **multilingualism** that underpin the book and which help you to understand the experiences of multilingual pupils in mainstream schools such as those you met in Chapter 1. As I said at the start of Chapter 2, theory has a crucial role to play in teaching. The theories discussed in this chapter are based on extensive international research, mostly classroom based and much of it carried out by teachers. They will help you to understand more about the multilingual and EAL learners you teach and to make informed decisions about the best ways to help them, and all your pupils, to succeed. The theories flow through the practical ideas presented in Chapters 4 to 7. To illuminate many of the theoretical perspectives in this chapter, there is an extended case study by Zofia Donnelly of one multilingual learner's experiences in school and community. There are also questions and activities interspersed through the chapter to help you think about how the theories relate to your own experiences, as well as their practical implications.

Following this chapter, which is the final one in Part 1, there is a set of 'key principles' for thinking about your planning and teaching, which will help you in planning and evaluating your own teaching strategies. These principles are illustrated by the practical examples in Chapters 4 to 7.

These are the main sections and subsections of the chapter.

1. **What does it mean to be multilingual?**
    1.1 The global context
    1.2 Being multilingual in mainstream education in England
    One multilingual learner's experience – case study by Zofia Donnelly

2. **Multilingualism in education**

    2.1 Policy constructions: assessment, achievement and the 2014 curriculum

    2.2 Cummins' theories: CUP, language interdependence, BICS/CALP

3. **The importance of learning outside school**

    3.1 Home, family and community learning contexts – 'funds of knowledge'

1. What does it mean to be multilingual?

1.1 The global context

If the stereotypic image of the monolingual English speaker who believed that they could make themselves understood by speaking English wherever they went ever had any basis in reality, it is rapidly becoming outmoded. While it is true that English is still the most widely used language in the world, its dominance has reduced substantially in recent years. English is spoken all over the world and is still the most popular language on the internet with 536.6 million users, but other languages such as Mandarin (currently with 444.9 million users) are rapidly gaining ground (Internet World Statistics, 2010). While it is now the third largest language in terms of native speakers (after Mandarin and Spanish), English is still probably the most commonly spoken language in the world. The British Council estimates that about 25% of people in the world (and rising) can speak English, but those who speak it as an additional language outnumber those who speak it as a first language by three to one. This means that about three-quarters of the conversations in the English language around the world are carried out by multilingual speakers. Around 80% of people in the world (and rising) are multilingual. So, for most people in the world, their normal everyday experiences are mediated in more than one language. Though people all over the world are interested in learning English, advancing their study and working in English-speaking countries, many more children around the world are educated in a second or additional language (most commonly English, Spanish or Mandarin) than in their mother tongue. Being multilingual is thus the normal condition, and people who see themselves as monolingual are increasingly in the minority.

It is now generally accepted that being multilingual brings benefits for educational success. Dutcher *et al.* (1994), in an extensive review of global research into multilingualism, drew some strong conclusions about the role of multilingualism in learning, which include the following:

- Development of the mother tongue needs to be encouraged to promote cognitive development and as a basis for learning the second language.

- Individuals most easily develop cognitive skills and master content material when they are taught in a familiar language.

- Individuals most easily develop literacy skills in a familiar language.

- Cognitive/academic language skills, once developed, transfer readily from one language to another.

- Success in school depends upon the child's mastery of cognitive/academic language, which is very different from the social language used at home.

- Parental and community support and involvement are essential.

These ideas are illustrated and explored through the research presented in this chapter. They have important practical implications for thinking about working with multilingual and EAL learners.

1.2 Being multilingual in mainstream education in England

In Chapter 1, there is a full discussion about multilingual and EAL learners in England, with vignettes and case studies of pupils in mainstream schools who fit in that category. When I use the term **multilingual** here, I include all those pupils who come under the 'EAL' umbrella, such as those that I described in Chapter 1, with their hugely diverse language experiences, knowledge, strengths and needs. I prefer the term 'multilingual' because I think it is broader and more inclusive than EAL. It is also more comprehensive than '**bilingual**', and includes those pupils who speak two languages. As I illustrated in Chapter 1, 'EAL' is a rather problematic term; for example, for many multilingual pupils in England (those who would be categorised as 'advanced bilingual learners'), English is not an additional language at all, but often their first and most dominant language. Using the term 'multilingual' also represents more accurately the important idea that, for such children, all their languages contribute to their knowledge of the world and their language repertoires, which they can use in communication. Multilingual children and adults do not keep each of their languages separate – they naturally switch and mix between the languages they have at their disposal. If you listen to groups of multilingual people talking to each other, you will often hear words, phrases or even sentences from English mixed with the languages they are speaking. This has been known as **codeswitching** and is increasingly frequently being described as **translanguaging**. It is especially common in children whose families have been settled in the UK for two or three generations, and who still maintain strong links with their countries of origin.

Research Focus

A new term, **translanguaging**, is currently being introduced into the literature, which moves our understanding of multilingualism beyond the term codeswitching. The term helps us to consider the ways that multilingual people can use their language resources, fluidly moving across the languages they know to express what they wish to say in the most effective ways. In Chapter 2, I argued that we need to appreciate the importance of identity for understanding language and learning; García (2009) suggests that the term translanguaging helps us think about a 'language identity' which is 'brighter and more intense' than a monolingual one, and is a reflection of the wider choices available to multilinguals to make meaning. She argues that children (and adults) switch from one language to another in order to accomplish what they want to do, and to reflect

→

their language repertoires and identities. In their communication, they are often not consciously thinking about which language to choose, but about what they want to communicate, and to whom. The following example shows this. It was collected in a small study I conducted of how children made links between their learning in **complementary** and in mainstream school settings. Sameena is an eight-year-old child, who is of third-generation Pakistani heritage. She was very proud that she gained level 3 in her KS1 maths SATs. Here she describes how she uses her knowledge of Punjabi to answer her class teacher's 'hot mental' questions at the start of the daily maths lesson. The children were asked to count in fives from 20 to 40:

> We had to count in fives, so I did it in my head in Punjabi then I said it out in English. Eek, do, teen, cha... twenty-five chey, saat, aat, nor... Thirty... Eek, do, teen, cha... thirty-five...

Her voice varies as she tries to demonstrate how the counting in Punjabi is going on silently in her head while the performance of the English numbers is producing the correct answers. She almost whispers when she says the numbers in Punjabi and then she says those in English out aloud. She repeats the counting from 1–4 and then from 6–9 in Punjabi and says the relevant number to count to 5s in English in between. In this way, she accomplishes the task, in English, set by the teacher. Sameena is focused on answering her teacher's questions in order to affirm her identity as 'level 3' by showing she is good at mathematics. The language she needs comes naturally from her repertoire, which includes both English and Punjabi numbers. Evidence like this makes us question the commonsense myth, mentioned in Chapter 1, that in learning a new language, you should not use the ones you already know as they might interfere.

Multilingual children in England often speak different languages with different family members as a perfectly normal part of their lives. They may speak English with their siblings, friends and perhaps their parents, and their home languages with uncles, aunts and grandparents, who may be living with them or contacted regularly by phone or skype. They will also, often, be learning the language of the religious books of their community and their **heritage languages** in a complementary class, which I discuss further in section 3 and in Chapter 7. In a research project that was undertaken in 2003, Aitsiselmi studied the ways that people living in one area of Bradford used languages (2004). He revealed the complex ways in which members of different ethnic minority communities use all the languages and dialects in their repertoires. He notes the complications that some of his respondents faced when asked to name the languages they spoke. One simply said, 'we just call it apni zabaan (our language)'.

Activity 3.1
Languages interview

Arrange to carry out an informal interview with a multilingual child, or preferably a small group of children, in your class (or another class, if there are no multilingual learners in your own class). The aim is to find out about the languages they speak at home, how they use them, who they speak them with, what other learning experiences they may have, etc. Here are some suggested questions. Do not turn it into a formal interview – try to have a conversation with your informants.

1. Tell me about the languages you know.
2. Do you speak other languages with members of your family? Which ones?
3. Can you remember how you learned the languages you know?
4. Can you read any other language besides English?
5. Do you go to a Saturday class or a class outside school to learn other languages?
6. Do you go to any special clubs or places of worship where you speak other languages?
7. Do you have relatives in other countries who you speak different languages with, or write letters, emails, etc?
8. Can you teach me a little bit of your language?

In talking about multilingualism in this way, we are not suggesting that EAL learners are fluent in all the languages they speak and write, but that – like the majority of people in the world – they have access to more than one language in normal and natural ways in their daily lives. The following is a useful working definition of this kind of multilingualism. It is helpful in understanding the experiences of many multilingual and EAL learners in schools in England. Hall *et al.* (2001) say that multilingual pupils are those who:

> *live in two languages, who have access to, or need to use, two or more languages at home and at school. It does not mean that they have fluency in both languages or that they are competent and literate in both languages.*

(p. 5)

This way of thinking about multilingualism makes clear the links between language and identity that were discussed in Chapter 2. An understanding and appreciation of these links is very important for success in education. Research into multilingualism and multilingual education by Cummins (2001), García (2009) and many others resonates with the view of languages that Aitsiselmi discovered in his research in Bradford, that multilingual people translanguage as part of their everyday ways of communicating. It also challenges the myth, raised in Chapter 1, that when learning a second language, the learner's first language can 'interfere' and should be avoided.

As discussed in Chapter 1, in school, pupils can very quickly pick up negative messages about the languages they speak at home, even when they are unintended. They can feel that the languages have no place, and that being multilingual is not of any value to their mainstream education and the ways they are assessed. This, after all, reflects in many ways the prevailing attitude in the wider society. I once had a long and interesting conversation with a group of Year 6 children about their languages, the ways they used Urdu, Punjabi, English, French and Arabic and how their 'monolingual' friends envied their knowledge. At the end, I asked them if they knew what the word 'bilingual' meant. One boy responded, 'is it something to do with support?', suggesting that he linked it with those pupils in school who needed support for their learning. It is essential that multilingual pupils recognise their own power and the potential for learning that being multilingual gives them – and if they don't begin to do this in the primary school, it will be too late. Underachievement at secondary school among minority ethnic pupils can be linked to the lack of support for their first languages as young learners, both in school and at home. This resonates with one of Nieto's key ideas about learning (see Chapter 2), that it grows from the cultural contexts in which the learner is situated. Instead of focusing on the 'problems' of having children in mainstream classrooms who speak different languages in other contexts, it is much more positive to consider the possibilities that could open out if we see the children's languages as resources for their learning. As demonstrated in Chapter 7, research is beginning to show that multilingual learners are eager to use their home languages for learning, and that this can have positive benefits across the curriculum, not just for learning English and for literacy. Chapter 7 gives many examples of the ways that home languages can be used as a resource for learning in mainstream schools.

One multilingual learner's experience – case study by Zofia Donnelly

Magda attends a primary school in rural North Yorkshire where just under 25% of the pupils are bilingual. She arrived from Poland in July 2013 and joined Year 6 at the beginning of academic year 2013–2014. She had learnt some English in Poland, but she felt this limited her initial interactions with her English peers as she found that they spoke too quickly for her to be able to pick up elements of a conversation. A translated version of Magda's report from Poland is shown below (see original in Figure 3.1).

Annual Learning Outcomes

Behaviour: The student is able to monitor her own behaviour independently. She is very sensitive. She is able to behave in conflicting situations. She controls her own emotions. She can concentrate for longer periods of time. Her behaviour is passive during lesson time. She works at a moderate pace. She can complete a group task. She respects group rules. She does not disturb other pupils during lesson time. She cares about her own safety. She speaks politely to her peers. She joins into various child and teacher-led activities.

Religion/Ethics: Very good.

Compulsory Education: The pupil answers questions in a full sentence, sometimes using just one word. She reads in full sentences. Sometimes she does not understand the text. Often she makes mistakes in aural tasks/exercises. Her written responses are short. She knows parts of speech. Her addition and subtraction is not always correct, she is able to add and subtract up to 100. She needs to develop her ability to form longer responses in written tasks relating to text. She is aware of her immediate environment. She can recall the names of animals and plants.

→

She is aware of 'stranger danger'. She knows the monuments in her locality. She completes artistic tasks carefully according to examples (demonstrated by the teacher). She is not a keen singer. She can play percussion instruments. She has wonderfully mastered all forms of physical activity. She cares for her personal hygiene. She is able to use a computer, the internet and various multimedia. She can recite longer versed poetry and can sing songs in English, remembering correct pronunciation; she can name objects and describe them.

WYNIKI KLASYFIKACJI ROCZNEJ

zachowanie *Uczennica samodzielnie dokonuje oceny swojego zachowania. Jest bardzo wrażliwa. Potrafi zachować się w sytuacjach konfliktowych. Kontroluje własne emocje. Potrafi się skupić na dłużej. Zachowuje się biernie na lekcji. Pracuje w umiarkowanym tempie. Potrafi przyjąć powierzone przez grupę zadanie. Przestrzega zasad obowiązujących w grupie. W czasie zajęć nie przeszkadza innym. Dba o swoje bezpieczeństwo. Grzecznie rozmawia z rówieśnikami. Włącza się do różnych form zajęć proponowanych przez kolegów i nauczyciela.*

religia / etyka   *bardzo dobry*

Obowiązkowe zajęcia edukacyjne

Uczennica wypowiada się pojedynczymi zdaniami, czasami na pytania odpowiada tylko jednym wyrazem. Czyta zdaniami. Czasami nie rozumie czytanego tekstu. Często popełnia błędy w pisaniu ze słuchu. Formułuje krótkie wypowiedzi pisemne. Zna części mowy. Nie zawsze poprawnie dodaje i odejmuje, mnoży i dzieli w zakresie 100. Należy doskonalić umiejętność rozwiązywania zadań z treścią. Orientuje się w najbliższym środowisku przyrodniczym. Potrafi wymienić nazwy roślin i zwierząt. Jest ostrożna w kontaktach z nieznajomymi ludźmi. Zna zabytki swojej miejscowości. Starannie według wzoru wykonuje prace artystyczne. Niechętnie śpiewa. Potrafi grać na instrumentach perkusyjnych. Wspaniale opanowała wszelkie formy aktywności ruchowej. Dba o higienę osobistą. Jest świadomym użytkownikiem komputera, Internetu i multimediów. Recytuje dłuższe wiersze i śpiewa piosenki w języku angielskim pamiętając o prawidłowej wymowie, nazywa obiekty z otoczenia i opisuje je.

Dodatkowe zajęcia edukacyjne

Indywidualny program lub tok nauki

Szczególne osiągnięcia

Figure 3.1 Magda's Polish report

The report evidences her personality and attitude to work. There is clear information about her performance in numeracy and literacy in her own language, as well as historical, geographical and general knowledge. This is crucial information for her new class teacher as it gives a bilingual overview of achievement for both the teacher and the student. These 'funds of knowledge' can help Magda immediately begin to feel that she is in a 'safe space' (Conteh and Brock, 2010) on her road to integration.

Importance of the mother tongue

Magda's 'buddy' (see p. 92) speaks Polish, has a good command of English and is also her best friend, enabling her to integrate more easily into school life. The interaction between them involves all four elements of language: speaking, listening, reading and writing. She understands what is going on around her, feeling safe in a multilingual teaching and learning environment. Other children are keen to be friendly with Magda and her buddy. This learning environment influences Magda positively and develops a 'safe space' linguistically for her, which she can relate to. The class teacher's strategies emphasise the importance of first language maintenance (Conteh, 2012). She feels that bilingual pupils benefit from being in a group in their own right. She acknowledges that language learning is gradual and therefore the first language is necessary for an extended period. She allows Magda to speak Polish as much as she needs to, which is a good example of translanguaging (García, 2009). Interestingly, the 'British' children are somewhat envious of Madga's and other EAL children's linguistic skills. This is positive for the EAL children as it raises their self-worth and sense of pride. The class teacher realises that different languages may share identical means of expression, for example personification in literacy, and that this can lead to effective teaching strategies in a particular subject. This provides a conceptual basis on which both the teacher and learner can linguistically and culturally build. Kenner et al. (2007) and Gonzalez et al. (2005) allude to this when they discuss the importance of 'funds of knowledge' (see pp. 44–45).

García's (2009) theory of 'translanguaging' – counteracting the idea of a **monolingualising** society – was very much evidenced when the class teacher suggested that a bilingual member of staff would have sensitivity to the linguistic difficulties and obstacles experienced by Magda. She recognised that this would also contribute to building the 'safe space' for learning. The lesson observation transcribed below (from January 2014) illustrates how easy it is to misjudge a conversation with a multilingual child who is at the early stages of learning English, if the means of communication is solely English. Magda and her teacher are discussing the Christmas holidays.

T: Good Christmas?
M: Yes
T: Stay here (pointing finger down) or Poland?
M: England
T: What presents did you get?
M: *Shrugs shoulders*

→

T: You get presents?

M: Ah, yes

T: What presents?

M: *Puzzled look*

T: You get book? Computer? Clothes (*pointing to pictures in First Thousand Words*)

M: Ah, yes, yes. Book, computer, trouser, big present. Christmas good (*smile appears on face*).

Following this, I, as a visiting teacher, continued the conversation with Magda in Polish. The responses were now in full sentences. Adjectives and verbs were included and a fuller picture of Christmas was gained, without prompting, which included the Christmas Eve dinner and the members of the family present at the event.

T: A jaka była pogoda podczas Bożego Narodzenia?

M: Było bardzo zimno. Padał śnieg. Sankowaliśmy się (*big smile*).

T: Było Was dużo na Wigilii?

M: Cała rodzina zjechała się. Wesoło nam było.

T: A co jedliście na kolację wigilijną?

M: Jadłam barszcz, pierogi, karpia, uszka, różne sałatki, makowiec i sernik. Pyszne!

T: Gdzie poszłaś o północy?

M: Cała rodzina poszła na Pasterkę gdzie śpiewaliśmy kolędy.

Translation:

T: What was the weather like at Christmas?

M: It was very cold. It was snowing. We went sledging.

T: How many of you were present at the Christmas Eve dinner?

M: The whole family got together. We were happy.

T: What did you have to eat for the Christmas Eve dinner?

M: I had beetroot soup, dumplings, carp, ravioli, various salads, poppyseed cake and cheesecake. Delicious!

T: Where did you go at midnight?

M: The whole family went to the 'Shepherd's Mass' where we sang carols.

The teaching assistant felt that while Magda needed to develop her competence in English, this had to happen alongside her need to maintain her appropriate, overall curriculum level. Staff agreed that the first language, where at all possible, should be accessed and maintained, rather than gradually dwindling to a level of general understanding, which could mean that the child's overall development and achievement could suffer. Interestingly, although Magda is fluent in speaking her own language, there is evidence in her written work that she has some difficulties (see her report from Poland, above). It emerged that, for approximately 10% of the time, she writes the words phonetically as she has heard them spoken. This then raises the issue of whether or not she is reading enough in Polish in order to internalise and memorise Polish phonics and spelling patterns to be able to maintain her written level parallel with her speaking and listening

→

levels. Following Conteh's (2012) theory of the importance of fostering the first language in order to develop the new language, it begs the question whether Magda's native language is suffering and what impact this may have on her overall learning. Magda's lessons, where possible, are translated into Polish and tasks for written work are also set in Polish. Magda has taken part in lessons involving discussion as a member of a peer group where Polish is the main means of communication. With the help of the teaching assistant, the tasks were explained and completed in Polish and then the pupils' responses translated into English. Then the class teacher marked them using the *APP (Assessing Pupils' Progress) Writing Tracker*. The teacher wrote positive and encouraging feedback in English, which was then translated into Polish. Assessment for learning was evident through peer group marking, traffic lights, smiley faces and thumbs-up.

Learning across the curriculum

Magda accesses the full school timetable, along with the rest of her class. She finds PE, games, music and drama similar to Poland and partakes fully in these activities, including performing in the school play about World War II. Magda felt it was easy to learn the songs for this because, as she said, 'the same thing was sung every time over and over, and it was easy to remember it' suggesting that repetition reinforced the meaning for her. The teacher is frustrated that there is insufficient time to devise tailor-made resources for a bilingual learner. In an ideal world, she sees the value of a language induction programme. She also feels that time constraints mean there is very little flexibility in shifting away from the National Curriculum in order to meet Magda's specific needs. There was a feeling that this was, to a degree, specialist work and the class teacher welcomed any support available from specialists.

As a visiting teacher, I was able to contribute to teaching in science and literacy. This paragraph gives brief examples of some of the outcomes. During a KS2 class-integrated science week, all the Polish-heritage children were grouped together and Magda worked with a Polish peer group, which gave a lot of opportunities for discussion. Tasks were explained and discussed in Polish and recording was done in English. Through this, Magda was able to understand deeply the notions of 'prediction' and 'result' relating to science experiments. This involved looking at which materials dissolve and do not dissolve e.g. soil, sugar, salt, sand and taking part in the filtering of these materials. Answers were recorded in English. The literacy lessons related to the topic of World War II. The class had been reading the *The Silver Sword* by Ian Serraillier (1956). Having learned about World War II in Poland, Magda was totally familiar with this area in literacy. She mentioned that she had spoken to her grandmother about the war, who was able to contribute historical information linked to the story's setting. This endorses Kenner *et al.*'s (2007) points about the important role that all members of a family play in teaching, learning and transcending knowledge through generations.

Learning outside the school

The involvement of her grandmother in Magda's learning is a positive example of linking home and school, a key element of the funds of knowledge philosophy. Moreover, as the theories

$\rightarrow$

presented in Chapter 2 illustrate, learning the first language nurtures and influences conse-quent learning. Pedagogy and policy strategies relating to the multilingual child are found not only at the chalkface but very much in the school as a whole and in the wider community. Magda's profile illustrates this clearly and also demonstrates practical ways in which multilin-gual children can access the right to foster their linguistic and cultural heritage. To support this further, Magda was informed of the Polish school in the nearby large town and of its benefits, including Polish reading and writing and keeping in touch with Polish culture and traditions. Her involvement in this would work very much in her favour, not just in maintaining and devel-oping her skills in Polish, but in developing her local knowledge, meeting more children from her background, learning and identifying with various groups and networks already in place. Magda's mum hopes to enable her family to uphold Polish values, celebrations and culture as she feels this is an important element of her children's identities. Being part of this com-plementary learning community supports a holistic approach to a child's well-being through family, school and community, echoing Bronfenbrenner's (1979) ecological theory relating to the role of the family and its links to community culture and language and identity. Magda has vis-ited the complementary school and hopes to start attending in the new academic year.

2. Multilingualism in education

2.1 Policy constructions: assessment, achievement and the 2014 curriculum

No child should be expected to cast off the language and culture of the home as he {sic.} crosses the school threshold, nor to live and act as though school and home represent two totally separate and different cultures which have to be firmly kept apart.

This much-quoted advice from the Bullock Report (DES, 1975: 286) is supported by what we know from research about the best ways to promote children's learning, and illustrated in Zofia's case study of Magda. We need to know about how children learn in different contexts, both in and out of school, and to use this knowledge to develop official policies and classroom practices which are truly inclusive. But, of course, to achieve inclusion through recognition and acceptance of diversity in this way is not easy.

The National Curriculum, first introduced in 1988, recognised above all that every pupil has an entitlement to learn English, but did not consider the importance of their heritage and home languages. Its key aim was that, by the age of 16, all pupils would be able to use spoken and written standard English confidently and accurately. Through all the years since its introduction, that aspiration has not changed. But it has been described as a 'monolingualising' curriculum, as no specific reference was made to pupils who may have two or more languages in their repertoires. There was no sense that, for such pupils, their entitlement to English might need to be secured in different ways from 'monolingual' children. The National Curriculum Council did produce some guidance about language diversity (NCC, 1991) but it epitomised what Safford (2003: 8) calls 'the contradiction at the heart of education policy in England' for multilingual pupils, i.e. that their home languages and cultures could be positively 'celebrated' in school in different ways, but not that they should form a central element in their learning of the curriculum. The circular welcomed language diversity as 'a rich resource', and went on to offer some guidance and support for teachers working with multilingual pupils. Essentially, it suggested that pupils could be encouraged to use their first languages for learning only until their proficiency in English was strong enough for them to move to the exclusive use of English. In this way, other languages were not seen as relevant to learning.

This approach to accommodating pupils' home languages and cultures in their learning has come to be known as **transitional bilingualism** by many writers. It is based on the assumption that English and knowledge of English should replace rather than grow from knowledge of other languages. Research has shown that transitional bilingualism can lead to restricted concept learning and problems with achievement. Instead of this, the theoretical and practical ideas in this book all promote a model of **additive bilingualism**. I believe that the best way to help multilingual pupils learn and achieve to their fullest capacity is certainly to value their multilingualism, but to go much further than this. The English language needs to be seen as part of their ever-growing language repertoires, not as a replacement for their other languages. There is a great deal of research that supports this idea, such as the work of Cummins (2001), which is described in the next section. The key practical implication of this is that we need to develop strategies that allow pupils to play to their strengths, using the languages they know best to take ownership of and manage their learning. This underpins the practical ideas discussed in the second part of this book, and particularly in Chapter 7.

When the National Literacy Strategy was introduced in 1998, there was still no recognition of the importance of multilingualism for learning. The first version of the Framework for teaching (DfEE, 1998) – the famous 'blue file' and its accompanying 'lunchbox' of training materials – made no mention at all of multilingualism as a possible factor, either positive or negative, in learning to read and write. An additional section to the files was later distributed, which included provision for EAL learners, together with those with SEN and those in vertically grouped classes in small schools. Making such a simple link between SEN and EAL was unfortunate. It masked the fact that many EAL learners actually have *language* needs rather than *learning* needs. It is no doubt true that they often need support, but this support can sometimes come from allowing them to use the languages they already know, rather than ignoring this knowledge. The same link between EAL and SEN was made in later versions of the National Curriculum, and has now become accepted, in many ways. Curriculum 2000 had an introductory statement about 'inclusion' (DfE, 2012) that talks about the 'potential barriers to learning and assessment' for pupils with SEN, disabilities and EAL.

Research Focus

Assessment

Cummins (2001) argues, based on his research with French-English multilingual pupils in Canada, that the merging of multilingualism with SEN can have negative academic outcomes. It can lead to multilingual pupils being assessed as having learning needs and then placed in SEN groups, when in fact their needs are for specific language support in order to develop their competence in listening, speaking, reading and writing in order to cope with the demands of the curriculum. His theoretical models can help us to understand the ways in which multilingual learners' experiences of language and learning need to be seen differently from those of children who do not 'live in more than one language'. Some of his key ideas are explained in the next section.

Safford (2003: 8) suggests that we have 'two conflicting policy paradigms' in curriculum and assessment in England:

> ...the celebration of ethnic and linguistic diversity, and the universal model of language development and assessment.

For teachers working with multilingual children, assessment is a complex issue, as Safford (2003) shows in her teacher's account of trying to assess pupils from a wide range of language and cultural backgrounds in following official requirements. Many writers (e.g. Baker, 1996) spell out the negative implications for children's learning when assessment policies demand that we treat children as if they are all the same and expect them to attain the same targets in the same ways. Ultimately, this denies multilingual learners the means to develop to their full potential and, in effect, closes the door to educational success for them. Providing 'equal access' does not mean that we should treat all children in the same way. Doing this means that we often ignore some of the things that some children can do and the skills they have. We need to recognise the ways that national testing procedures do not give us a 'fair test' of all our children's full capabilities.

Imagine what the fish and the seal are thinking and feeling as they listen to what they have to do in the so-called 'fair' test in Figure 3.2! Can you also think about what skills and expertise they have, which they cannot use in climbing a tree? These skills are ignored in the 'universal' test. Allwright and Hanks (2009: 21) also point out the negative effects on teachers' views of their pupils, arguing that 'when teachers are constrained to operate standardised assessment procedures, they will find it difficult to resist the associated view of the learner'. In Chapter 6, you will find a full discussion of assessment across the curriculum in relation to multilingual learners.

The 2014 curriculum

Despite the recent, and continuing, rapid growth in numbers of multilingual pupils in our schools, there is very little reference to EAL learners in the new National Curriculum, or guidance about how to meet their needs. In a document of 224 pages, there are 94 words that make direct reference to English as an additional language. To repeat what I say in the introduction, here they are:

Figure 3.2 A universal approach to assessment?

4.5 Teachers must also take account of the needs of pupils whose first language is not English. Monitoring of progress should take account of the pupil's age, length of time in this country, previous educational experience and ability in other languages.

4.6 The ability of pupils for whom English is an additional language to take part in the national curriculum may be in advance of their communication skills in English. Teachers should plan teaching opportunities to help pupils develop their English and should aim to provide the support pupils need to take part in all subjects.

(DfE, 2012: 8)

Moreover, the model of language that underpins the curriculum is very different from the one that I presented in Chapter 2, where I argued that we need to think about the ways that languages are used, and who uses them, i.e. the functional model (see pp. 35–39). Instead of this, the National Curriculum has what I call a 'naming the parts' model of language, where terminology and definitions take precedence over thinking about texts in their contexts of use. An example from the extensive glossary in the 2013 curriculum document illustrates what I mean:

The surest way to identify nouns is by the ways they can be used after determiners such as 'the': for example, most nouns will fit into the frame "The ___ matters/matter."

Nouns are sometimes called 'naming words' because they name people, places and 'things'; this is often true, but it doesn't help to distinguish nouns from other word classes. For example, prepositions can name places and verbs can name 'things' such as actions.

Nouns may be classified as common (e.g. boy, day) or proper (e.g. Ivan, Wednesday), and also as countable (e.g. thing, boy) or non-countable (e.g. stuff, money). These classes can be recognised by the determiners they combine with.

(DfE, 2013: 9)

Such an approach can drive teachers to think that they need to teach through disconnected words, phrases and sentences to make sure that their pupils can reproduce the definitions and identify the **word classes** in formal tests. This is unhelpful, not just for EAL learners, but for most pupils. It is essential that we take a critical approach to the curriculum and recognise that, if we are genuinely committed to helping multilingual learners to succeed, a much more theoretically informed approach to pedagogy is needed. The limited 'guidance' does begin to point the way forward, by indicating two key issues.

- First, it suggests the importance of knowing about where our EAL pupils come from, about the languages they speak and their educational backgrounds.

- Second, it makes the important point about how EAL pupils' subject and conceptual knowledge may be ahead of their knowledge of English.

The second is a key issue in planning and assessment, particularly at secondary level, and there is extensive coverage of this in Part 2.

Before we get too depressed, it is important to remember that, as teachers, we have the professional knowledge and authority to make informed decisions about how we interpret official policies – teachers are the experts, and the ones who know their pupils best. Zofia's case study above is just one illustration of the ways in which skilled and committed teachers can develop learning opportunities for their EAL pupils that benefit their learning in positive and creative ways. The following section is a brief example of how, starting from a principled theoretical position, teachers can use policy documents to develop effective learning for their EAL pupils in one curriculum area.

Making links in the curriculum – the KS2 Framework for languages

It is very important to make links whenever possible across curriculum requirements in order to play to the strengths of multilingual learners. An example of where this can be done very fruitfully is in the teaching of other languages and in literacy. Pupils categorised as EAL learners bring positive resources into this area of the curriculum, if the approaches to teaching and learning are designed to help them make links between the languages they know and the new languages they are learning. Since 2002, the KS2 Framework for Languages (DfES, 2002) has offered new ways of thinking about language to primary teachers, and some of the ideas have been extended into secondary. This is the policy document underpinning the introduction of modern foreign languages into primary schools (PMFL), as part of the New Labour reforms. The approach it advocates is very different from the way that 'foreign languages' are mediated in the 2014 KS2 curriculum, which is more akin to traditional secondary MFL teaching. Rather than seeking to develop proficiency in a specific language, PMFL is much more about building generic strategies for language learning and developing the positive values, attitudes and awareness that learning languages provides. The framework has two 'cross-cutting strands', Knowledge about language (KAL) and Language learning strategies (LLS). These are intended to stimulate children's creativity and ensure an international dimension in learning across the curriculum. Different languages can even be used for different learning intentions across the strands.

The objectives in the two strands lend themselves to a wide range of activities that, besides promoting children's learning of different languages, can get them exploring their local communities and the wider society as they develop global awareness and understanding. They can be met in ways that include families and affirm their funds of knowledge as well as those of multilingual staff in the school. These kinds of activities promote the best kinds of learning for multilingual pupils, and examples of these can be found throughout Chapters 4, 5 and 7. In Chapter 5 (pp. 117–119) there is an extended example of how Years 5 and 6 pupils used familiar stories to develop KAL as part of their literacy lessons.

Activity 3.2
KS2 Framework for languages: making links

Get hold of a copy of the KS2 Framework for languages – it is online, if you cannot find a hard copy (see the reference below for links to the three parts). Read the guidance on page 11 about the structure of the framework, in particular the information about the Knowledge about language (KAL) and the Language learning strategies (LLS). Then, look at the KAL and LLS objectives for one of the years (it doesn't matter which, but you could do this with colleagues and each focus on a particular year, then share your findings). Think about how they link with children's learning of literacy, and what activities you might do, to help your children achieve them.

2.2 Cummins' theories: CUP, language interdependence, BICS/CALP

Research Focus

Cummins' ideas are well known throughout the world, and provide powerful explanations for many distinctive features of multilingualism. They show how the learning of first and additional languages is always linked, and how academic language proficiency needs time to develop. The key difference in Cummins' thinking and writing from many other writers about second language acquisition is that he includes learners' first languages in the processes of learning a new language. This is why his work is more relevant for understanding the needs of multilingual learners in England than models taken from other models of language learning such as **Second Language Acquisition (SLA)** and **English Language Teaching (ELT)**. I will discuss three of his main ideas that are very relevant to understanding the needs of multilingual and EAL learners; the first two, **Common underlying proficiency (CUP)** and **linguistic interdependence**, are helpful in understanding the ways that multilingual learners process and use their languages and the third, **BICS/CALP**, is a way of thinking about the kinds of language that successful learners need to know.

CUP and linguistic interdependence

It used to be believed that moving between different languages could be confusing for multilingual individuals. So, in teaching, one of the main 'myths' that developed (see Chapter 1,

p. 25) was that the languages had to be kept separate in order to avoid the first language 'interfering' with the new language being taught. Cummins proved how wrong this was by observing the ways that multilingual children actually used their languages, both in oracy and literacy. He recognised many years ago that languages were not kept separate, but that multilinguals switched between their languages in ways such as those described in section 1.2 above. So he concluded that, instead of a separate proficiency for each language that they could speak, read or write, all human beings have some kind of common underlying proficiency (CUP) for language. This could be imagined as a sort of reservoir of language understanding, knowledge and skill, which is drawn on to make the meanings that the language user needs in the context in which they are situated. This clearly links with the ideas about language repertoires and choices that I discussed in Chapter 2.

Cummins' famous 'iceberg' diagram represents the CUP. My version is in Figure 3.3. The horizontal line is the boundary between the language user's inner capacity in their brain, and the outside world. The tips of the iceberg represent the languages being used, whether it is LI, L2 or any further languages. These draw on the part of the CUP iceberg which is hidden, but which supports all the language choices that the user makes.

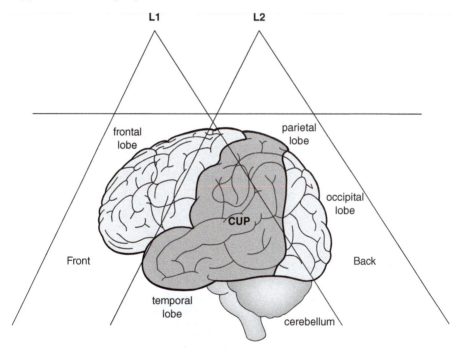

Figure 3.3 Cummins' iceberg diagram of the CUP

The idea of the CUP clearly links with the notion of language repertoires. It also underpins the theory of linguistic interdependence, which Cummins describes as follows.

> *Knowledge and understanding of one language links to knowledge and understanding of new languages – this is especially significant in relation to literacy.*

The reference to literacy is very important in education. The following vignette, of a nine-year-old 'new arrival', provides compelling evidence of the ways that literacy in his first language opened up his learning of English.

Vignette

Making links

Mushtaq was nine years old when he arrived in England from Bangladesh, unable to speak any English at all. On his first day in school, he was sent to join my 'language support' group where we were doing some story-based activities. He spent the whole lesson in silence while the rest of the group worked on an African story about the sun and moon. The next day, Mushtaq gave me a piece of paper covered in neatly written script. I did not know what the script was, and was amazed when I discovered that on the paper was the sun and moon story, written out in Bengali. His classmate had re-told the story to him, and he had written it out for me. So it turned out that Mushtaq was already highly literate in Bengali. The following week, he contributed to a trilingual book that we made about the story. The writing in the top right-hand corner of the page is his (see Figure 3.4).

Over the next few weeks, Mushtaq contributed to several other trilingual books like this, and also made some story tapes where he read stories in Bengali for other children to listen to. Within six months, he was one of the best readers in his class – in English.

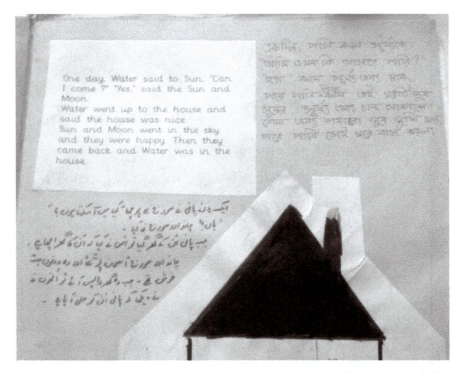

Figure 3.4 Children's trilingual book

Once again, the key message here is that we must find out about the languages that our pupils can speak, read and write outside the mainstream classroom. It does not matter if we cannot speak, read or write them ourselves – I cannot speak Bengali, and did not even know what language it was when I first saw the script on Mushtaq's paper. We must value the knowledge that our pupils bring to the classroom and help them find spaces in which they can construct their own ways of learning, beginning from what they already know.

BICS (Basic Interpersonal Communication 'Skills')/CALP (Cognitive Academic Language Proficiency)

These well-known, but sometimes misunderstood, acronyms underpin an important idea that Cummins has developed over the years, about the ways that languages are learnt and used. It has relevance for all pupils, but is of particular relevance for multilingual and EAL learners. BICS/CALP are sometimes described as 'skills' or even specific features of language to be taught and tested, but this does not really reflect what they are. It is sometimes said that BICS is more to do with spoken language and CALP with written, but again this is not really what Cummins meant.

Basically, BICS refers to all the social, everyday things we do with language, embedded in familiar contexts, such as greetings, conversations, retelling, describing, recalling, and so on. CALP, on the other hand, refers to all the – usually more cognitively demanding – things we need to do with language in order to achieve academic purposes, such as explaining, analysing, arguing, and so on. BICS relates to the kinds of language which develop first, usually in face-to-face, highly contextualised situations. CALP develops through engaging in more decontextualised situations and discussions, and so is often seen as more complex. CALP has two main dimensions: it is the **cognitive language** which we need in order to think and do cognitively demanding things, such as investigating, exploring ideas, analysing, hypothesising and solving problems. It is also the kind of **academic language** that we find in textbooks, lecture notes and so on, and which we need to learn to write in order to succeed, as we progress through the education system. This often has features such as the passive voice, vocabulary with Greek and Latin roots, the use of metaphor and personification and the use of abstract nouns, such as 'information' from 'inform' and 'hunger' from 'hungry'.

Cummins has developed the notions of BICS and CALP over the years, and he now writes of them as a continuum, rather than as two separate aspects of language. Educated adults move back and forth across the continuum according to what they are trying to do with language, and we should be aiming to develop this capacity and confidence in the children we teach. The BICS/CALP model is relevant for all children – all children need opportunities to use a wide range of language and languages in different ways in their learning. The model also has implications which are specific to multilingual learners. Cummins found that children entering school with very little English would develop BICS (i.e. fluency in the kinds of language interactions suggested above) quite quickly, usually within 18 months to two years. But full capacity in CALP would take a lot longer. Cummins concluded that this could take at least seven years. It is also clear that the progression from BICS to CALP is not automatic, and that children need to be supported as they move from learning through context-embedded activities to the more context-disembedded tasks they are expected to perform as they move through primary school and on to secondary.

The BICS/CALP ideas can help us to see through the confusion between language needs and learning needs that I talked about in section 2.1. Children enter school unable to speak English and at first, they can seem to do very well. They learn to do all the social things they want to do in English, and everything seems very promising. Then, things slow down as the long slog to develop CALP begins. Sometimes, pupils do not seem to make progress at all. This is because their thought processes are still largely in their first language, and they are – literally – learning to think in a new language. Unfortunately, it is at this point, usually, that the assessment wheel starts turning and pupils find themselves placed in SEN groups and even diagnosed with learning difficulties. Worse still, in secondary schools they can be placed in sets where they do not have the opportunity to attain high GCSE grades, no matter how hard they try. Often, all they need is time and the opportunity to continue using their first language to support their thinking in the new language.

3. The importance of learning outside school

3.1 Home, family and community learning contexts – 'funds of knowledge'

As I explained in Chapter 1, it is important to remember that, for many multilingual learners, formal learning does not end when they go home from their mainstream school in the afternoon. Many attend community-based classes in mosques, synagogues, churches, temples and other settings where they learn to read and write their heritage languages and the languages of their religions. These are known as 'supplementary', or increasingly commonly 'complementary' schools. Many students go on to take GCSE and A-level exams in Urdu, Gujerati, Bangla, Polish, Chinese and other languages. There is a growing body of research into the ways that children learn in their complementary classes, and the links that they can make between their complementary and mainstream learning, such as the example of Sameena in section 1.2 of this chapter. In Chapter 7, you will find an extended discussion of learning in complementary schools, and examples of activities of the kind that could easily be developed in mainstream classrooms.

Many multilingual pupils experience learning in different contexts, but often, their teachers in one system know very little about what goes on in the other. There is no link between their different learning contexts, and children are left to make their own sense of the learning demands on them. One Year 6 boy, whom I interviewed as part of a small research project, talked about his learning in the mosque in a very insightful way, describing the different things his teachers did in his mosque school and his mainstream school. He ended with a very powerful and deeply felt comment:

> I think the mosque and school should be together ... it's like the same thing ... you're teaching something, you're getting knowledge from people.

As well as finding out about the languages that the pupils in your class speak, it is very worthwhile to find out about the different schools they attend, and what they are learning there. This will make them feel that you are interested in them and value them as individuals. It will also increase your knowledge of your pupils' home and community experiences.

Activity 3.3
Learning in home and community

In a school with EAL learners, find out what the policies are for working with parents and families to support their children's learning. Think about how they might help to access family 'funds of knowledge'.

Find out if the school has a home–school liaison officer (HSLO) and ask if you can talk to them about what they do, and how they work to develop links between home and community and school. If you can, try to visit a community or complementary school.

We also need to be aware of the ways that children are learning in the home, and of how this contributes to the 'funds of knowledge' (see Chapter 2) that they bring to their learning in more formal, mainstream settings. Children are often involved in interpreting and translating for family members who may have very limited English; they take part in extended family activities such as weddings and celebrations for Eid and other religious events. They sometimes travel to their countries of origin or to visit relatives in other parts of the world. All of these experiences offer possibilities for learning, with the added benefit of affirming the children's identities as members of dynamic, diverse communities. Families mediate every child's first learning experiences, and it is the responsibility of the school to build on this in whatever ways it can. Ideas for this, related to learning across the curriculum, are provided in Chapters 4, 5 and 7.

Learning Outcomes Review

The four learning outcomes for this chapter are all to do with understanding the language and cultural experiences of the multilingual and EAL learners you will be teaching. Here are some questions to consider in thinking about these outcomes.

Self-assessment questions
1. How have your views about multilingualism and multilingual learners been changed by the ideas you have read about in this chapter?
2. How do your personal experiences of language diversity and multilingualism in school compare with the ideas you have read about in this chapter?
3. In what ways could we assess multilingual and EAL learners' learning without depending on their capacities in English? Can you think about how you could do this with children that you teach?

Further Reading

Conteh, J. (2003) *Succeeding in Diversity: Culture, Language and Learning in Primary Classrooms*. **Stoke-on-Trent: Trentham Books.**
Based on research with successful multilingual KS2 learners and their families, this book develops many of the ideas discussed in this chapter and includes evidence from interviews with families and teachers and classroom observations to illustrate the arguments developed.

Hall D., Griffiths D., Haslam L. and Wilkin Y. (2001) *Assessing the Needs of Multilingual Pupils: Living in Two Languages*, **2nd edn. London: Fulton Books.**
A clear, practical and concise account of the tensions between 'EAL' and 'SEN', with useful guidance for planning. This will help you ensure that the language and cognitive demands of your activities provide support and progression for multilingual learners.

References

Aitsiselmi, F. (2004) *Linguistic Diversity and the Use of English in the Home Environment: a Bradford Case Study*. Department of Languages and European Studies, School of Social and International Studies, University of Bradford.

Allwright, D. and Hanks, J. (2009) *The Developing Language Learner: An Introduction to Exploratory Practice*. London: Palgrave Macmillan.

Baker, C. (1996) *Foundations of Multilingual Education and Multilingualism*, 2nd edn. Clevedon: Multilingual Matters.

Bronfenbrenner, U. (1979) *The Ecology of Human Development*. Cambridge, MA: Harvard University Press.

Conteh, J. (2012) *Teaching Bilingual and EAL Learners in Primary Schools*. London: Learning Matters/Sage.

Conteh, J. and Brock, A. (2010) 'Safe spaces'? sites of bilingualism for young learners in home, school and community, *International Journal of Bilingual Education and Bilingualism*, 14(3): 347–60.

Cummins, J. (2001) *Negotiating Identities: Education for Empowerment in a Diverse Society*, 2nd edn. Ontario, CA: California Association for Multilingual Education.

Department for Education (DfE)(2012) *Including All Learners*. London: DfE. www.education.gov.uk/schools/ teachingandlearning/curriculum/b00199686/inclusion (accessed 21 February 2012).

Department for Education (DfE)(2013) *The National Curriculum in England: Key Stages 1 and 2 Framework Document*. London: DfE. https://www.gov.uk/government/uploads/system/uploads/attachment_data/file/244216/English_Glossary.pdf (accessed 21 December 2014).

Department for Education and Employment (DfEE) (1998) *The National Literacy Strategy: Framework for Teaching*. London: DfEE.

Department of Education and Science (DES) (1975) *A Language for Life* (The Bullock Report). London: HMSO.

Department for Education and Science (DfES) (2002) *Key Stage 2 Framework for Languages*, parts 1, 2 and 3

http://webarchive.nationalarchives.gov.uk/20130401151715/http://education.gov.uk/publications/eorderingdownload/framework%20for%20languages%20-%20part%201.pdf

http://webarchive.nationalarchives.gov.uk/20130401151715/http://education.gov.uk/publications/eorderingdownload/framework%20for%20languages%20-%20part%202.pdf

http://webarchive.nationalarchives.gov.uk/20130401151715/http://education.gov.uk/publications/eorderingdownload/00171-2007dom-en.pdf (all accessed 17 November 2014).

Dutcher, N., in collaboration with Tucker, G.R. (1994) *The Use of First and Second Languages in Education: A Review of Educational Experience*. Washington, DC: World Bank, East Asia and the Pacific Region, Country Department III.

García, O. (2009) *Bilingual Education in the 21st Century: A Global Perspective*. Chichester: Wiley-Blackwell.

Gonzalez, N., Moll, L. and Amanti, C. (eds) (2005) *Funds of Knowledge: Theorizing Practices in Households, Communities and Classrooms*. New York: Routledge.

Hall, D., Griffiths, D., Haslam, L. and Wilkin, Y. (2001) *Assessing the Needs of Bilingual Pupils: Living in Two Languages*, 2nd edn. London: David Fulton.

Internet World Statistics (2010) *Internet World Users By Language: Top Ten Languages* http://www.internetworldstats.com/stats7.htm (accessed 17 November 2014).

Kenner, C., Ruby, M., Gregory, E. and Al-Azami, S. (2007) How research can link policy and practice: bilingualism as a learning resource for second and third generation children. *Naldic Quarterly*, 5(1): 10–13.

National Curriculum Council (NCC) (1991) *Linguistic Diversity and the National Curriculum*, circular number 11. York: National Curriculum Council.

Safford K. (2003) *Teachers and Pupils in the Big Picture: Seeing Real Children in Routinised Assessment*. Watford: NALDIC.

Principles for planning for multilingual learners

These six key principles for planning lessons and activities for multilingual learners have been developed from the ideas discussed in Chapters 1 to 3. In Chapters 4 to 7, I will use these principles to present practical examples of activities and strategies to promote multilingual children's learning in speaking and listening, reading and writing across the curriculum.

1. Developing a positive ethos that reflects language and cultural diversity at whole-school level supports home–school links, and encourages families and schools to work in partnership.

2. In the classroom, providing opportunities for multilingual pupils to use their first languages in everyday activities opens out potential for learning and affirms their identities.

3. Pupils need every possible opportunity to explore ideas and concepts orally in all subjects across the curriculum.

4. Before beginning extended writing activities, pupils need plenty of chances for collaborative discussion and practical experience.

5. Promoting awareness of language systems and structures by allowing multilingual pupils to analyse and compare the different ways of saying things in the languages they know helps develop their CALP and also promotes language awareness among their monolingual classmates.

6. Providing extensive opportunities for hands-on experience enhances language learning and learning more generally.

PART 2
PROMOTING LEARNING – PRACTICAL APPROACHES FOR MULTILINGUAL AND EAL LEARNERS

4 Planning across the curriculum for multilingual and EAL learners

> ## Learning Outcomes
>
> This chapter will help you to achieve the following learning outcomes:
>
> - develop understanding of how to plan to promote learning across the curriculum that links with pupils' home and community experiences;
> - develop awareness of different ways to plan and organise group work to promote learning for multilingual and EAL learners;
> - gain greater understanding of the importance of speaking and listening for learning generally and for multilingual and EAL learners in particular.

Introduction

All of the ideas presented here build on the theories about language and learning that are introduced in Chapters 2 and 3. The learning outcomes for the chapter are linked with the six principles for planning at the end of Part 1. In this way, you can see how oral language is a central factor in learning, and how you can build it in to your planning for all subjects across the curriculum. This, of course, is important for all pupils, not just multilingual and EAL learners.

Interspersed through the sections of this chapter, there are three case studies by practising teachers which illustrate some of the key themes in the chapter: first, Pete Ruse and Linda Sandler discuss joint planning between an EAL specialist and a subject coordinator; then Catherine Porritt gives an overview of the Talking Partners Programme and finally Ana Korzun describes the way she developed differentiated planning for a new arrival. There are also questions and activities to help you to think further about the ideas that you are reading about as well as to think practically about your planning in all subjects across the curriculum. There are some suggestions for further reading at the end of the chapter.

These are the sections and subsections of this chapter:

1. **Planning across the curriculum**

   1.1 Starting points – developing plans

   1.2 The Cummins' quadrant

   1.3 The importance of joint planning

   Planning an RE lesson – case study by Pete Ruse and Linda Sandler

2. **Organising classes and groups for learning**

    2.1 Planning for collaborative talk

    The Talking Partners Programme – case study by Catherine Porritt

    2.2 Including new arrivals in your lessons – buddies and mentors

    2.3 Differentiation in planning

    Differentiation in planning for one EAL learner – case study by Ana Korzun

1. Planning across the curriculum

1.1 Starting points – developing plans

Developing medium-term plans or units of work and short-term plans to promote the learning of multilingual and EAL pupils is complex. Do not be tempted simply to depend on plans you find on the internet or in published schemes of work. They may give you some starting-points and resources, but you need to spend time thinking about the pupils you will be teaching and constructing your own planning to meet their needs. Then you will understand much more fully what you are proposing to teach, and why. This will pay off in the quality of your lessons as well as in the learning and behaviour of your pupils. You will also build up a stock of ideas and strategies that you will be able to use over and over again.

For pupils who are at the early stages of learning English, there are always two strands involved in their learning. They need to learn:

- the curriculum content;

and they also need to learn to use…

- the English language in increasingly academic ways in order to access the curriculum.

Of course, this is true for all pupils, but it is clearly more important for many EAL learners who often need to catch up with their peers in terms of their knowledge and use of English. Maggie Gravelle (1996, p. 8) explains this point thus:

> *Bilingual learners need both the curriculum that motivates and has relevance for them and the systematic language development and feedback that enables them to achieve within it.*

It is sometimes the case that some multilingual learners will be ahead of some of their classmates in their understanding of the concepts and content in particular curriculum subjects, but they may not have the English vocabulary and grammar to show you what they know. This is often the case with mathematics. Such pupils can find it quite frustrating if they are given tasks to do that are far below their academic capability in a subject. It is very important that you find out whether your 'new to English' pupils have been to school in their countries of origin, and try to get some idea of what they may have learnt. There are some ideas in Chapter 6 (section 3) that can help you to do this. You need to think about teaching the curriculum content in interesting and challenging ways, alongside making sure you accommodate the time necessary to teach the specific English language that your pupils need in order to access and express their understanding of that content.

The functional model of language and grammar introduced in Chapter 2 will help you to clarify the language demands of the subjects you are teaching. It reminds us that we need to be clear about two important language-related elements in planning, which are:

- what we are expecting our pupils to be able to *do* with the language they are learning;
- the *kinds* of language they will need to do these things.

In order to do this, we need to go beyond thinking about just the key vocabulary that our pupils may need in order to learn concepts and content in different subjects across the curriculum. We also need to think about how to help them become familiar with the ways the language is organised grammatically and textually – in other words, the kinds of spoken and written texts (or **genres**) they will be using and constructing in their learning. For example, in science, they will no doubt be following instructions – as well as making up their own – and perhaps writing reports; in history and other humanities subjects, they will be taking part in discussions and debates, writing narratives and so on.

Remember that texts are spoken as well as written. We now feel very familiar with the idea in literacy of teaching the different text types pupils need to know for their writing, but the suggestion that we can also teach them the different ways in which they need to use language in speaking is a fairly new one. This will be discussed further when we introduce the Cummins' quadrant in the following section.

Activity 4.1
Text types for learning

Make a table like the one below showing the main text types that pupils are expected to learn about in literacy. In the second column, list the subject areas for which you think each text type is relevant. Remember that the text types can apply to different subjects. In the third column, list some of the different kinds of texts that you think pupils need to be able to learn and use in different subjects across the curriculum. Include spoken as well as written texts. There are some examples to start you off.

Text type	Curriculum area	Example of text
Reports	science, history	• A written report of a 'fair test' that the pupils have conducted. • An oral role play of warriors reporting to their chief what happened in a Viking raid on a Northumbrian village.
Discussion texts		
Reference texts (explanations)	geography	• A weather forecast as part of a radio or TV programme.
Persuasive texts		
Recount		
Instructions		

Relating different text types to areas of the curriculum in this way helps us to think about the language demands of all the different subject areas and of the particular tasks we are asking our pupils to do. If we combine this with the first principle for planning (p. 70) and identify ways in which we can make the curriculum content build on the prior experiences of our learners, this will help in working out how to make the content and the language of the tasks we plan more interesting and relevant for multilingual and EAL pupils – indeed for all pupils. There are ideas in Chapter 5 for strategies and resources that help you to do this.

An excellent way to begin planning a topic or a new area of the curriculum is to make a **KWHL** grid. This is a variation on the well-known KWL grid – '**K**now, **W**ant to find out and **L**earn – the '**H**' stands for 'How can I find it out?'. This encourages you to ask four rather than three questions about the new area for learning, to clarify the main elements to be included in your planning, as well as begin to think about how you might teach it.

- What do my pupils already *know*?

- What do I *want* them to find out? (check the curriculum requirements)

- *How* will they find this out?

- What will they *learn*?

Figure 4.1 depicts a KWHL grid, which a trainee teacher made to begin planning for his Year 3 class to do a science-based topic about the life cycles of plants and animals. Notice how he included in the first column both the *content* knowledge and the *language* knowledge from different areas of the curriculum that he knew his pupils had done and so would be able to bring to their new topic.

What we know (K)	What we want to find out (W)	How we will find this out (H)	What we will learn (L)
• The *hungry caterpillar* story • Words to describe family members: *mum, dad, grandma, brother, baby, sister,* etc. • Names for animals and their babies: *sheep/ lamb; dog/puppy; cat/ kitten* • How to write instructions	• Life cycle of butterflies and moths • Different parts of a plant • Stages of development in plants • Stages of development in animals • Life cycles of different kinds of animals	• Plant seeds in the classroom and observe them growing • Look carefully at plants and compare to illustrations in books or on the internet • Use information books to find out about animals in other countries • Outing to Butterfly World	• How to draw butterflies, plants and animals • How to read carefully to find out specific information • How to put pictures, words and sentences in the correct order to provide information

Figure 4.1 A KWHL grid

When you complete the first column, spend a bit of time thinking about both the language and the content knowledge that your pupils already have. This will help you to generate a bank of both content ideas and language for planning your activities. The language functions from Wolfe and Alexander, quoted in Chapter 7, section 1.2 (p. 162), will help you do this. The next step is to think about how to sequence the activities to develop appropriate progression in your planning. The Cummins' quadrant is very helpful for this.

1.2 The Cummins' quadrant

Cummins' ideas about the common underlying proficiency (CUP), basic interpersonal communication 'skills' (BICS) and cognitive academic language proficiency (CALP) are explained fully in Chapter 3. They are important in your planning process for thinking about how to structure activities and sequences of activities to promote learning. The learning highlighted in this sequencing has three dimensions, namely:

- conceptual development;
- language development;
- progression in learning.

Cummins' concept of the CUP emphasises *all* the knowledge of any and all languages that pupils bring to their classrooms and how this can be seen as a resource to support their learning of any subject. We need to find ways to tap into the full repertoire of our pupils' language resources. There are many ideas in this chapter to help with this.

The BICS and CALP concepts have many implications for medium-term planning and also for lesson planning. Activities need to be structured and sequenced in order to support pupils' progress in their learning from context-based, cognitively less demanding activities that mainly use informal language (BICS) to the more academic and cognitively demanding tasks that require more academic language (CALP). We need to start with activities at the level where pupils can use their BICS-related language skills, and gradually move into activities which are more demanding cognitively and where CALP-related language capacity and knowledge come into play. In this way, we will be scaffolding pupils' academic learning and providing the means for them to develop deep and rich conceptual understanding of the subjects they are learning. At the same time, we will be providing increasingly demanding and language-rich activities that will scaffold pupils' learning of English and enhance their confidence as speakers and writers of English in a wide range of ways.

Cummins developed a quadrant framework to show how BICS and CALP could be fed into planning and teaching through identifying, developing and sequencing appropriate tasks in different curriculum areas for all pupils, and especially for multilingual learners (see Figure 4.2).

Each axis can be thought of as continuum, with contextual support on the horizontal axis and cognitive demand on the vertical. The horizontal axis, moving from left to right, encourages you to think about sequencing your activities from context-embedded learning, with lots of hands-on activities, artefacts and so on to activities which are less dependent on the immediate context. The vertical axis relates to the degree of cognitive demand in a task, which closely relates to the language demands. It moves upwards, from tasks that are not very demanding to increasingly cognitively challenging activities.

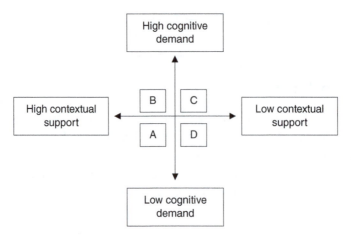

Figure 4.2 The Cummins' quadrant

Good planning for concept learning and language development will ensure that pupils always move from activities with strong contextual support to those which are less contextually supported in these ways. At this higher level, activities will be much more dependent on the linguistic cues and the pupils' own knowledge of language, as well as what they have already learnt. The following vignette, in mathematics, shows how your activities could progress through the quadrants.

Vignette

Progression in mathematics in Reception

If you are teaching children in Reception or Year 1 about the properties of different shapes, the progression from activities with low cognitive demand and high contextual support to activities with high cognitive demand and low contextual support might look something like the following.

- *Quadrant A*: activities which involve pupils in touching and handling plastic shapes, talking about them, making patterns and pictures with them, describing, matching and beginning to compare them.
- *Quadrant B*: activities which move pupils to seeing and talking about the shapes as visual representations, such as matching shapes to pictures, finding objects in the classroom which are particular shapes, talking about what is the same, similar or different about a collection of shapes or pictures.
- *Quadrant C*: activities which encourage pupils to think and talk (and perhaps write and draw) about the shapes without immediate visual or concrete support, such as answering questions (or making up their own questions) about a square and how it is different from a triangle, making a chart about the similarities and differences of shapes, drawing shapes following instructions given by the teacher or other adult, or their peers.
- *Quadrant D*: there should be no activities in this quadrant as they would not promote the pupils' learning.

In Conteh, 2006 (p. 11), I described this progression through the three quadrants in Cummins' diagram like this:

> *Beginning with context-embedded activities and gradually moving, with talk and action, towards less embedded activities means that children are never left without support, and at the same time are being encouraged to move to the new knowledge which is the object of the activity.*

The kinds of activities that fit into each quadrant, defined by their conceptual and language demands, are categorised in Figure 4.3.

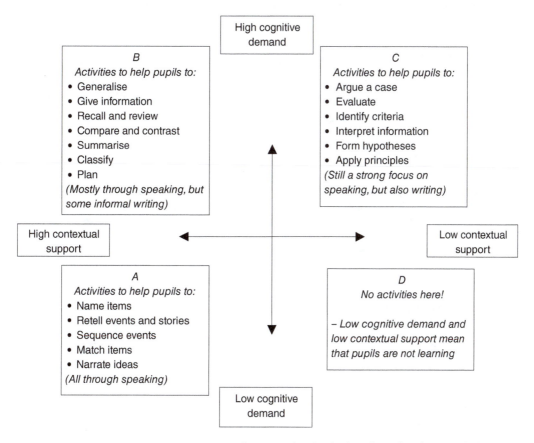

Figure 4.3 Planning for learning using the Cummins' quadrant

Oral language is clearly important for activities in quadrant A, but it remains just as important as we move to activities in quadrants B and C. At all stages, talk remains a key vehicle for learning. It is vital that you plan activities which provide opportunities for pupils to use talk in more sophisticated and adventurous ways, at the same time as supporting them in trying out ways of speaking which may not be familiar to them. This helps them both to develop confidence as speakers of English and to think about and learn the new concepts in the subject you are teaching. Pauline Gibbons (1998) talks about the 'teacher-guided reporting' stage of the activity. This equates to quadrant. Wells and Chang Wells (1992) discuss the 'three modes of interaction' which pupils need to develop through talk, and which they regard as essential for learning:

A: Shared understanding

B: Expert guidance

C: Reflection

These also correspond in many ways to Cummins' quadrants A, B and C. At the reflection stage, pupils will be talking in much more formal, discursive and analytic ways than they were at the start. Thus, their understanding of the content is enhanced and they are also using the language they will need for writing.

To illustrate this, let us think about planning a set of story-based activities in literacy, which is relevant for both primary and secondary pupils. The key learning objective may be to have pupils write their own version of a story or write from a particular character's viewpoint. A sequence of activities based on the story that helps pupils to progress through quadrants A, B and C might look something like Figure 4.4. The pupils may not actually get down to any formal writing at all in the first three or four lessons, but when they do come to the task of writing, they will have a rich stock of words, structures, ideas and understanding of the story to bring to it.

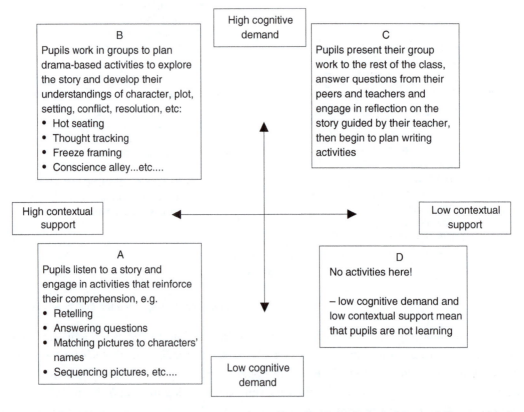

Figure 4.4 Cummins' quadrant and literacy planning

Hall *et al.* (2001) have some examples of planning using Cummins' quadrant which show the progression of activities in science and there are examples of planning using the quadrant diagram on the NALDIC website (Franson, 2011).

Activity 4.2
Planning for progression

Using the Cummins' quadrant and the ideas and diagrams above, look at some of your planning in a particular area of the curriculum. See if you can identify which activities might fit into each of the four quadrants, and consider whether you could re-order the activities to build in better progression or whether you need more activities in any quadrant.

1.3 The importance of joint planning

Increasingly in schools, there are teachers and Higher Level Teaching Assistants (HLTAs) who have specific responsibility for EAL learners. It is essential that they have time to work together with subject coordinators, subject teachers in secondary schools and class teachers in primary schools to develop joint planning which meets both the language needs and curriculum needs of pupils. This takes time, but the benefits are considerable. The following case study, written by a subject coordinator and an EAL teacher in a secondary school, shows how this can be done.

Planning an RE lesson – case study by Pete Ruse and Linda Sandler

At a regular hub meeting, a Local Authority (LA) EAL consultant and EAL co-coordinators from across the LA decided to embark on a project to video examples of good practice as part of a training resource. In order to give the project the attention it required, the head of EAL in one secondary school negotiated its completion as a target in her next Performance Management (PM) cycle in a way that fitted in with whole-school priorities related to literacy development. The focus would be talk as a rehearsal for writing in science and RE. The head of EAL involved one of her team to work with the Science Department and she herself worked with the Humanities Department.

The Head of EAL, Head of Humanities and the teacher with responsibility for RE decided that Year 11 were the priority for the Humanities Department, given the critical importance of exam results to the school. A group was selected that included some International New Arrivals (INAs, with fewer than four years in the UK), some of whom were at an early stage of acquiring English language. The head of EAL was already supporting this group. The language priority identified was writing answers to GCSE exam questions that required an extended response. The topic to be covered in the weeks that fitted in with the project timetable was 'The causes of war', using Darfur, Sudan as a case study, a part of the 'Peace and Conflict' module of Edexcel GCSE RE.

The chosen Year 11 group consisted of 11 boys and 18 girls. One learner had a statement of special educational needs. Learners had a range of attainment from a predicted F grade to a B. Nine learners were INAs, five of whom were in the early stages of English language development. Three of these were at very early stages and of these, two had had full schooling in their country of

$\rightarrow$

origin and had good academic skills in their first languages (L1). Both were being entered for GCSE RE, one for the full GCSE and the other for half a GCSE due to having missed too much content to be entered for the full one. In a planning meeting, the two teachers looked at learner grouping, deciding on groupings that supported language development and encouraged talk for learning. The criteria taken into account were mixed levels of English language development; target grade; gender; friendship (or not); and previous engagement with content. The two early stage EAL learners, for example, had high target grades, reflecting their academic competence in their L1s.

This grouping represented a departure from usual practice in the RE teacher's classroom, where the early stage INAs were usually grouped together at the front of the classroom so that the EAL support teacher had easy access to them. As an outcome of the project, this subject teacher has now reconfigured her teaching space to facilitate group work and talk for learning. As head of RE, she is in a position to influence the practice of other RE teachers in the department by incorporating the frameworks, activities, techniques and strategies explored in this project into the schemes of work for next year. Joint planning naturally led to joint lesson delivery, building on existing ways of working in a more considered and explicit process than is generally possible in the bustle of daily life in a busy school. Both teachers felt that this further deepened their teaching partnership. This resulted in a stronger voice for the EAL practitioner, which led to a clearer language focus in the curriculum generally. Both agreed that pupils' learning behaviour improved as a consequence, with the early stage EAL learners working more independently and all learners being more engaged.

The videoed lesson had the following learning objectives (notice how they include both curriculum and language):

- To identify reasons why countries go to war.
- To analyse reasons behind a recent conflict.
- To reflect on your own view and to explain whether you think that war is the best way to solve conflict.
- To become more confident in using PEEL in an extended answer question. (PEEL is a model paragraph structure – Point Evidence/Example Explanation Link back to question – used by the English Department, see Figure 4.5)
- To unpack models of appropriate academic language.
- To use the four language skills (listening, speaking, reading and writing) in context.
- To practise academic language in both speaking and writing (explanation and analysis).

The first phase of the lesson activated learners' prior knowledge of the topic. The task was to select four possible justifications for war from eight possibilities, which included some red herrings. This involved reading for meaning, having a purpose for talk and engaging with good models of spoken and written English in a supportive group dynamic. It introduced subject and topic specific vocabulary in context as well as formal academic English language and grammar patterns.

The main phase of the lesson involved reading a case study of the conflict in Darfur, Sudan and identifying four causes of conflict. Less confident readers were supported by more confident ones and there was a clear purpose for reading. The text itself was challenging enough to generate talk about what it meant. Later on, in a videoed evaluation conversation between the two teachers, they explored the tension between how accessible a text is and how challenging it is. Challenging texts provide good models of academic English and can be made accessible through the activities packed around them. Texts made accessible by stripping them of more complex language structures deny learners experience of the kinds of language they need to achieve highly.

→

The main phase went on to an activity where learners had an empty grid of four rows, each representing a paragraph, and four columns, one each for Point, Evidence, Explanation and Link back to the question. Early stage EAL learners also had sentences on cards to fill the grid with. Put together correctly, this resulted in a model text of four paragraphs (see Figure 4.5).

Explain the causes of a recent conflict. (8 marks) A conflict is .... There are several reasons why countries and communities go to war.				
	POINT	**EVIDENCE**	**EXPLANATION**	**LINK BACK TO QUESTION**
Firstly	Historical conflicts between countries or communities are sometimes left unsolved and lead to war or civil war.	For example, in Sudan during the conflict of 2003–2007 the Government were accused of persecuting non-Arabs.	Thus, religious and ethnic issues and disagreements were deepened and made worse.	Therefore, non-Arabs were involved in the conflict in Darfur because they were persecuted by the Sudan Government.
In addition	Some countries or communities go to war to protect their own natural resources, or are attacked so that others can take control of their natural resources such as oil or land.	For example, in Sudan in 2003–2007 there were food and water shortages because of drought and people were forced to move to different areas and start new lives.	Thus, the original people living in these new areas had fewer resources because there were more people.	Therefore, because people in Darfur were unhappy with this happening they felt forced to fight back to protect their land and fight against the Government for allowing it to happen.
Furthermore	Some countries or communities go to war because they feel they need to protect their interests and identity.	For example, in Sudan in 2003–2007 the people living in the west were segregated and felt they were being treated unequally by the Government.	Thus, the people of the western districts wanted to be independent of the Sudan Government and set up their own state.	Therefore, people in Darfur being segregated and marginalised led to conflict because they felt they had to fight to protect their interests and identity.
Finally	Some countries or communities go to war because of conflict between different groups battling for power and status.	For example, in Sudan in 2003–2007 some ethnic groups were armed by the Sudan Government and encouraged to attack other ethnic groups and take their land.	Thus, many people were unable to defend themselves and were killed or displaced into refugee camps, where they remain.	Therefore, some groups being armed and supported by the Sudan Government at the expense of other groups caused conflict in Darfur.

Figure 4.5 PEEL Grid for the lesson

Evidence sentences all start with 'for example'; explanation sentences all start with 'thus' and link back to the question sentences, which all start with 'therefore'. This 'filling a grid' activity enabled early stage EAL learners to move bits of text around and try them out in various places

→

in the process of deciding what goes where. This is an example of minimal production demands allowing focused engagement with text instead of the pressure to fill the grid with writing, which might distract early stage EAL learners into copying chunks of text. More advanced learners had the opportunity to fill the grid with their own notes. In this way the task was easily differentiated.

This activity generated lots of task-focused talk among the pupils. The two teachers could circulate and listen in to each group to identify individual and common issues. In this instance, this Assessment for Learning (AfL) process resulted in the early stage EAL learners being encouraged to use their bilingual dictionaries to look up words they had identified as key words. This allowed them to make connections with their L1 and access the content of the text efficiently, especially where vocabulary was not concrete. It allowed them to make connections with what they already knew, bringing this to the reading of the text. Listening in to group talk also identified common issues with words and expressions. 'Plagued by' and 'drought' were two notable examples in this lesson. There was also discussion about what reading strategies learners were using. Encouraging a 'meta-stance' on their learning in this way helps learners identify what they are doing and this enables them to get better at it. The main phase was concluded with a self-assessment activity which encouraged learners to evaluate what they had done and how confident they felt about it and consider the next steps they might take to make progress. The final phase of the lesson was writing an answer to an extended answer question, giving learners the opportunity to use the text structure and language that had been modelled in the lesson. The resulting texts provided the 'grist for the mill' for the next lesson.

Both teachers valued the way that having language objectives for the lesson as well as content objectives organised the lesson. Learners had the opportunity and support to engage in task-focused talk that prepared them for engaging with a challenging text that modelled the type of writing demanded by the curriculum. The two teachers noted how the organisation of the classroom and the nature of the activities had a positive impact on learning and language development. For example, embedding the use of appropriate sentence starters for specific purposes (e.g. 'thus' for explanation) allowed the teachers to use them as prompts for eliciting appropriate sentences. The pre-planning resulted in a more equal teaching partnership. The resulting video material is proving to be a useful training resource, for example, for newly qualified teachers and those undergoing initial training, where grouping for purpose and integrating language development objectives into lessons can be highlighted.

A key point that emerges from thinking about planning in this way is that, alongside planning the content and progression of the teaching activities, we need to think carefully about ways of organising classes and groups of pupils to facilitate their learning, and this is the focus of the following section.

2. Organising classes and groups for learning

2.1 Planning for collaborative talk

If you want to provide as many opportunities as possible to promote talk for learning, you need to have flexibility in organising both the classroom space and the seating and positioning of your pupils, as Pete Ruse and Linda Sandler's case study shows. In this section, we will consider ways of grouping pupils for talk. But simply placing pupils in groups around tables does not mean that they will engage in learning through talk. Your activities need to be structured so that you progressively build your pupils' understandings of the content and concepts they are learning. The kinds of talk that your pupils need to do should become increasingly complex as they move through the activities. They should be expected and able to talk in increasingly well-informed, thoughtful and independent ways about the topic, and to engage in increasingly sophisticated discussions with their classmates. The activities you plan need to provide pupils with clear aims and purposes for their talk, clear structures to guide their work and clear outcomes so that they know what they are expected to achieve. The following vignette illustrates this.

Vignette

Planning for progression in oral activities

Figure 4.6 shows part of a medium-term plan developed by a trainee teacher on the popular classic narrative poem *The Highwayman*, followed by two extracts of talk from different activities in the unit of work. The plan was designed to be carried out over two weeks with a Year 5 class. Notice how the key learning objectives are in terms of pupils' understanding and knowing, and how they are linked with the outcomes, which are in terms of what pupils will be able do (at different levels, of course) at the end of each set of activities. Notice also how there is a strong focus on oral work, and a mix of whole-class and group activities across the plan.

Key learning objectives	Main activities	Resources	Assessment/ outcomes
Understand the structure and key features of narrative poems, and ways of performing them	• Introduce *Highwayman* poem with pictures and artefacts – focus on setting, events, characters (mainly whole class, some group work) • Develop performance of whole poem, in groups	• Story sacks, artefacts from poem, pictures on IWB • Audio or video recorder to record performance	All pupils take part in performance of poem
Understand the differences between literal and figurative language	• Pupils in groups explore different characters in poem (using drama techniques) • Pupils in groups explore literal and figurative language used to describe characters, write prose description of their own character • Pupils consider main events in the narrative from range of viewpoints, and write narratives from different viewpoints	• Large cut-outs of different characters from poem, thesauruses, dictionaries, simple props for role-play work	All pupils produce a piece of narrative writing based on the poem

Figure 4.6 Medium-term planning for The Highwayman

Here are two examples of talk, one from a lesson at the start of the plan and one from halfway through. Read them and then reflect on them using the questions in Activity 4.3 (see below). The first example of talk comes from the first lesson the trainee taught. She was introducing the poem to her class, and began by discussing the history of roads and stagecoaches, and the ways that highwaymen held up coaches. After this, she showed her pupils pictures of the characters and setting of the poem (the pictures by Charles Keeping are excellent) and then read the first section to them. She wanted to make sure that her pupils had remembered the main facts of the poem, so she led a whole-class discussion.

Teacher: Who do you think is the main character in the poem?
Child 1:   The highwayman.
Teacher: That's right … who are the other important characters?
Child 2:   Bess, the black-eyed daughter.
Teacher: That's right, and who else?
Child 3   Tim, the ostler.
Teacher: Who can tell me what an ostler is?
Child 1:   Someone who looks after the inn.
Teacher: Not quite … he works in the stables, so he looks after the…
Child 4:   Horses.
Teacher: That's right. Who can find a simile to describe Tim the ostler?
Child 3:   Hair like mouldy hay.
Teacher: That's right.

The second example of talk came in the middle of the second week of work. The class had rounded off the first week by carrying out a performance of the whole poem, which had been videoed, and which they enjoyed very much. Following this, the pupils had been divided into mixed ability groups, and each group was given a different character to study. They did **hot seating** activities in their groups to explore the decisions made by their characters in the poem. Following this, the teacher reorganised the groups so that each group included pupils who had studied different characters (this is called **jigsawing**). Each jigsaw group was given a different section of the poem to discuss from the viewpoints of the different characters, in such a way that the whole poem was covered. Then the class came together to review their findings about the different characters. This was to be followed in the next lesson by a writing task – each pupil was to plan a piece of writing where they wrote a narrative from the point of view of one of the characters in the poem: Bess, the landlord's beautiful daughter, Tim the ostler, King George's men or the highwayman himself. Here is part of one jigsaw group's discussion – they were talking about the end of the poem, after King George's men had killed the highwayman.

Child 1:   I don't think the highwayman should have come back for her, he should have known he would get killed.
Child 2:   But how was he to know that King George's men would come to the inn and set a trap for him?
Child 1:   It was really sad when he died … they shouldn't have killed him.

Child 3: I think he deserved to die, highwaymen killed a lot of people … It shows you about Dick Turpin in York Museum and how he killed people on the roads.

Child 1: But he really loved Bess, and he made a promise to her.

Child 3: He should have realised that they would be out to get him.

Child 2: They shouldn't have killed Bess the black-eyed daughter as it wasn't her fault.

Child 4: They should have got Tim with the tatty hair.

Activity 4.3
Planning for collaborative talk, understanding *The Highwayman*

When you have read the two examples of classroom talk, think about the following questions.

1. Which quadrants in Cummins' framework do you think the discussions fit into?
2. What do you think are the teacher's objectives in the first discussion?
3. What roles do the pupils take in this discussion?
4. What do you think the teacher needed to do in order for the pupils to take part in the second discussion?
5. What role does the teacher take in this discussion?
6. What roles do each of the four participating pupils take in this discussion?
7. What are some of the differences between the kinds of language the pupils use in each extract?
8. Do you think the second discussion is successful? Why?

In the *Highwayman* activities, there were several different kinds of groupwork:

- *Whole-class*, with a teacher-led question and answer session.

- *Mixed ability groups*, where pupils were sharing ideas about something they all knew about.

- *Mixed ability (jigsaw) groups*, where pupils had to share knowledge about different parts of the poem.

At other points in the *Highwayman* plan, the pupils would be engaged in different kinds of group work in order to complete different tasks.

- *Talking partner (pairs)*, for recalling and reinforcing knowledge and sharing ideas quickly at different times.

- *Friendship groups*, for the oral performance.

- *Ability groups*, for the writing task, so that support could be provided to meet the different needs of the pupils.

Other ways of grouping your pupils could be as follows.

- Pair to four, pupils are given a task to do in pairs, and then join up with another pair to make a group of four to share their findings – this can be a good way to form mixed-sex groups by having the pairs same-sex, then joining pairs of boys with pairs of girls.

- Listening triads: three pupils work together. Child A and child B carry out a task, which could be following instructions, telling a story, etc. Child C's role is to be the observer. They have to make careful notes of what is said, then report back to the rest of the class in the plenary part of the lesson.

The Talking Partners Programme – case study
by Catherine Porritt

Talking Partners is an intervention developed in Bradford in 1999, initially to address the needs of EAL pupils, although it has been shown repeatedly to benefit all learners. Pupils who are included in Talking Partner groups typically make two or three times the progress that would be expected over a year, but within the period of a ten-week intervention. What follows is a description of the Talking Partners programme, after which there is a more detailed description of how Talking Partners as an intervention was introduced into one primary school and the results that were achieved. Investment in training is an integral part of the programme: all adult partners, teachers, TAs and so on, need to be trained to deliver the programme. They learn about the rationale behind the programme as well as the methods and successes of past work, joining in the activities to experience the programme first hand. At the end of the training, they are asked to work collaboratively as a group to produce plans.

Talking Partners comprises a range of talk-related activities which are particularly beneficial for EAL learners. The key aim is to provide opportunities for pupils to hear, use and most importantly to rehearse meaningful language in supportive contexts. The demands for performance are deliberately reduced to enable students to experiment and thus extend the repertoires of English language structures which they understand and use. Comprehension is supported through the use of concrete objects, artefacts, puppets, high quality images or short extracts of selected text. This means that interest and enquiry are provoked separately from the language to be taught. In this supportive context, and through careful modelling of target language, the pupils hear and rehearse language, developing and extending beyond the known into the unknown. For each activity the cognitive challenge is designed to remain high while the language demands are carefully constructed to become increasingly precise as confidence in speech and comprehension in English grows. This progressive development allows for support initially to be provided and then withdrawn step by step as the child's confidence and ability grow, following Cummins' terminology, from context embedded to context reduced learning.

The range of activities covers the spoken language demands of the English curriculum and focuses on the functions of the language. For example in *Picture Talk*, the pupils work with their partner to build a group description of the selected picture. In *Same and Different*, the group identify the features that two objects or images share, and compare and contrast the differences. In *Question Circles*, the group collaborate to produce long lists of questions that could be asked of a picture, character, or expert. There are ranges of picture sequencing activities, *What is it?* and barrier games, that allow the pupils the chance to think and practise language, always in fun contexts. The materials and activities can be used in class with assorted groups of pupils across a range of needs including EAL. With concrete objects

→

to discuss and carefully modelled speech to rehearse, this approach has been used effectively in many schools. Small group work is an essential element of the programme, where the Talking Partner (TP) works with groups of three pupils to scaffold and encourage more sophisticated uses of language. Three is judged to be the optimum size allowing enough chance for rehearsal and practice whilst maintaining interest, as no child has to sit and listen for extended periods without the chance to interact. Three 25-minute sessions are spread across the week. Here are some typical activities.

Picture Talk: A group of Year 2 pupils is working on a Picture Talk activity based on an illustration from *The Pirates Next Door* story, showing a pirate ship parked outside a house.

TP: Let's look carefully at this picture. There is Tilda, riding her bike, and then look, she sees that pirate ship! She is surprised! What else can you see?

Ch. 1: It's got wheels

TP: Oh yes, the pirate ship is on a trailer with wheels.

Ch. 2: There's a shooter, its got ... um ... um ...

TP: Yes, on a ship there are big guns, they are called cannons, and they shoot cannon balls like those (pointing to illustration) Do you want to say that?

Ch. 2: Cannons, the ship got cannons ...

TP: Who is this in the picture?

Ch. 3: Um ... he is up ...

Ch. 2: He is Jim lad

TP: Yes, it's Jim, the pirate and he's up the ladder.

The discussion continues for a few minutes until everything in the picture has been considered, or the time available runs out.

Character Role Play stage 1: A group of Year 2 pupils (who are all advanced bilingual learners) is working on *The Pirate Next Door*, exploring character. They are taking the role of the neighbour telephoning complaints to the council. The children and TP together develop ideas of the imagined problems caused by the pirates and formulate one or two as complaints to the council. With a telephone prop, the pupils take turns to ring up the council officer played by the TP, who responds in role, clarifying and agreeing with their complaints, and modelling back the complaints to be addressed.

Ch 1: They got swords, big swords.

TP: Oh, they are carrying swords, I see, they are carrying sharp swords, that could be dangerous.

The next child is invited to make a complaint, either the same sword issue, or another. Such interaction enables precision, differentiation of the scaffolding provided and allows TPs to consider each child as an individual. For this group, the priority is increasing the range of vocabulary used; other groups may focus on language structures. The same materials can be used for pupils to develop curriculum-relevant spoken language and comprehension in parallel, small-group activities. This provides ideal opportunities for pre-teaching the vocabulary and language structures that will be necessary to allow pupils full access to the cognitive academic language necessary for the whole-class lessons.

→

Introducing Talking Partners into one school

This section describes how the programme was introduced into one primary school which was faced with a rapidly changing intake of pupils. In describing the school's experience of introducing the programme, we can consider the reasons they adopted the programme, their experience of delivering it and the impact on pupils' progress. The school felt they needed to address three particular needs: firstly to help the recently arrived EAL pupils move beyond the very early naming stages of English; secondly to support the significant number of pupils in the school with speech, language and communication needs; and thirdly to address the need across the school to help all pupils to learn to speak and listen to each other more effectively.

In the first term, a LA specialist EAL teacher visited the school for a morning each week. For three weeks all the teaching assistants were withdrawn from class for a course of three mornings training in the programme. The lead teacher for oracy was also trained in order to support and advise the teaching assistants during the programme delivery, and assist in the initial and final assessments. Following the training, the teaching assistant partners spent an additional morning together with their oracy coordinator planning the first few weeks of their programme and sourcing support materials such as images relevant to the curriculum to be studied in class, picture sequences to illustrate scientific or story sequences, artefacts to describe, puppets and small world figures for story-building activities, and texts rehearsing academic language vocabulary that would need explanation and modelling. The oracy coordinator liaised with class teachers to ensure the plans and resources would support the topics to be studied in each year group, so that the plans once resourced could be further developed to support the curriculum in class.

The large number of pupils identified for the project gave the opportunity for initial collection of data, to be compared with post programme data for those pupils within and without the programme. An additional comparison was possible within the data assembled: between EAL pupils and the English first language (E1L) pupils, who were identified as having additional communication needs. One group of pupils was selected to receive the programme immediately. The intervention was built of three sessions a week covering six different activities, each selected to rehearse a different aspect of language. The week typically included news telling, story telling, describing and comparing, question circles, character study and reporting. The teaching assistants reported that the pupils really liked the variety of activities. Pupils really enjoyed going out in their little groups of three with an adult on a regular basis. For this project, each trio of pupils was selected to contain at least one EAL child, someone each child could build a relationship with, a possible friend, and a child who may have an additional speech language and communication need for whom additional rehearsal is so necessary. Frequently visitors would overhear pupils asking teaching assistants 'Is it Talking Partners today?'

The programme materials provide a staged model of introduction for each activity, initially with high levels of support through modelling, concrete artefacts and pictures to describe, gradually reducing stage by stage as pupils built confidence and language skills. In this way, dependency on the adult partners was reduced. The adult role gradually changed to one of formative assessment and recording. They recorded which activities pupils could do independently, which with support and how frequently. This colour-coded record indicated clearly where the pupils were developing, and where more support was needed. The teaching assistants commented how

$\rightarrow$

simple the recording was to complete. At the beginning of the programme all pupils identified for the programme were achieving only very low scores on published tests. Teaching assistants leading the groups began to notice changes in the children quite quickly, and during the course of the programme, class teachers and parents frequently became aware of their child's increased confidence in experimenting with spoken English. But observed, recordable evidence is needed to check progress, as well as more subjective observations. This is where the recorded sampling of pre and post intervention speech and responses to class activities provides evidence.

The contrast between their responses from the beginning and from the end of the programme showed clearly the children's progress. For example, one picture showing a mother about to remove wellington boots asks, 'What is the mother going to do?' A reception class child answered at the beginning of the programme, 'Off your shoes'. At the end, her response was, 'taking girl's shoes off, no boots, they off'. Where initially her response was telegraphic, using single words to convey meaning together with phrases collected from the classroom, by the end of the programme she had learned how to nominate people, how to indicate possession, she knew some different verbs and parts of verbs, she had an increasing range of vocabulary and was self correcting. In another activity, shown a picture of a man climbing a ladder to rescue a cat, she was asked, 'What is the man doing?' She replied initially, 'Up cat, tree up'. At the end of the programme, her answer, 'Man getting cat down on up the house', shows she is now able to nominate people, use prepositions, use appropriate participles of verbs, knows positional vocabulary and has an increasing vocabulary.

An older EAL boy, asked the same questions requiring a future tense response, initially said, 'He's putting the girls' shoes', by the end of the programme, 'Take the boots off the girl'. When asked about rescuing the cat, he replied initially 'Man he get cat' and when prompted added, 'and going up'. After the programme his response was 'Going into the ladders and trying to get that cat', and with a further prompt, 'house'. The completeness of the phrases, with appropriate use of tenses, determiners, articles and demonstratives, together with the increased range of vocabulary, all demonstrate the increased range and control of spoken English he had gained during the course of the ten-week programme.

One teaching assistant reported the change in the pupils, which reflected their growing social confidence as well as their learning, in the following comments:

> You saw with your own eyes. A lot of the pupils were insecure, the pupils had problems in class, but when you worked in the small talking partners group, after they were so much better in class. It was not just one thing, it was the package. The Czech pupils stayed only with the Czech pupils but when they were in mixed tiny groups they made links with other pupils and stayed friends with these pupils which was even better.

Another teaching assistant commented:

> The fast paced short activities were appealing, moving on from one stage to the next. Having something in front of them to talk about gave them confidence, and let them build on what they already know.

The statistical data collected in the pre and post assessments confirmed these observations. Testing at intervals allowed comparison between two periods, before and after the intervention.

$\rightarrow$

Whilst all pupil groups made most progress when on the intervention, it is interesting to note that for EAL and E1L pupils, many of whom have communication difficulties, they all continued to make considerable progress after they had completed their course of Talking Partners. This is in marked contrast to the pupils who for a variety of unforeseen reasons were not included in any group, where their age-related spoken language scores showed that they continued to make little or no progress.

Further analysis of these results confirms what specialist EAL teachers have long observed: that if the needs of EAL pupils are properly considered and addressed, they are not the only pupils in classes to benefit. Pupils from English-speaking backgrounds who can find difficulties in decoding verbal communication also progress. The tasks can be planned and scaffolded in different ways for both EAL and E1L pupils.

2.2 Including new arrivals in your lessons – buddies and mentors

One of the main decisions that a teacher needs to make when a new-to-English pupil arrives in their class is what ability group they should join. Many teachers feel intuitively that new arrivals will be best placed in a low-ability group, perhaps because they feel they will be supported by additional staff and the activities will not be too demanding. But new arrivals are not necessarily of low ability and they may be hampered in their learning by being placed in a group where they are not given interesting things to do which provide some cognitive challenge. They may also feel that their prior knowledge and experiences are not valued. It is often better to place new arrivals in a middle-ability group, so that they can begin to tune in to the discussions taking place and pick up models of classroom language.

As they settle into school and their social English begins to develop, new arrivals need to hear academic English being used fluently and competently in the development of learning. It is often a tricky balance to provide new arrivals with cognitively demanding activities at the same time as supporting them in understanding and using the language that this might entail. One of the key implications of this is that new arrivals must never be assigned to a group permanently. Their progress needs to be monitored to make sure they are being challenged. They need to be moved to a different group if it helps. They must also have the opportunity to mix with other pupils and engage in activities with different levels of language challenge.

It is often helpful to team a new arrival with a buddy or peer mentor. This may be a child who speaks the same home language and is more fluent in English and can therefore communicate readily as well as translate, or it may be a 'monolingual' child who is confident and curious and willing to assume responsibility for someone else for a while. The buddy's role could be shared by different pupils. For example, a 'language buddy' may be someone who shares the same first language as the child and who can act as an interpreter. If there is no other child in the class who can do this, the language buddy could be from another class or even a sibling or other relative who does not attend the school, but who comes in from time to time. Then, there may be a 'school buddy' who helps with getting to know the routines of the school, where things are, when things happen and so on. There may be a 'learning buddy', or different ones for different lessons or areas of the curriculum. The kinds of things buddies can do include:

- help familiarise the new arrival with where things are such as toilets, cloakrooms, dining hall, assemblies;
- explain who's who in school and what they do, e.g. secretaries, dinner ladies, TAs;
- support the new arrival in making friends;
- introduce the new arrival to other members of the school.

2.3 Differentiation in planning

Differentiation in planning for one EAL learner in secondary school – case study by Ana Korzun

Kristof arrived in the UK at the end of Year 6 with no level of English. In September, when he started his secondary school joining the other English-speaking Year 7 students, he seemed very withdrawn and did not participate in his lessons. He would not talk or produce any independent writing and did not show any engagement in the school life at all. His English teacher thought that Kristof was very reserved as a person naturally and did not push him to participate in their lessons.

In October a teaching assistant, Mrs T, started supporting Kristof in his English lessons and he started coming out of his shell, engaging in some conversations but with Mrs T only. Six months later Kristof still could not produce any independent writing but could speak some English, although not openly in front of the class but to selected teachers only. In April Mrs T left the school and Kristof felt very upset about it.

In March I started supporting Kristof in his mainstream English lessons. At that time, twice a week he would also have individual EAL tuition with a Polish-speaking family support worker. At that time Kristof's vocabulary had expanded and one of his favourite exercises in English lessons was labelling pictures with the words. I think he liked this exercise because it was something that matched his level of English and he could complete the task. Kristof, as much as the other pupils in class, enjoyed having a complete final product at the end of each lesson.

March

In March all Year 7 pupils were studying Macbeth, written in the English language, and hard enough for native English speakers to understand. Kristof could not participate in the lessons without differentiated work, so alongside the class reading, I provided differentiated and less complicated tasks for him. When the whole class was asked to write a paragraph imagining being present in the castle, Kristof had to copy out the story of Act 2 of Macbeth filling in the blank spaces with words from the list. He also was asked to copy it as neatly as possible into his neat writing book. Here is a summary of the lesson plan:

→

Lesson topic: Macbeth

Main differentiated tasks: labelling, matching words with definitions.

Target: to engage Kristof in lessons and provide him with ability appropriate tasks.

Purpose: to enrich Kristof's vocabulary, engage him in lessons, improve and check his reading comprehension.

Reason: Kristof would not write in full sentences independently but was able to show understanding and work at individual word level.

Target for the next month: start practising independent writing.

Kristof produced some vivid labelled drawings of the play, which showed his strong engagement with it (see Fig. 4.7). At the end of March, Kristof began to translate the key words into Polish using his bilingual dictionary on a daily basis.

Figure 4.7 Kristof's drawing of Macbeth

April – May

In April Kristof was fully engaged in his English lessons, produced independent writing and demonstrated a great ability in critical thinking. He was introduced to writing in PEE (Point, Evidence, Explain) paragraphs which he seemed to understand. With some help from a teaching assistant Kristof managed to produce some excellent paragraphs. Most of the differentiation was based on using writing frames and completing them with the information from a list or particular book pages. Kristof demonstrated great comprehension of the book and films of the play and could successfully complete comprehension-based tasks but still was not able to write independently, which is why writing frames worked really well. Then the class read the Roald Dahl story called 'A Lamb to the Slaughter' which Kristof read along in his lessons together with

$\rightarrow$

the whole class, and he also read it in Polish at home. After that Kristof wrote a diary entry in Polish, based on the events in the story and then he translated it into English with the help of a Polish-speaking family support worker. At first, he was confused about why he was asked to write in Polish, but then he found it helpful and enjoyed writing in his home language (see Figure 4.8). He said that it was 'great writing in his home language' because he could write everything that he thought and also because he loved Polish.

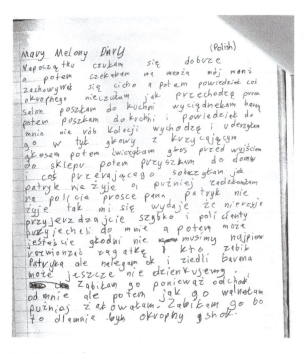

Figure 4.8 Kristof's Polish diary (a retelling of the Roald Dahl story 'A Lamb to the Slaughter')

Here is a summary of Kristof's tasks for the month and his responses:

Topics: 'Private Peaceful' film, 'A Lamb to the Slaughter' story.

Kristof produced his first independent writing piece, a comparison paragraph of two war films that students had watched in the class. He wrote a paragraph of approximately 50 words and used capital letters and full stops correctly. Kristof omitted some main verbs, especially 'to be' and prepositions (e.g. 'This film nearly same film Private Peaceful'), however he used the past simple tense describing one of the films ('Morpurgo was soldgiers') but did not use the past tense in the other sentences.

Differentiated tasks: Writing frames in English. Independent reading and writing in Polish.

Target: continue working on reading and listening comprehension, use Kristof's home language to accelerate the process of creative writing and translate the key words of the lesson into Polish in order to get used to the process of using a dictionary. Practising independent creative writing using Polish language to get the ideas written down.

Purpose: to help Kristof become a confident writer and generate the process of creative writing and critical thinking in both languages.

→

Sub-purpose: to preserve and develop Kristof's home language.

Outcomes: Kristof had become a more confident writer and managed to produce a large piece of creative writing in two languages.

Next month's target: to continue writing independently in English.

June

In June, Kristof demonstrated a continuous improvement in his independent writing. He read the Scottish tale 'Selkie's Wife' in English and used a google translator to translate it into Polish and showed later a very strong understanding of the story. He re-read and translated the tale in his own time independently and managed to answer in English all questions given to the whole class (in writing). He showed his understanding of the story, again labelling and storyboarding as well as drawing some key images from the story. Kristof did not have any new differentiated tasks but was very confident with what he was doing on a regular basis at that time. He immediately looked up the key words, used the translator or a dictionary and even kept writing in Polish, which did not stop him from writing in English. By this stage Kristof's confidence had grown a lot, he was doing well in his mainstream lessons even without a teaching assistant, he put his hand up when he knew the answer and even performed reading a poem out loud in front of the class.

July

In July, Kristof was able to analyse poems and write in simple PEE paragraphs if the writing frame was provided for him. For example, the teacher asked him to use sentences such as: 'In this poem, the poet describes … as …. This suggests that ….'.

Using these sentence frames, Kristof produced the following PEE paragraph:

> In this poem, Island Man, the poet describes London as 'grey and metalic'. This suggests that London is not beautiful and the island man does not like.

He wrote all his PEE paragraphs without using his dictionary and did not pre-write in Polish. Kristof was proud of the writing that he was producing and even asked if he could take his book home to show to his parents. His main teacher and I were very happy with the progress that he had made over the year and he seemed to be a different boy compared to the one he was when he started. Kristof's rapid progress over a period of a few months was very pleasing and, on the whole, largely due to one-to-one attention, which was gradually reduced as he developed confidence and independence.

Learning Outcomes Review

Together with the principles introduced after Chapter 3, the learning outcomes for this chapter give you some criteria to evaluate your planning to ensure that you have used every opportunity you can to promote learning for your multilingual and EAL learners in the activities you provide for them. To review how well you have understood the ideas in this chapter and used them to underpin your own planning, use the following checklist to evaluate your planning in any subject area of the curriculum. This will help you to see how far you have been able to find ways to promote learning for your multilingual and EAL learners, and also to identify points in your plans where you could perhaps improve provision. If you do this for one element of your planning, you could work with colleagues to evaluate all the planning for your class, year group or key stage.

Planning checklist
In your planning, have you:

- clearly identified the language demands of the activities (not just the key vocabulary, but the kinds of structures and texts that pupils will be using)?
- included content that will be meaningful, relevant and interesting to your pupils?
- made links with your pupils' prior knowledge in terms of both language and content?
- made sure that the sequence of your activities supports your pupils' progress from context-embedded, cognitively undemanding learning to more cognitively demanding and less context-embedded learning?
- provided plenty of opportunities for speaking and listening in ALL your activities, not just the introductory ones?
- identified ways in which your multilingual and EAL learners could use their home languages for their learning?
- planned different kinds of group work to provide opportunities for your pupils to engage actively with the concepts and content they are learning?

Further Reading

Gibbons, P. (1998) Classroom talk and the learning of new registers in a second language, *Language and Education*, 12(2): 99–118.
This article, along with other materials written by Pauline Gibbons, gives very clear examples of the ways that concept learning and language learning go side by side, and how teachers can scaffold children's learning through oral activities across the curriculum.

Gravelle, M. (ed.) (2000) *Planning for Bilingual learners: An Inclusive Curriculum*. Stoke-on-Trent: Trentham Books.
This helpful book includes a comprehensive and clear introduction which outlines principles for planning, and chapters written by different experienced teachers which give examples of planning for new arrivals and for learning across the curriculum.

References

Conteh, J. (ed.) (2006) *Promoting Learning for Bilingual Pupils 3–11: Opening Doors to Success*. London: Paul Chapman.

Franson, C. (2011) *Bilingualism and Second Language Acquisition*. Reading: National Association for Language Development in the Curriculum (NALDIC). http://www.naldic. org.uk/eal-initial-teacher-education/resources/ite-archive-bilingualism (accessed 21 December 2014).

Gibbons, P. (1998) Classroom talk and the learning of new registers in a second language, *Language and Education*, 12(2): 99–118.

Gravelle, M. (1996) *Supporting Bilingual Learners in Schools*. Stoke-on-Trent: Trentham Books.

Hall D., Griffiths D., Haslam L. and Wilkin Y. (2001) *Assessing the Needs of Bilingual Pupils: Living in Two Languages*, 2nd edn. London: Fulton Books.

Wells, G. and Chang-Wells, G.L. (1992) *Constructing Knowledge Together: Classrooms as Centers of Inquiry and Literacy*. Portsmouth, NH: Heinemann.

5 Strategies and resources for learning across the curriculum

---

Learning Outcomes

This chapter will help you to achieve the following learning outcomes:

- develop understanding of ways of linking language learning and content learning for multilingual and EAL learners;
- develop awareness of the diverse ways in which literacy and learning across the curriculum can be promoted through reading for pleasure and stories;
- understand the importance of promoting language awareness for all pupils.

Introduction

This chapter provides practical examples of strategies and resources to promote multilingual and EAL pupils' English language learning and learning across the curriculum. They are all based on the theories about language, multilingualism and learning discussed in Chapters 2 and 3, and the principles listed at the end of Part 1 of the book. Cummins' ideas related to the common underlying proficiency, linguistic interdependence and BICS and CALP were introduced in Chapter 3 and they underpin the examples in the first section of this chapter, which give you some ideas about linking language learning and concept/content learning in different subjects across the curriculum. There are two case studies in this section; the first, by Oksana Afitska, highlights the important role of talk in learning science at KS2 and the second, by Pete Ruse, illustrates the ways that subject teachers and EAL specialists can work together in secondary science and geography. Section 2 provides a discussion about the importance of reading for pleasure in literacy and of story as a vehicle for learning across the curriculum. This is illustrated by a case study by Ali O'Grady about reading with teenage boys. There are also many practical examples of the ways that familiar stories can be used to promote learning. The final section of the chapter introduces the idea of languages as a resource for learning for all (both teachers and pupils), and is illustrated by a case study from Anita Conradi about a languages club in a London primary school.

All of these approaches are particularly valuable for multilingual and EAL learners, as they ensure that their learning is always grounded in meaningful contexts and experiences. At the same time, they are equally valuable for all pupils. Throughout the chapter, there are discussion points and activities to help you think about the ideas you are reading about, and there are some suggestions for further reading at the end of the chapter.

These are the main sections and subsections of the chapter:

1. **Linking language learning and content learning**

    1.1 Focusing on language demands

    Teaching science to EAL learners at KS2 – case study by Oksana Afitska

    1.2 Working with colleagues – skills for EAL specialist teachers

    Partnership teaching – case study by Pete Ruse

2. **Literacy, learning and story**

    2.1 The importance of 'reading for pleasure'

    Reading for pleasure with teenage boys – case study by Ali O'Grady

    2.2 Stories for language learning

3. **Promoting language awareness for all pupils**

    The Languages Club in a primary school – case study by Anita Conradi

1. Linking language learning and content learning

1.1 Focusing on language demands

The Principles for Planning for Multilingual Learners (pp. 70, 222) emphasise the importance of speaking and listening and of hands-on activities to provide pupils with rich opportunities for learning that can meet individual needs in a range of ways. Equally important is the need to think carefully about the language demands of the activities you are planning for your pupils. This means asking two key questions of your activities.

1. What language is involved in the particular concept and/or content that is the objective of the learning?

2. How can pupils be supported through the activity in developing their understanding and capacity to use the language independently?

We can think of language demands, essentially, in two ways. First, pupils need the key vocabulary – the words – that underpin the concepts they are learning. Second, they need to understand the words in context – in other words, as part of whole texts.

Words, words, words

Many words in English have different levels of meaning or different meanings in different contexts. This can be confusing for all pupils (and many adults), not just EAL learners. Think of the meaning of the word 'relief' in a geography lesson, or on the label of a bottle of cough medicine. Think of the word 'materials' in a science lesson or in a dress shop. Think of words that we use every day in particular phrases that can seem contradictory – 'running fast' is about moving quickly, but 'sticking fast' is about staying still. Many words have everyday meanings that pupils will be familiar with, but then very particular meanings when they are used in school subjects.

Research Focus

The meaning of 'half'

One of the early KS1 mathematics SATs questions (for seven-year-olds), set in 1997, was about pupils having soup for lunch. On the test paper, there was a simple picture of four pupils sitting round a dining table with bowls of soup in front of them. The question read something like:

> Half the pupils had chicken soup and half the pupils had tomato soup. Draw a circle round half the pupils.

The examiners were surprised to find that almost 70% of the pupils who took the test got this problem wrong, as mathematically it was not difficult. When the scripts were analysed, it was found that many pupils had drawn a circle round half of each child in the picture, rather than two out of the four pupils.

(Example from an examiners' moderation meeting)

All pupils develop semantic strength and capacity by having the opportunity, in a language-rich environment, to play with words, to encounter words in a range of contexts and texts and to make their own connections in word meanings. Here are some simple activities and ideas that can make your classroom a language-rich environment and encourage your pupils to be enthusiastic, curious and analytic about words and their meanings.

- **Displays**: find as many ways as possible to have vocabulary related to the concepts you are teaching on display round the classroom – word mats, word walls, labels, word banks and so on. Change them regularly to maintain pupils' interest. From time to time, mix up the labels and have pupils sort them out. Use multilingual lists and labels whenever you can. Ask your multilingual pupils to provide equivalent words and encourage your class to compare the different words for particular things and ideas.

- **Washing lines**: this is a good activity to reinforce pupils' understandings of words and develop awareness of shades of meaning. Prepare sets of words that show different degrees of meaning, e.g. size (minuscule, tiny, small, middling, big, huge, gigantic); volume (whisper, mutter, mumble, grunt, shout, scream, screech). Other categories could be heat, probability, speed, and so on – relate your words to concepts and content that the pupils are learning across the curriculum. Pupils in groups put the words in order, discussing and justifying their choices. Then they stand in line, so the class can see the words, and explain their decisions. Finally, the words are pegged on a washing line strung across the classroom so that everyone can see them and use them in their speaking and writing.

- **Odd one out**: this activity is based on sets of three or four words, which all have something in common, but there is always a feature shared by two but not all three. The point is that pupils make their own decisions and justify them. Here are some examples.
  - Sea, river, canal: they are all bodies of water, but 'sea' is the odd one out because it has three letters; 'canal' is the odd one out because it is man-made; and 'river' is the odd one out because it has a 'v' in it.

- Knight, sword, stone: they are all from traditional stories, but 'knight' is the odd one out because it does not begin with 's', 'stone' is the odd one out because it ends with a vowel and 'sword' is the odd one out because it is an object made of metal.

- Bird, fly, feather: they are all to do with birds, but 'fly' is the odd one out because it is a verb and the others are nouns; 'feather' is the odd one out because it has four phonemes and the others have three; 'bird' is the odd one out because it ends in a consonant sound.

As you can see, there can be a range of answers, to do with phonics, spelling, meaning or grammar. The important point is that pupils have to explain and justify their own answers. Groups of pupils can be given sets of words to discuss and come up with answers to, then the words can be given to another group. Once they get the hang of it, pupils can be asked to come up with their own sets of words to challenge their classmates. One of the benefits of this game is that it encourages pupils to think of meanings above individual word level, and this helps to develop their understanding of texts.

Words, sentences and texts

As we saw in Chapter 2, words cannot be fully understood in isolation. Key vocabulary is not enough to help pupils develop the deeper understandings that are needed to promote the academic language required for real, powerful learning and achievement. Pupils need rich experiences of words used in a wide range of authentic **texts** (both spoken and written) in order to develop as capable speakers, readers and writers. They need to analyse texts in order to understand how they work and how to make the right choices in their own writing. The '5Ws' questions introduced in Chapter 2, linked to the functional approach, are helpful in analysing the language demands of the concepts and content that pupils are learning across the curriculum.

The most important principle here is to make your literacy teaching cross-curricular. When you are teaching about non-fiction text types, use topics for pupils' writing from different areas of the curriculum in which they already have practical experience and knowledge. This will help to make their writing meaningful, authentic and purposeful. For example, after studying electricity in science, pupils can write instructions to make a circuit in literacy. After finding out about the Vikings in history, they can write a newspaper report about a raid on a village.

Here are some ideas for activities, which, in a language-rich learning environment, help pupils to develop academic language and independence as readers and writers.

- **Reference texts**: don't depend on computer dictionaries and spell-checkers – they often contain errors and can prevent pupils from developing strategies for using reference texts including dictionaries, thesauruses and so on. Make sure you have a range available in your classroom, including picture dictionaries, multilingual dictionaries and subject dictionaries. Model their use, and encourage pupils to use them independently in checking their spellings and finding the best words to express what they want to say or write.

- **Text frames (graphic organisers)**: these are usually employed as supports to help pupils structure their written texts. They can also be a useful resource for developing reading skills and understanding of academic language. They are a visual way of helping pupils understand how ideas are linked in different texts, and how to report, explain, justify, discuss and argue about the concepts they are learning. Alice Washbourne (2011: 124–5) provides some simple examples of graphic organisers to illustrate cause and effect, processes, cycles and so on, which pupils could complete after a science task with the information they have learnt, or after reading a non-fiction text in a particular genre.

- **Text reconstruction**: these activities, which are sometimes called **DARTs** (directed activities related to texts), are where pupils are expected to put back together a text that has been disrupted in some way. They are all about getting pupils to think beyond word level about what they are reading. They provide excellent opportunities for discussion, as an introduction to writing. A text can be cut into sections, and pupils have to work in a group to agree on how it goes together again. Pupils can be given the first part of a sentence, and then asked to choose the correct ending from a selection on the interactive whiteboard (IWB). Again, the emphasis needs to be on their explaining and justifying their choices.

Activity 5.1
Content and language

Choose a short non-fiction text from a topic you are planning to teach or a book or other resource you are using in your teaching. Using the 5Ws (see p. 31), analyse the type of text it is and consider what language demands it would place on EAL learners. Prepare a graphic organiser that would help pupils analyse and understand the text.

If possible, try your ideas out with a group of pupils; review and adapt for use in a future lesson.

This case study is taken from a larger dataset of 20 lessons collected as part of the EAL Science Project (a collaborative project between the University of Sheffield and Sheffield City Council, 2013–2015) in five primary schools in Sheffield, South Yorkshire. Lessons were observed and recorded and the transcripts were then analysed to identify the strategies the teachers used to integrate science and language learning.

Teaching science to EAL learners at KS2 – case study by Oksana Afitska

The 'Keeping warm' science lesson reported here was observed in a Year 4 class in a school where 90% of pupils are categorised as EAL, a mixture of advanced and intermediate bilingual

→

learners, with some pupils new to English, from Roma backgrounds. Between them, they speak nearly 20 different languages and come from a range of different minority-ethnic heritages, with pupils of Pakistani heritage being the prevailing ethnic group. The lesson lasted 90 minutes and included many examples of effective teaching strategies that can be employed by teachers in different settings, both primary and secondary.

The lesson began with a warm-up activity where the pupils were asked to put cards into two separate categories, the names of which were not provided. As the teacher gave the instruction she used gestures alongside her verbal instruction to reinforce the points of the task. As she said:

... two separate categories, please

she showed her hand with two fingers outstretched to reinforce the meaning of the word 'two'. This supported those pupils who might not be familiar with the English numerical system and also reinforced the instruction. She kept using this strategy consistently throughout the lesson.

The pupils completed the card-grouping activity and identified that the two categories were 'hot' and 'cold'. The teacher then asked them to come up with their own words to be put into the 'hot' and 'cold' categories. She said:

I want you to think of any words or any vocabulary related to keeping warm that you might know ... it does not matter whether you got one word two words twenty words ... I want you to talk to the person sitting next to you...

By giving instructions in this way, she was using a range of strategies and achieving the following teaching and learning objectives:

- activating further the pupils' existing knowledge and vocabulary on the topic;
- identifying any possible gaps in their knowledge prior to introducing the new topic;
- using the paraphrasing technique to increase the chances of pupils understanding her instruction (and also expanding their vocabulary repertoire);
- reinforcing the idea that it doesn't matter how much or little learners say, thus putting beginner and less confident EAL learners at ease;
- encouraging peer support in learning.

All these strategies helped the teacher to integrate science and language learning, to promote a positive, welcoming ethos in her classroom and a safe and friendly environment for learning. For example, the peer-led learning allowed pupils to try out their 'new' linguistic knowledge (for example, a word from their passive vocabulary) and 'scientific' ideas. The strategies also gave the teacher an opportunity to monitor individual pupils' work more closely and provide them with targeted one-to-one help where needed. Of the 90-minute lesson the learners spent 16 minutes doing peer-work activities. Having discussed a few examples of suitable words with the teacher in a plenary session and having completed this activity in their pairs, the pupils called the words out one by one and the teacher clarified, exemplified and put them into context as needed to support the pupils' comprehension of these words and the ideas behind them. These strategies are exemplified in the following excerpts:

→

Preparation for peer-work, eliciting and clarifying examples (Sweating episode)	Monitoring peer-work, eliciting specific vocabulary items from the learners (Freezing episode)	Plenary work, collecting pupils' responses, clarifying and exemplifying the answers (Chilli episode)
P1: Glasses T: Glasses … sunglasses […] P2: Sweating T: Sweating … A man sweating on a hot day. [Teacher pretends to be wiping sweat of her forehead.] Sweating. Good.	T: What's the word? Hot ____ P3: Boiling T: Boiling, lovely […] T: Cold – what's the word for cold [Teacher wraps herself with her hands and makes a movement as if she is shaking] … you are cold, you are ___? P4: Freezing T: Freezing … write it down.	P5: Chilli T: Chilli. Do you mean chilly as in cold. You are chilly or [teacher wraps herself with her hands as if trying to make herself feel warmer] or do you mean chilli as if you eat and it is hot? [Teacher makes a movement pretending that she is eating something.] P5: Hot T: Hot, hot chilli that you might eat … sensation, heat. OK.

During the lesson the teacher paid close attention to the elicitation of samples of the learners' spoken language and she also provided them with opportunities to practise their skills in writing. Throughout the lesson the learners produced different kinds of written language, starting from simply copying the lesson topic from the board into their books and drawing spider diagrams using single words, to gradually progressing to writing their own questions in full and instructions in the form of bullet point lists. Whenever the learners were asked to produce written language, the teacher gave them an example or two of what to write and how to write it. For example, in the following extract the teacher reminded the learners to use sentence starters to help them construct their sentences.

Sentence starters episode	
T: I want you to think of five questions that you might want to find the answer to, so you can use the sentence starters to help you – who, what, which, how, does or when. […] You might ask a question like erm … how do we measure heat or how do we measure temperature, OK? You might ask a question like erm … what happens when we leave an ice cream out in the hot weather, OK?	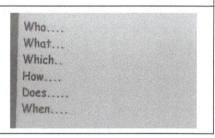

Once the learners finished writing their questions, the teacher elicited a wide range of responses. The importance of such contributions, particularly for beginner EAL learners, is that they gain much needed support from the teacher as well as reassurance that they, just like anybody else in their class, have valuable ideas and content to contribute to the lesson. During this activity the teacher provided extensive feedback to the learners on their questions and invited them to elaborate on their responses further, both linguistically and conceptually in relation to science, as is illustrated in the following example:

$\rightarrow$

Elicitation of responses and provision of teacher feedback	
P1: *How do you measure the heat?*	P6: *… in a … in a…*
T: *How do you measure ___?*	T: *Does ice cream melt when you are in an igloo? It may be different than when you are in a sun. OK. [...] P7?*
P1: *Heat*	
T: *Heat. How do you measure heat? OK. P2?*	P7: *What would happen if you left an ice cream in a sun?*
P2: *How does the [inaudible]*	T: *Good. What would happen if you left ice cream in the sun? P8?*
T: *How does the sun ___?*	
P2: *How does the snow melt*	P8: *Why does the chocolate melt in the sun?*
T: *Ah, how does the snow melt? or Why does snow melt? Excellent. Well done.*	T: *Why does chocolate melt in the sun? P9?*
[...]	P9: *Why does ice melt?*
P5: *How does temperature grow?*	T: *Why does ice melt? P10?*
T: *How does temperature grow? or What makes temperature rise? OK. Anybody else got a question, P6?*	P10: *[shrugs his shoulders]*
	T: *Come on [in encouraging voice]*
P6: *Does the ice cream melt?*	P10: *How do you measure heat?*
T: *Does ice cream melt? Where? Be a bit more specific. Does ice cream melt ___ … Where?*	T: *How do you measure heat? OK, pencils down…*

It is important to note that the teacher accepted 'repetitive' responses (i.e. responses that had already been given by other learners in the class) just as readily as the original ones and acknowledged them as equally valid contributions. For less confident EAL learners, the simple act of uttering a sentence in an unfamiliar language in front of the whole class is a major achievement and contribution to the lesson, and they learn a great deal from listening to their more advanced peers. Having elicited and discussed the learners' questions, the teacher invited them in a plenary session to think about and explore their ideas about certain scientific facts. As she elicited the pupils' responses she encouraged them to produce answers in full sentences, in this way maintaining the dual focus of her science lesson – teaching scientific concepts and supporting learners' English language development.

Full sentences episode
T: *P13, what happens when the ice cream is left out in the sun?*
P13: *It melts.*
T: *Right. Full sentence please.*
P13: *When you leave an ice cream <u>outside</u> <u>where it is boiling weather</u> it melts.*
T: *OK. It melts. Anyone else can answer this question. P14, full sentence please.*
P14: *Ice cream – What happens when an ice cream is left in the sun? [P14 reads this question from the board] Ice cream – When you leave ice cream in the sun it will melt <u>into a liquid</u>.*
T: *OK. Anybody else got an answer?*
P15: *When you em … leave ice cream em … <u>outside</u> in <u>a really</u> hot weather it turn into a <u>really runny</u> liquid.*
T: *OK. Right. Second question then [...]*

→

This example also shows how creative pupils can become in forming their full sentences, sometimes providing fuller syntactic structures in their answers than are actually needed (e.g. P13 and P15's responses). As the lesson progressed, more good teaching strategies were observed. Firstly, the teacher spent some of her lesson time eliciting specific vocabulary items from the learners. This practice is linked to **formative assessment** in that it allows teachers to probe their pupils' knowledge, identify gaps in it and instantly adjust their teaching, where needed, to address the needs of the class. Here are some examples.

Temperature episode	Ice episode	Thermometer episode
P3: The decking will feel very cold or cold because at night it will be very windy and colder than in the day. T: … OK _I am looking for one word in particular_ let's see if anyone can get it into their sentence, P11? P11: it will be cold or very cold because the sun erm … got erm… Class: down P11: and then the moon will come and it won't be hot T: OK P16: the temperature [inaudible] T: Um? (referring to P16's utterance) P16: the temperature will [go down] T: Excellent. Good boy. The temperature changes at nighttime. What happens during the nighttime? P16: The temperature goes down. T: Yeah, the temperature falls (teacher makes a hand movement downwards) at nighttime.	T: _I am looking for one word in particular._ P7: it's when you put water into this erm… T: (Shakes her head), P20? P20: [inaudible] P13: frozen water (on the background) T: No (referring to P20's answer) What did you say, P13? P13: frozen water T: Ice is frozen water. OK. Ice is frozen water. So when water freezes it gets that cold it freezes […] **Defrost episode** P21: It goes soft [talking about frozen fish fingers] T: It goes soft as they ___? _I am looking for the word._ P21: Cook T: No, they do not cook, you put them into oven to cook. They de___ Class: Defrost	T: _What do you think this bit of a thermometer might be called?_ Make a guess- P2: it might be top T: Top. Could be. Now you should all know answer to this. _What is this bit called_ (points to the body of the thermometer)? Make the link to maths. What this bit is called? P15: Value T: No, not value P27: Length T: What would it be in maths? P19: Scales T: Scales. Scale part of the thermometer. _Does anybody know what this bottom part is called?_ I'll give you a clue. The gardeners at the moment are planting them in the garden in the school. P20: Soil T: It's not called soil. P1: Bottom T: Bulb. Its called bulb. It's like a flower that has a bulb. A flower. Same name but different meaning. This is called a bulb of a thermometer.

→

Secondly, throughout the lesson, the learners were observed actively enquiring about unknown or unclear words as they came to their attention. This practice is very important for EAL classrooms as it demonstrates the learners' active and meaningful engagement with the lesson, and that the teacher was able to create a safe classroom environment where her learners felt safe to produce questions and queries. In this class, learners also felt free to provide help to their peers not only in group work but also in plenary sessions, as is evidenced in the 'Temperature' episode above, demonstrating yet again the level of their concentration and the extent of their engagement with the activity.

Ice episode (in part)	Tarmac episode	Distorted episode
T: Very interesting question here. Say your question. P4: _What is ice?_ T: What is ice? Tell me what ice actually is. _P4's question is what is ice?_ P14: Water T: _P16 see if you can tell what ice is [...]_ P13: frozen water T: Ice is frozen water. OK.	T: Tarmac P17: _What?_ T: Tarmac. The concrete, the ground. The tarmac.	T: if you are reading the temperature and you are reading it like this (teacher holds the reading line of the thermometer below her eye line) it's distorted. P8: _What is distorted?_ T: It means you won't read it properly.

At certain points in the lesson the teacher chose not to probe the learners' knowledge but to provide them directly with the explanations of specific vocabulary items, perhaps to save the lesson time for the discussion of more 'important', fundamental scientific concepts, related directly to the topic. She did so in two ways: implicitly, by rephrasing her utterance, or explicitly, by providing contextual synonyms and actually showing what the item meant.

Occurring episode
T: _something is happening, the change is occurring_ ... it is either heat is added or heat is taken away from something

Decking and tarmac episode
T: Decking, so the decking is here (shows), the steps [...] The tarmac – which means the concrete (makes a hand movement parallel to the floor)

Finally, the teacher made extensive use of the whiteboard throughout the lesson to provide visual clues to the learners to support them in:

- learning new vocabulary items;
- reading in the target language;
- comprehending instructions and core lesson information in the target language.

→

Learning new vocabulary and subject related concepts

T: OK, most of you agree that temperature means whether something is hot or cold. OK, let's find out. (Teacher reveals the definition on the board.) Temperature is a measure, right, well done who said this, of how hot or cold something is.

P26: Thermometer

PP: Ah, that's what I was gonna say!

T: Shh! We measure temperature with the thermometer. And those who do not know, this is just one example of a thermometer (teacher reveals a picture of a thermometer on the board.)

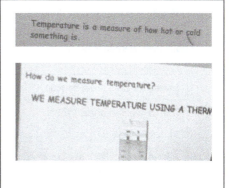

Comprehending instructions

T: OK, so, question – What happens when an ice cream is left in the sun? Question number two – How are ice cubes made? Talk to the person next to you, see if you can come up with the answer straight away.

T: Can anybody think of another example when heat is either added or taken away from something?

Reading in the target language

T: OK, reading the thermometer. Eyes on board. [...] Right, at the moment these one, two, three, four, five, six statements are all mixed up (statements are written on the interactive whiteboard). This is how to read the thermometer properly. What I'd like you to do with your partner is read them. We will read them together. And I want you to shuffle them in a right order [...] (Teacher reads the statements one by one and learners follow.)

Labelling activity

T: This is a thermometer. We have to label the thermometer. Scale – is this bit (teacher writes label on the picture on the interactive whiteboard). Stem – the big long part (teacher shows the stem and labels it).

P8: Stem

T: And a bulb

P7: is at the bottom.

P12: Bulb

T: Bulb. Stem (shows). You have to imagine – like the way the flower grows – bulb is at the bottom, stem is the bit that comes up (shows). OK.

→

Notice how in the 'labelling activity' excerpt, the learners repeat the names of parts of the thermometer to themselves after the teacher. This behaviour suggests that 'noticing' and active learning are taking place. The teacher ends the lesson by implementing a quick summative assessment procedure to monitor the extent to which the lesson's learning objectives were achieved.

Summative assessment episode
T: What is temperature, P7?
P7: Temperature is ___
T: What is the definition of temperature?
P10: Temperature is it measures hot or cold.
T: Good. Temperature measures how hot or cold something is. OK. What do we measure temperature in?
PPs: Celsius
T: Celsius degrees and ___?
PPs: Fahrenheit
T: Good. What instrument measures temperature?
P2: [no response]
T: What do you handle? What have you been learning about all afternoon?
P2: Thermometer
T: Good. Thermometer measures temperature. Full sentences please […]

1.2 Working with colleagues – skills for EAL specialist teachers

One of the essential skills in EAL pedagogy is the ability to work with colleagues to plan and implement teaching that allows pupils the opportunities to learn both the concepts of the subject being studied and the English language required to think, talk and write about the subject. This is especially important in secondary schools. In the 1980s and 1990s, there was much research and development of the concept of partnership teaching (NALDIC, 2014). This showed, among other things, that time spent by subject and 'EAL specialists' working together in careful planning was always of benefit to the quality of the pupils' learning and always time well spent. If one of the colleagues is bilingual or multilingual themselves, the partnership can be even more beneficial; in Chapter 7 (section 3, pp. 172–178) there is a discussion of ways of working with multilingual colleagues. The following case study, written by a secondary EAL specialist teacher, illustrates the benefits of subject and EAL teachers working together.

Partnership teaching – case study by Pete Ruse

I work as an EAL support teacher part-time in a number of schools. I see building partnerships with subject teachers as a core part of my practice and strive to create a balance between supporting learners' learning directly within lessons and, outside of lessons, having an impact on the curriculum they experience so that it is more organised with language development objectives in mind. Explicitly and implicitly acting to increase subject teachers' knowledge and skills in this area is a fundamental aspect of this, especially as new teachers join the profession.

In one school, I was timetabled to support a Year 10 science class, one lesson out of five per week. This group was a challenging one for me from a number of perspectives. It was a low attaining group (a 'lower ability set') with a number of learners presenting with challenging behaviours that suggested they were hostile towards school. It was relatively large with around 26 pupils. Four of the group were International New Arrivals (INAs) in the early stages of acquiring English language. These INAs had varied educational backgrounds but all were literate in their first language (L1) and all had had full schooling before they arrived in the UK.

The teacher was in his second year of teaching. There was also a student teacher attached to the group, observing it before she started teaching it as part of her initial teacher training, and a teaching assistant attached to a pupil with a statement of special educational needs. Much of the teaching effort was aimed at managing behaviour and keeping control, rather than covering content and fulfilling school and department requirements for assessments and GCSE exam preparation. It seemed important to me not to disrupt the fragile order the science teacher had created but at the same time to find ways to enhance the English language development experience of the pupils. My most acute challenges, though, were that one early stage EAL learner refused to have anything to do with me, apparently feeling the stigma of 'needing help', and that the curriculum topic (genetics) was very conceptually sophisticated and difficult to engage with, especially for one of the INAs, who had only just arrived. It seemed that a significant number of learners perceived me as having lower status than the other teacher(s) and I was finding it hard to establish myself in that classroom.

The approaching end-of-topic assessment gave me the opportunity I was looking for. I negotiated with the science teacher that I would take on the task of making the test more accessible and engaging for all the class, including the early stage EAL learners. The test itself was a series of questions on genetics requiring one word or short phrase answers together with having to draw a couple of diagrams. I decided to supply learners with the answers, but randomised, so that they had to look at each question and find the appropriate answer to write in and then cross off. I thought this would both reduce the language demand for the early stage EAL learners and be somewhat engaging for the rest of the class, if only for its novel approach.

→

I prepared the materials and the science teacher set up and organised the lesson. We thought this was the least disruptive approach to take. Initial thoughts on the learners' part that this would be easy because they had the answers soon gave way to a realisation that it was actually a challenging activity. All engaged with the activity to such an extent that I was able to support some learners, who would previously have avoided talking to me, with specific questions. That they asked for support was, to me, a measure of how motivating they found the exercise, though it probably reduced the validity of the test somewhat. This seemed a small price to pay for the chance to establish a dynamic of purposeful activity in that classroom and to give me a chance to establish a good relationship with the group.

The early stage EAL learners accessed the test with the help of a first language dictionary. This included the most recent arrival, who showed he had a better grasp of scientific knowledge than anyone suspected from the information we had of his educational background. His progress through the test was slow, however, and he had only half completed it by the time the bell went. But he had avoided the fate of sitting with a standard test in front of him and not being able to engage with it in any way. Along with the rest of the class, he had achieved something to feel good about. The atmosphere in the class was perceptibly happier and more relaxed at the end of the lesson than it was at the start.

In another school, where I was working on a temporary basis, I was timetabled to support a Year 10 geography class taught by the Head of Geography for one lesson a week. Not only was she a very experienced Head of Geography, she had extensive experience of working with EAL practitioners. Circumstances dictated that while she knew I was going to turn up, we did not have a chance to have a conversation. On arriving in her classroom, she invited me to sit down and look through a pile of test scripts that the class had completed the lesson before. She was particularly concerned about their answers to extended answer questions, in that many learners seemed not to have grasped what the questions were asking of them.

Reading carefully through the scripts and making the occasional note, I was able to tune in to the class and the teaching and learning dynamic in the classroom. Having all chosen geography as an option, all the learners seemed motivated and engaged. They had a range of attainment from predicted 'A*' to 'E' grades at GCSE. There was one International New Arrival (INA) who had been in the UK for three years and who was able to communicate in English verbally quite effectively, though his written English was at a much earlier stage of development. From his test script, he clearly had problems identifying what the test questions were asking him to do.

I negotiated with the geography teacher that I would prepare a lesson on reading exam questions for the following week. This seemed to be a good place to start. I knew that the class had had lots of practice doing exam type questions so I tried to think of another way to approach the matter. I decided to 'reverse engineer' a test, where I would supply a set of answers and the activity would be to write the (possible) questions. I calculated that this would really focus learners on close reading of answers (a useful model) and generating an appropriate form of question for that answer. If you can write something you can read it.

The first slide of the presentation was the starter activity – to match terms with their opposites – to introduce the concept of an 'anti-quiz':

$$\rightarrow$$

	The Antartic
A cyclone	
	An anti-quiz
A syncline	
The Arctic	
	An anticline
A quiz	
	An anticyclone

Then a quick anti-quiz – what are the (possible) questions to these answers:

1. Name of school
2. 11 o'clock
4. 1050m
3. 250 miles
5. A corrie

This further established the idea of making up the question to match the answer. Then, some real life geography GCSE examples: first some one-mark questions, for example:

1. Study **Figure n** on the insert, a 1:50 000 Ordnance Survey map extract of [*a river in England*].

a) ....

18–22m

b) ....

Possible answers:

- There is a confluence.
- A tributary joins the [river].
- It meanders.
- A bridge crosses it.

The real question to a) being:

What is the approximate height of the [river] in grid square xxxx?

And to b):

What happens to the [river] at [grid reference] xxxxxx?

Followed by some two-mark questions. For example:

5 ....

→

Weather is the day-to-day variation of features such as rainfall, temperature and wind, whilst climate represents the average weather conditions over a long period of time – at least 30 years.

The real question being:

What is the difference between weather and climate?

There was some animated discussion during the activity, followed by feedback and unpacking some of the language issues, focusing on the links between the structures of the questions and the structures of the answers.

For me, the common feature of these two examples is that between us, the teaching staff, we created some space for ourselves. In the first example, we created space for the science teacher to set up an activity that really engaged learners and allowed me room to engage with learners in a positive way that increased my credibility with them. In the second example, the geography teacher had room to reflect on the class and their learning from a different perceptual position, and I had room to put together an activity that focused learners on useful language development objectives. I am aware that in both cases I was benefiting from the credibility and goodwill created by the EAL practitioners who had gone before me as well as building the foundations of further EAL–subject teacher partnerships.

Best practice would involve collaborative planning to embed language development objectives in schemes of work, as well as the production of suitable learning materials and activities presented collaboratively. Real world constraints on time and opportunity mean that this is not always possible. Producing materials for other teachers to use and taking lessons are useful strategies for EAL teachers, enabling them to put language development on the agenda. Showing subject teachers that it is possible (and desirable) to build language development objectives into curriculum content lays the foundations for more collaborative planning and joint delivery of lessons.

2. Literacy, learning and story

2.1 The importance of 'reading for pleasure'

Over recent years, official policies related to literacy have demanded the teaching of the discrete skills of reading, with a heavy emphasis on phonics. This has led in many situations to the real aims and purposes of reading becoming sidelined or even forgotten, adding to the difficulty of the task of learning to read for many pupils, especially for EAL learners. The following case study, written by a secondary teacher, illustrates how 'reading for pleasure' can be restored to the classroom – even for teenage boys who are often, albeit unjustifiably, seen as unwilling readers.

Reading for pleasure with teenage boys – case study by Ali O'Grady

I teach in a very diverse secondary school, which over the last seven years has changed cohort dramatically. Currently there are 27 languages spoken by our students, many of whom have arrived new to English. One of my responsibilities is to manage EAL, although I am an English subject teacher.

At the beginning of the Year I was given an Alternative Curriculum lesson on my timetable – one hour a week with a Year 10 class who were taking a reduced number of option subjects. The group consisted of seven boys, with four out of the seven categorised as EAL learners. We were later joined by a new arrival, new to English. For the first term an outside agency was brought in to teach the group numeracy skills and I was asked to focus on literacy skills in the following two terms. The boys were clearly disengaged after the numeracy lessons, so we sat down and discussed what they wanted to do. I suggested reading a book and they were open to this. I searched for a book I thought would engage them. The boys were really sporty, in fact one of them was out of school for a day a week to train with a football club, so I looked for a novel with a sporty theme. Coincidently we had been sent six copies of *Now is the Time for Running* by Michael Williams. After reading some reviews I decided this would be a good place to start. The novel is a story of survival that opens with a soccer match in the dusty fields of Zimbabwe. Things change when the soldiers arrive and the two brothers in the story are the only survivors. The plot follows them to South Africa and their experiences as illegal immigrants. The World Cup of street soccer features later in the novel, with some very hard-hitting and realistic themes.

We started reading the novel together. I had decided that we would discuss themes and plots, but we would not study the novel in as much detail as we would if we were studying it for GCSE. Instead, we would read the novel for enjoyment, and I would not expect any formal work. The students were keen that I read the novel to them and so this was what I did. I asked at various points if they wanted to read but they were adamant, as a group, that they wanted me to read to them. We discussed the novel as we went along. This started as me checking that they were not just sleeping with their eyes open as I read. I found they followed the plot with interest and had strong awareness of some of the hard-hitting themes. Some of the students in the group came from countries where they could have been exposed to violence and were happy to talk, not about personal experiences, but general situations in their countries. We also talked about issues that were in the news at the time that related to the themes of the novel and I asked them to watch the news if they could so that we could all join in the discussion.

The boys enjoyed me reading the novel to them and discussing current affairs, asking questions about situations they were unsure of. The size of the group meant that they asked questions openly and without the hesitation that sometimes comes when they are

$\rightarrow$

part of a large group. The mix of the group, and the number of EAL students meant that they were confident to ask if they were unsure of words or phrases. The English-speaking students supported by explaining meanings. This demonstrated to me the power of allowing the students to read for enjoyment. Taking away the pressure of exams or controlled assessments meant that we could take as much time as we needed, and allowed us to spend that time on discussion that really supported their English language development. I certainly feel that the students expanded their vocabulary, but also their knowledge of world affairs and awareness of situations around the world.

The students' engagement with the sessions was strong. We would read for the majority of the hour, quite often in the library, and various staff who walked through the library during those times commented on how the students seemed to be enjoying the experience of being read to. My decision not to do any formal work on the novel took away the stress of completing written activities and any work we did was discussion.

We read the novel over the course of a term. The students continued to enjoy reading and indeed continued to ask me to read to them. They had discussions with various members of staff who were interested in what they were doing and were very articulate in explaining what the novel was about. When we had finished the novel they asked me to find another one to read and so I started to research similar novels. I decided to try to find one set in England as a contrast.

The novel I chose was *After Tomorrow* by Gillian Cross. Its premise is that the banks have crashed and currency has become worthless. In the Britain of this novel, families go hungry and live in fear of armed raiders. The answer for some people is to leave Britain and this is what the family in the novel do. They go to France and end up in a refugee camp, facing similar problems that we see on the news about refugees and asylum-seekers. Again this was a novel that engaged the students. They were keen to understand how banks could crash and what the impact would be. The idea of currency being worthless fascinated them, as the novel talked about how the prices for fresh food rocketed. The shortages of food and the lawlessness fascinated them, especially as it was set in this country. They could also relate the experiences of the refugee camps to what they saw on the news. This allowed us to discuss the plight of people in camps, fleeing their countries for whatever reason. These discussions led nicely to some discussion of current affairs and also fitted nicely into the SEAL themes of empathy and thinking about others. Those students who were more aware of world issues, maybe because of personal experiences, were keen to share their knowledge, and others were keen to learn. Culturally it was a very mixed group from a number of different countries with very differing experiences and they were very keen to learn from each other. In this context reading allowed us to share personal experiences, and learn about the very real experiences of others.

My brief had been to work on literacy skills with the students and I feel this approach benefited them, especially the EAL students. They enjoyed reading the books without the pressure of GCSE in a small group environment. They would ask about vocabulary they didn't understand and so developed their vocabulary. They were exposed to books they perhaps would not ordinarily have read in the English language, and their confidence in

$\rightarrow$

speaking English certainly developed. For some of the students, the SEAL aspects of the work were really important and helped develop relationships with other students.

I was lucky to have the time and opportunity to read with my group without the formalities of studying for an exam. I believe that reading for enjoyment is vital, especially for EAL students and being read to can improve the experience. If there are opportunities to read for pleasure I would highly recommend this approach; indeed I feel it should be an element of the curriculum for EAL learners.

2.2 Stories for language learning

As the previous case study shows, pupils respond to stories in a variety of ways, intellectually, emotionally and imaginatively, and many come to the classroom with a variety of traditional stories – in some cases from a range of cultures and languages – in their heads. The use of familiar stories can be highly motivating in validating pupils' existing linguistic and cultural knowledge, even though the story may be encountered in an unfamiliar language. Prior knowledge of plot helps pupils work out the meanings of unfamiliar words. Well-known, traditional stories can be used in interesting and imaginative ways with pupils in primary and the early stages of secondary schooling to achieve high levels of literacy learning.

Vignette

Little Red Riding Hood in different countries

As part of their literacy teaching on their first school placement, two trainees, who were in a Year 5 class where about 70% of the pupils were multilingual, were asked to teach the Primary Literacy Framework unit of work 'Stories from other cultures'. They began by finding several different versions of the *Little Red Riding Hood* story, and discussed these with the pupils, thinking about the differences in settings, characters and plots. They identified the key features of the story, then moved on to think about the ways it could be changed to fit into different countries and language and cultural contexts. Then the pupils developed Little Red Riding Hood fact sheets for different countries, such as that shown in Figure 5.1.

The pupils were then arranged in groups and each group given a country and its fact sheet. The task was for the group to write the story of *Little Red Riding Hood* for their country. They were allowed to use words from any languages they knew in their writing and provided with this writing frame to help them organise their ideas.

Many pupils used words from their home languages, thinking carefully how to spell them in the English alphabet. They were learning French in MFL, and some of them used vocabulary they had learnt in these lessons in their stories. Figure 5.3 is one of the pieces of writing the pupils produced.

(Continued)

(Continued)

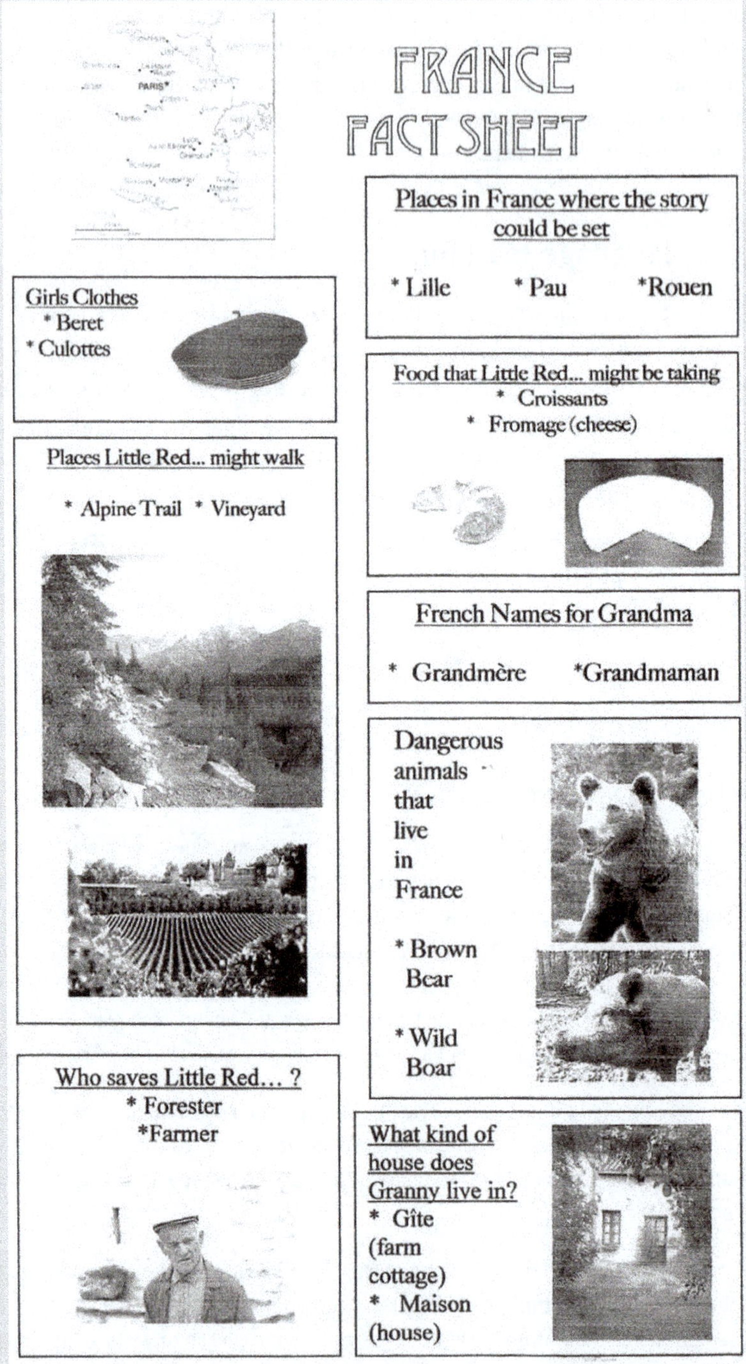

FRANCE FACT SHEET

Girls Clothes
* Beret
* Culottes

Places Little Red... might walk

* Alpine Trail   * Vineyard

Who saves Little Red... ?
* Forester
*Farmer

Places in France where the story could be set

* Lille   * Pau   *Rouen

Food that Little Red... might be taking
* Croissants
* Fromage (cheese)

French Names for Grandma

* Grandmère   *Grandmaman

Dangerous animals that live in France

* Brown Bear

* Wild Boar

What kind of house does Granny live in?
* Gîte (farm cottage)
* Maison (house)

Figure 5.1 Pupils' fact sheet about France

My Tale from Another Culture Story Choices

The country where
my tale will be set is _____

The place where the
characters live is _____

My character will
be wearing red_____

So her name will
be Little Red_____

In their language,
Grandma is called_____

The food she is taking
to her Grandma is_____

On her way to Grandma's
she goes through a _____

On her way she meets a friendly
(but secretly deadly) _____

Her Grandma lives in a _____

Little Red… is saved by a_____

Figure 5.2 Story frame for Little Red Riding Hood

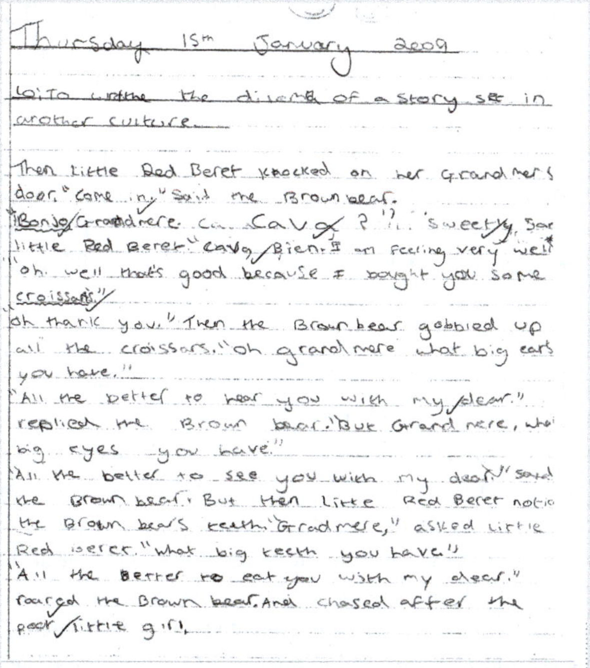

Thursday 15th January 2009

LO: To write the diary of a story set in
another culture.

Then Little Red Beret knocked on her Grandmer's
door. "Come in," said the Brown bear.
"Bonjo Grandmere ca Cauve?" "," sweetly, Sar
little Red Beret "cavg, Bien. I am feeling very well."
"oh well, that's good because I bought you some
croissons."
"oh thank you." Then the Brown bear gobbied up
all the croissons. "oh grandmere what big ears
you have."
"All the better to hear you with my dear,"
replied the Brown bear. "But Grand mere, what
big eyes you have."
"All the better to see you with my dear," said
the Brown bear. But then Little Red Beret notio
the Brown bear's teeth. "Grandmere," asked Little
Red beret. "what big teeth you have."
"All the Better to eat you with my dear."
roared the Brown bear. And chased after the
poor little girl.

Figure 5.3 Child's 'multilingual' version of Little Red Riding Hood

Activity 5.2
Writing with traditional stories

Choose a familiar traditional story and think about how you could use it to develop some activities, which would help to improve multilingual and EAL learners' writing, using their knowledge of other languages. If you can, try out your activities with a small group of pupils, then review and adapt so that they can be used in your future planning.

3. Promoting language awareness for all pupils

The final case study in this chapter shows the positive value of regarding language diversity as a positive feature of school life and a resource for all pupils, using many strategies that follow **language awareness** principles. It reports work done in a school with a high number of multilingual pupils, but similar work can easily be done in schools where most pupils are monolingual, though it would need to be organised in a different way. Indeed, the important messages about language diversity that the case study illustrates are even more important in such settings.

The Languages Club in a primary school – case study by Anita Conradi

Context

I work as a part-time EAL teacher in a primary school in southeast London: almost half of our 450 pupils are from ethnic minority families. I have counted 27 languages spoken by the families, who come from at least 38 different countries. Although in the course of every year some pupils arrive at the school who are new to English, many of our multilingual pupils have lived most of their lives in the UK, and the majority have done all their schooling in English.

Our recent Ofsted inspection report was satisfied that: 'Pupils who speak English as an additional language make similar progress to their classmates because they are well supported by teachers and other adults', but I felt that many of our multilingual pupils had the potential to achieve even more in school. With the introduction of the new primary curriculum, with its emphasis on the teaching and memorising of facts, I was concerned that there would be even fewer opportunities for class teachers to draw on the vast linguistic experiences of our pupils, or to raise the profile of multilingualism in their classes, even though research has shown what a positive impact this can have on pupils' self-esteem and sense of identity, and therefore on their learning. In spite of the welcoming ethos of the school, many class teachers seemed unaware of the languages spoken by their pupils,

$\rightarrow$

unless they are recent arrivals and relatively new to English. Even during the first week of the school year, when the whole school focuses on diversity and what makes each of us unique, I noticed that language skills were rarely mentioned. I am always struck by the reticence of the multilingual pupils themselves to talk about the other languages they speak and how surprised they seem if anyone asks them about 'their language'. This is not the case, however, when I have the opportunity to work with pupils in a small group situation. Then I find they are keen to read one of the dual-language books from the library, or to talk about their languages with other multilingual pupils, and they are usually very happy to help out by translating for a new arrival.

So as a first step in developing a more 'multilingual approach' to learning, I decided to set up an after-school Languages Club. I sent a letter of invitation to about 25 pupils from Years 4–6 (aged 9–11) who I knew to be multilingual. As I wanted groups of pupils from the same language background to work together if possible, I concentrated on speakers of eight of the most widely spoken languages in the school: Arabic, Spanish, Portuguese, Yoruba, Russian, Ukrainian, Mandarin and Albanian. The club was to take place for an hour on a Wednesday after school, in the second half of the summer term when the SATs exams were over and few other clubs were running. I was not surprised to find that the majority of the 14 who chose to attend were pupils who had previously worked with me in small groups, and who therefore already knew that I was interested in finding out about the other languages they spoke.

Activities

As this was a voluntary after-school club, it was important that the pupils enjoyed themselves and wanted to attend. Some of my ideas came from the language awareness work that I had done many years ago when teaching Modern Languages in a secondary school, and some from my more recent reading about activities to promote learning for multilingual pupils. I had already decided that we would have a quiz every week, and I also invited some of my multilingual colleagues to come along to read a story in their first language. In the first session we brainstormed other ideas for activities, as I wanted the pupils to feel some ownership of the club; there were many interesting suggestions, some more practical than others!

The quizzes proved to be the most popular of the activities, and ranged from naming different flags, to identifying the scripts from the languages spoken by the pupils. The favourite, however, was a quiz where the pupils looked at clips of different traditional songs, which I was able to put together from the internet, and then worked in groups to work out which language was which.

Storytelling was also a popular activity: our first invitations were to one of the class teachers who is a Spanish speaker, and to one of the teaching assistants, whose first language is Arabic. I was also able to arrange for one of my ex-students, a Chinese speaker, to come along to read a traditional story in Mandarin. In our first session I started the storytelling with a French children's story that I have often used in my teaching, chosen because it contains a large number of cognates with English.

The pupils were fascinated by the different scripts they saw in both the Chinese and the Arabic story. As the story chosen in Arabic by our teaching assistant was a version of *Goldilocks*, we initially discussed which words we would expect to be in the story and then each group was asked to identify one of the words and produce it in Arabic at the end of the reading. This activity also enabled the Muslim pupils in the group, who were themselves not Arabic speakers, to identify a number of other words which they recognised from attending classes at the local mosque.

Before listening to the traditional Chinese story, our visitor explained a little about the writing system and the pupils enjoyed learning the numbers from one to ten and practising how to write them. After we had heard the Mandarin version, the pupils focused on picking out and recognising numbers as they occurred in the written text. I was delighted when two of the Year 4 pupils, Paula, a Spanish speaker from Bolivia, and Djoumana, a girl of Algerian origin who speaks both Arabic and Kabyle, a Berber language, subsequently asked if they could present stories themselves. Paula chose to read a dual-language book from the school library, which I scanned so that the whole group were able to follow the text in both Spanish and English as she read it to them, and together we spotted cognates, identified vocabulary and discussed possible meanings. The other Spanish speakers were very keen to give their interpretations and particularly to point out how the word order differed from that of English. Djoumana played us a typical Kabyle poem set to music which she had found on the internet; she explained the meaning of the words as well as telling us the traditional story on which it was based. The other pupils were very interested and some were able to think of similar stories that they knew; they were also most impressed when our 'expert' showed us how to write some of the words in the distinctive Kabyle script.

As the pupils seemed just as keen to find out about the other languages spoken by their peers as they were to talk about their own, I included a number of language awareness activities. One of the more successful focused on the concept of language families and involved the pupils comparing counting systems in a range of different languages. I was struck by how quickly they spotted similarities between the numbers and by their interesting theories as to why this should be the case. The pupils wanted to have a party in our final session of the term, which also happened to be someone's birthday. As we shared the birthday cake, we talked about what you would say in the different languages and the pupils enjoyed talking about how birthdays were traditionally celebrated in their families. I also took the opportunity to get some feedback about the club and to give the pupils the chance to give suggestions for activities they would like to do on future occasions.

Impact

I was not expecting to see much impact on the pupils' school work after only seven sessions, but I was pleased with the enthusiasm of the pupils for the club – 12 of them attended every session. Whenever I saw the pupils around the school they were keen to assure me that they would be at the club that week, and, in their final feedback, all said

→

they would attend again if the club ran in the next school year. Other pupils came up to me in the playground to ask why they had not been chosen – being invited to the Languages Club was definitely seen as a privilege!

One of the Year 6 boys, Ahmed, a Yoruba speaker who was generally viewed as 'difficult' in class, surprised us all by coming back to school to attend the club after a day out at his new secondary school. The enthusiasm of Xiao Yu, a Year 4 girl with a Chinese background, was also unexpected; painfully shy in class, she rarely shared any of her home experiences with her close friends, let alone with her teachers. Xiao Yu attended every session of the club and amazed the other pupils by not only being able to introduce herself in Mandarin, but also by seemingly effortlessly writing whole phrases in Chinese, in spite of previously maintaining that she only spoke English! Although she was not confident enough to chat to our Chinese visitor, she clearly understood the language of the traditional story and was heard to explain some of the words to her friends and to help them with the pronunciation.

Feedback from the parents was also very positive: two mothers told me that their younger children, who would be in Year 4 the following year, were really looking forward to attending the club in the future. Another parent spoke to me about how her daughter, who had previously not been interested in speaking anything but English at home, had been asking to have stories read to her in Russian. I felt it was important that all the languages spoken by the pupils were given equal emphasis during the sessions and I believe that this is one of the reasons why the club was so successful – the look of delight on each child's face as they recognised their own language in one of the activities made the sometimes difficult task of finding examples in Albanian or Yoruba worthwhile! In their feedback, the pupils also said that one of the reasons that they enjoyed the club was that they were able to make new friends and learn something about their languages, and I think this experience was enhanced by the fact that the sessions provided an opportunity – and a reason – for the pupils to talk about their own languages in the company of other multilinguals. For once, speaking another language was being presented as both normal and even an asset.

Future plans

There are plans to run the club again in the next academic year. The pupils have asked to do presentations to the rest of the group on typical foods (with tasting sessions!), on traditional games and music, and on places to visit in the other countries they know well. As they become more confident in speaking about their own languages, I hope that they will be able to take part in school assemblies, especially in the International Week we are planning in school next year. Some of the older pupils are also keen to add a section to the school website with information about the different languages spoken by pupils in the school. After the success of the storytelling sessions, I plan to work with some groups of pupils to produce some dual-language books of their own, to display and to add to the school library. Perhaps the pupils' obvious enthusiasm for such activities will even encourage the class teachers to find the time in an already overcrowded curriculum to develop a more multilingual approach in their own teaching.

Learning Outcomes Review

The three learning outcomes for this chapter are all to do with linking the theories you read about in Chapters 2 and 3 to your thinking about the kinds of strategies and resources that will promote learning for your EAL and multilingual learners. You may be able to take some of the specific ideas described in the chapter into your own planning, but it is more likely that you will use your professional judgement to adapt them to your own classroom setting and the pupils you are teaching.

Self-assessment questions

1. Think about why it is important to draw out the language demands of the curriculum subjects you are teaching for EAL learners. Analyse some of your lessons in different areas of the curriculum to identify their language demands.
2. Why is reading for pleasure important as part of children's experiences of reading? What other kinds of reading would be of value to them in their learning across the curriculum?
3. In what ways might 'language awareness' be important in schools where there are few pupils learning EAL? How might you develop language awareness in such a setting?

Further Reading

Creese, A. (2005) *Teacher Collaboration and Talk in Multilingual Classrooms*. Bristol: Multilingual Matters.

This book looks in detail at the interactions between subject and EAL teachers in multilingual classrooms and shows their importance for learning in secondary schools. It also shows how policy statements and multilingualism ideologies position teachers and learners in particular ways. Different chapters consider the links between languages, different pedagogic approaches and teacher identities in secondary classrooms.

Hawkins, E. (1987) *Awareness of Language: An Introduction*. Cambridge: Cambridge University Press.

Eric Hawkins was the originator of the concept of language awareness, over 25 years ago, and his books still provide the best explanations of the concept and its value in languages teaching and learning, including modern foreign language and EAL. The principle also links to 'Knowledge about language', part of the KS2 Primary Languages Curriculum.

References

National Association for Language Development in the Curriculum (NALDIC) (2014) Partnership Teaching video. Available online: http://www.naldic.org.uk/eal-advocacy/eal-news-summary/140212 (accessed 20 November 2014).

Washbourne, A. (2011) *The EAL Pocketbook*. Hampshire: Teachers' Pocketbooks.

6 Assessing multilingual and EAL learners across the curriculum

> ## Learning Outcomes
>
> This chapter will help you to achieve the following learning outcomes:
>
> - understand the differences between standardised, **summative assessment** of attainment, assessing **achievement** and assessment for learning;
> - understand the issues related to assessing the attainment of multilingual and EAL learners using standardised assessments;
> - understand the importance of assessment for learning for multilingual and EAL learners;
> - gain knowledge of some practical strategies for assessing the strengths and needs of EAL and multilingual learners.

Introduction

In Chapter 3 (section 2.1, p. 41), issues connected with developing an inclusive approach to assessment were raised. While it is no doubt useful to be able to assess all pupils according to the same standards, if this is the only way in which they are assessed, the diversity of their experiences, knowledge and skills will not be recognised and understood. We may never find out about the things that individual pupils can do, which may be crucial to their ongoing development, learning and future attainment. In order to plan the best opportunities for learning for multilingual and EAL pupils, it is important to know about their current achievements as well as their summative attainments, in ways that recognise and value the full range of their experiences, knowledge and skills.

This chapter begins by offering some key principles for assessing multilingual and EAL learners, taken from the QCA (2000) document *A Language in Common*, which is still the most definitive official statement about assessing multilingual and EAL learners. Following this, issues are discussed related to the official, standardised ways of assessing attainment, and how they fail to recognise the distinctive needs of multilingual and EAL learners. In the third section of this chapter, there are suggestions for practical strategies to assess the learning and achievements of multilingual and EAL learners, and using the outcomes to support their future learning, including a case study by Dianne Excell, who describes her work in a secondary school in developing a range of assessments for secondary pupils from Year 7 to GCSE. The final section of the chapter deals with the need to understand the views of those most directly involved in assessment, the pupils, their teachers and their parents. This includes two case studies, one by Oksana Afitska based on interviews with teachers and pupils in Years 3, 4, 5 and 6 and one by Pete Ruse and Linda Sandler on pupil voice in secondary schools. These are followed by suggestions for ways of consulting with the parents and families of multilingual and EAL learners about their pupils' achievements and attainment.

Throughout the chapter, there are discussion points and activities to help you think through the ideas you are reading about, and there are some suggestions for further reading at the end of the chapter.

These are the main sections and subsections of the chapter.

1. **Principles for assessing EAL and multilingual learners**

2. **Standardised assessments of attainment**

    2.1 Issues in national assessment procedures for multilingual and EAL learners

    2.2 Language need or learning need?

3. **Assessment for learning**

    3.1 Profiling and sampling

    Assessing multilingual and EAL learners across the curriculum in a secondary school – case study by Dianne Excell

    3.2 Observing as a tool for assessment

    3.3 Pupils' and teachers' views

    Talking about teaching and learning science in the EAL context: interviewing teachers and learners in primary classrooms – case study by Oksana Afitska

    Learner voice – case study by Pete Ruse and Linda Sandler

    3.4 Consulting with parents

1. Principles for assessing EAL and multilingual learners

The national tests of attainment, the Standardised Assessment Tasks (SATs), were first introduced in the mid-1990s. At the time, there was a great deal of discussion about how to assess pupils who did not have English as their first language, as well as other pupils who were considered to have particular 'barriers to learning'. It was recognised that, for pupils new to English, it could be difficult to assess their understanding of different concepts, say in mathematics or science, without placing demands on their knowledge of English. So sometimes, it could be difficult to find out what pupils actually knew, in different subjects across the curriculum. It was also recognised that the content of the tests could never be culture-free, and so there could be difficulties with comprehension or with the fairness of the tests. Certain content or ideas might be strange to pupils from different cultural backgrounds, or could be interpreted in different ways. Given what we know about the importance of contextual support for pupils' learning and for multilingual and EAL learners in particular, this presents something of a paradox – in trying to provide contextual support, we may actually be making things harder for some pupils. Zaitun Varian-Roper illustrates this beautifully in her chapter about mathematics in Gravelle (2000). Joshua, a child from Uganda, was asked the following question as part of a mathematics test:

I ate half an apple and half of it was left. What was left?

(p. 70)

Joshua's written answer was, 'seeds', and later he asked the teacher, 'But what is an apple, Miss?' There are clear sensitivities in this aspect of testing, and care must be taken not to make assumptions, which could lead to unwitting stereotyping or even racism. These general issues will never be fully resolved, and must always be taken into account in interpreting the results of SATs and other kinds of **summative assessment**. It also has to be remembered that assessment instruments such as the SATs are developed by professional testers and commercial testing agencies in order to provide a final, externalised measure of attainment. There are many other reasons and purposes for assessment, which are available to teachers, and which are the main focus of this chapter.

A document produced in 2000 by the Quality and Curriculum Authority (QCA) *A Language in Common* provides an excellent general overview of the language issues underpinning formative assessment for EAL and multilingual learners. It also makes suggestions for ways of taking their levels of language development into account. It begins by stating some principles for all teachers to consider:

- Be clear about the purposes of the assessment, distinguishing summative, formative and diagnostic aims.
- Be sensitive to the pupil's first or main other language(s) and heritage culture.
- Take account of how long the pupil has been learning English.
- Assess in ways that are appropriate for the pupil's age.
- Focus on language, while being aware of the influence of behaviour, attitude and cultural expectations.
- Recognise that pupils may be at different levels of attainment in speaking, listening, reading and writing. (QCA, 2000: 8)

The first principle is crucial – it is vital to remember always to be clear about the reasons why you are assessing pupils and what you intend to do with the outcomes. The remaining principles stress in different ways the importance of understanding about pupils' knowledge of other languages, and also their community and cultural contexts. They recognise that, for many multilingual and EAL learners, their learning of their new language of English will not be progressing in the same ways as for pupils whose first language is English. As Cummins' BICS and CALP concept informs us, any pupils learning English as an additional language may quickly become competent and confident speakers, but their reading and writing may take much longer to develop. But for some, particularly older pupils, their reading and writing may be much better developed than their speaking. In assessing multilingual and EAL learners, no matter what the subject area, always bear in mind their language experiences and prior knowledge.

The recent Bew Review of testing at KS2 (DfE, 2011a: 10–11) points out the dangers of trying to assess pupils' mathematical ability with questions where their reading capacity may prevent them understanding the maths required. This is, of course, an issue for many pupils, not just some EAL or multilingual learners. As suggested in Chapter 5, it can be very revealing to assess multilingual pupils' knowledge of mathematics or science in their first language, with the support of multilingual colleagues or pupils.

2. Standardised assessments of attainment

2.1 Issues in national assessment procedures for multilingual and EAL learners

SATs are designed to test pupils' attainments in very specific ways. The 'fair test' cartoon in Chapter 3 (p. 60) raises issues about having one such universal means of assessing the attainment of every pupil at each stage of school. Not only does it mean that some pupils (like the fish or the seal in the cartoon) simply cannot do whatever the test might demand, but – just like the fish and the seal – they may have skills and expertise which the test does not recognise. It is crucial not to assume that because a multilingual or EAL pupil cannot do the standardised task, they cannot understand or do not know the concepts being tested. Over the years since the SATs were introduced, a wide range of intervention and assessment procedures have been developed, aimed to support the assessment of multilingual and EAL learners. These are sometimes attached to funding arrangements in the same way that special needs assessments can lead to statementing. As Safford's (2003) paper clearly demonstrates, they can often be very difficult and time-consuming to manage. And the outcomes may not always be very helpful for the pupils or their teachers.

Activity 6.1
Language and testing

Get hold of some old SATs papers in any subject. You may find some in school, or download some from the free SATs website (http://www.sats-papers.co.uk/). Think about the language demands of the tests. Here are some points to consider.

1. Does the layout of the papers help or impair comprehension?
2. Are the instructions clear? Note down any you think may be difficult to interpret and think about how you might re-word them.

3. Is the wording of the questions clear? Are there any possible ambiguities or confusions?
4. Is the content of the questions appropriate? Can you identify any cultural issues or possible ambiguities that may cause problems?
5. Are the illustrations clear? Do they support the understanding of the questions, or make them more difficult?

2.2 Language need or learning need?

Since the Education Act of 1981, there has been a categorical requirement that pupils who speak other languages besides English at home must not be categorised per se as having special needs (SEN):

> *A child is not to be taken as having a learning difficulty solely because the language (or form of language) in which he {sic} is, or will be, taught is different from a language (or form of language) which has at any time been spoken in his home.*

Despite this, there is often confusion between EAL and SEN. In assessing pupils, language needs can become interpreted as learning needs. EAL in itself can become constructed as a learning difficulty, which – of course – it is not.

Pupils who speak other languages besides English at home or who arrive in school from another country, new to English, are often at earlier stages of acquiring English than 'monolingual' pupils of the same age. So they are behind their peers in this area of their learning. They often very quickly develop confidence and skill in conversational language (BICS), but their capacity to understand and use academic language (CALP) takes much longer to grow. Of course, it is also true that young 'monolingual' pupils are at the early stages of developing CALP too. But, because their acquisition of English is usually more advanced, they can move ahead more quickly in a classroom where English is the only means of communication and of learning.

If these aspects of language development are not well understood, there is a risk that the multilingual or EAL learner is assessed as having learning needs or special needs, whereas in fact they more accurately have language needs. There may also be cultural factors that are affecting their learning, which the school is not aware of. The answer to providing for their needs and promoting progress in their learning is *not* to set them to do cognitively simplified tasks and give directed teaching of simple English. It may instead be much more helpful to ensure that they have the opportunities and the support (including using their home languages) to engage in increasingly cognitively challenging activities in contextually supported ways, as is suggested in the discussion on planning in Chapter 4. It may be helpful not to rush to intervene in any way, but simply to spend a bit of time in observing the child and thinking about his or her behaviour, as the following vignette, taken from Gregory (2008: 20–1), illustrates.

Vignette

Tony – EAL and/or SEN?

Tony, a Chinese-heritage child who lived with his parents and grandparents, was very bright and eager when he joined the Reception class of his local school at the age of 4 years 10 months. For a while, all went well. He was very alert and constantly asked, 'What's that?', pointing to things in the classroom. This amused the teacher and reminded her of a much younger child. He loved to draw, and spent a long time carefully and methodically copying the covers of books. After a while, Tony changed. His enthusiasm seemed to evaporate, and he would wander round the classroom aimlessly. His constant 'What's that?' worried the teacher, who began to think he lacked ability or was not getting encouragement from his family. A researcher who was studying Tony's literacy development visited his home. She was surprised by the frosty reception she received from Tony's grandfather, who showed her an exercise book with pages filled with rows of immaculately written Chinese characters. This was the product of Tony's work at the Chinese Saturday class he regularly attended. The grandfather compared this with a drawing Tony had done on the back of a shop advertisement, where he had written his name in poorly formed English letters, some capital, some lower case, in the corner.

At his Saturday class, Tony was clearly a capable and assiduous pupil, who could sit for long periods, carefully copying characters until the strokes were perfect, which is very important in Chinese calligraphy. At his mainstream school, he seemed unable to pay attention for a few minutes, and the work he produced often looked careless and messy. In discussing the home visit with the researcher, Tony's teacher began to understand that he was a very intelligent and hardworking child who needed to have the space to learn in different ways from the other pupils in the class, who were mostly 'monolingual'. Placing him in a special needs group would not help him develop to his full ability.

Activity 6.2
Reflection – EAL or SEN?

Consider the issues raised in the vignette above about Tony. Think about pupils you have worked with, who may have been identified as having SEN, and pupils categorised as EAL. Use these questions to reflect on the possible confusions between EAL and SEN.

1. From what you read above, how would you have assessed Tony's capabilities when he began school?
2. What might have helped the teacher to understand Tony's behaviour when he began school?
3. Why do you think Tony's grandfather was unhappy when he met the researcher?
4. What does the vignette tell you about the ways that multilingual pupils might learn literacy and how does this relate to the theories you read about in Chapter 3?
5. What does the vignette tell you about the links between home and school?
6. If you were Tony's teacher, what would you do, now that you know something about his experiences of literacy learning in his home community?

3. Assessment for learning

3.1 Profiling and sampling

In essence, assessment for learning is the process of making informed, diagnostic judgements about the pupils you teach, in order to decide what to do next. To help them make progress in a particular area of their learning, you need to know what your pupils can and cannot do. Collecting the information you need to make these judgements takes thought and time. Profiling and sampling are important strategies in assessment for learning. With multilingual and EAL learners, the first and most essential kind of profiling you need to do should take place as soon as – or even before – they enter school, whether as a new pupil in Nursery or Reception, or as a new arrival further up the school. Hall *et al.* (2001) suggest the information that schools need to know about pupils' languages and cultural backgrounds, and they provide a useful photocopiable form (pp. 76–7), which could be used for the purpose. Ideally, this kind of information should be collected as part of normal, everyday whole-school routines, and made available to teachers. If this is not the case in your school, you could collect it in your classroom. Here is a slightly adapted version of Hall's list:

1. Name child is called at home

2. Name to be called in school (if different)

3. Place of birth

4. Arrival date in UK

5. Family members who the child lives with

6. Length of previous schooling (in country of origin, and elsewhere, including UK)

7. Religion and festivals observed

8. Languages spoken at home to:

    a.   Mother

    b.   Father

    c.   Siblings

    d.   Grandparents

9. Languages used by family members to child

10. Languages other than English that child can read/write

11. Is the child right- or left-handed?

12. Does the child attend any school or class in the community:

    a.   Supplementary/complementary school

    b.   Religious school

    c.   Any other?

13. What languages are used and taught here?

14. Contact name(s) and details for the organisation(s)

15. Is an interpreter needed for teacher to talk to the parents?

16. If so, who and how can they be contacted?

Another aspect of profiling is the sampling of progress through the work that pupils produce. This can be done for any subject across the curriculum, in different ways. The aim is to collect evidence of pupils' achievements at different stages of their learning of a particular topic or concept. Their development in speaking, listening, writing or reading can also be evaluated in this way to help you decide what to do to help them to make progress. The idea of sampling is one of the key principles behind the *Assessing Pupil Progress (APP)* materials (DfE, 2011b). For example, to assess a child's progress in writing, samples of their written work are collected over a set period of time. Then they are assessed according to criteria that lead not just to assigning a level, but also to indicating what can be done next, to promote learning.

The vignette below (taken from Edwards, 1995) shows the rapid progress that can be made by a multilingual learner, in a supportive classroom environment where he is allowed to use his literacy in his first language to support his development in English.

Vignette

Shahed's writing

Shahed was ten years old when he arrived in England from Iran. He had a high level of literacy in Farsi, the official language of Iran, but very little English. For the first few months of his time in England, he was given the opportunity to write in Farsi while the other pupils in the class were doing their normal literacy activities. The teacher was able to find out what he wrote about with the help of his father. Figure 6.1 is an example of one of his early Farsi texts.

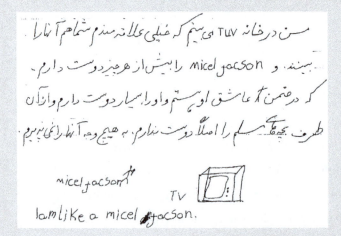

Figure 6.1 Shahed's Farsi writing

In common with many other biliterate pupils, Shahed is beginning to use his knowledge of different scripts to express his meanings in his writing. After six months in the school, Shahed was still writing in Farsi, but his writing in English was developing fast. Figure 6.2 is taken from his writing journal.

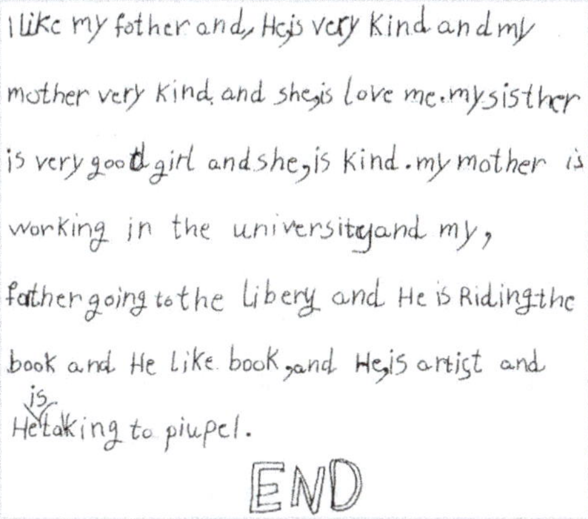

I like my fother and, He is very Kind and my
mother very Kind, and she is love me. my sisther
is very good girl and she is kind. my mother is
working in the university and my,
father going to the Libery and He is Riding the
book and He Like book, and He is artist and
is
He taking to piupel.

END

Figure 6.2 Shahed's writing, six months later

Three months later, he was taking a full part in most lessons, and literacy was one of his favourites. In a lesson where the pupils had been looking at picture books in order to write a story for younger pupils, *Not now Bernard* by David McKee was a favourite. Shahed wrote a letter to Bernard's parents (see Figure 6.3).

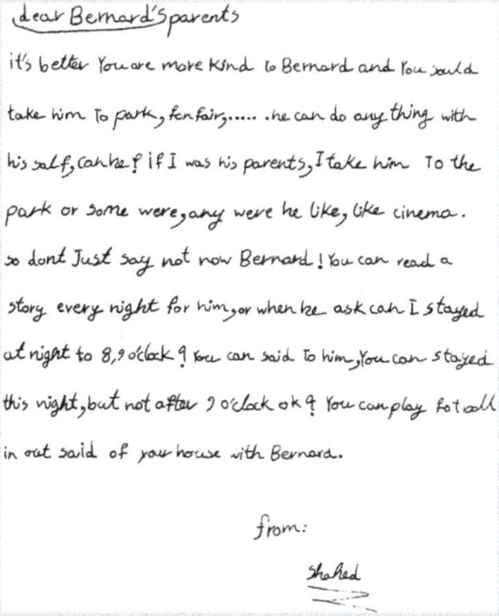

dear Bernard's parents
it's better You are more Kind to Bernard and You sould
take him To park, fonfairs...... . he can do any thing with
his self, can kee f if I was his parents, I take him To the
park or some were, any were he like, like cinema .
so dont Just say not now Bernard ! You can read a
story every night for him, or when he ask can I stayed
at night to 8,9 o'clock ? you can said to him, You can stayed
this night, but not after 9 o'clock ok ? You can play fot ooll
in out said of your house with Bernard.

from:

Shahed

Figure 6.3 Shahed's writing, three months later

Activity 6.3
Assessment for learning and writing

Here are the Assessment Focuses for KS2 writing from the APP materials.

AF1: Write imaginative, interesting and thoughtful texts.

AF2: Produce texts that are appropriate to task, reader and purpose.

AF3: Organise and present whole texts effectively, sequencing and structuring information, ideas and content.

AF4: Construct paragraphs and use cohesion within and between paragraphs.

AF5: Vary sentences for clarity, purpose and effect.

AF6: Write sentences with technical accuracy of syntax and punctuation in phrases, clauses and sentences.

AF7: Select appropriate and effective vocabulary.

AF8: Use correct spelling.

Using the Assessment Focuses, analyse Shahed's two pieces of writing in English. Think about what he can do in each piece, and also what he seems to be trying to do. Think about these questions.

1. What progress do you think he shows from the first piece to the second?
2. What do you think are Shahed's strengths and weaknesses?
3. If you were his teacher, what would you do to help him make further progress in his writing?

The following case study is written by a secondary school teacher who works in a school with pupils with a very diverse range of languages.

Assessing multilingual and EAL learners across the curriculum in a secondary school – case study by Dianne Excell

The results from KS2 SATs in English and maths, which secondary schools usually receive before the end of the summer term, provide information for teachers to place students arriving in September in appropriate sets for the core subjects. But more information is always needed. As part of the transition process, at the beginning of the autumn term, reading tests are often used as a baseline assessment (along with spelling, writing, speaking and listening) to provide more specific information about each student for subject teachers. Are these standardised tests a clear indication of ability for students learning English as an additional language (EAL)? The

→

observations shared here are the result of many years of experience in trying to overcome the issues which can create a barrier to achievement for EAL students in these tests.

At one girls' secondary school in inner city Bradford, most students have ethnic origins in Pakistan but were born in Bradford. Additionally, a few students each year arrive from a wide variety of countries such as Algeria, Bangladesh, Egypt, Greece, Hong Kong, India, Iraq, Japan, Jordan, Libya, Saudi Arabia, Spain, Sudan and Tanzania. Most are, by the 2005 Ofsted definition, 'multilingual learners', as they have been taught in the English education system for at least six years. However, all have English as an additional language to two others such as Urdu, Punjabi, Hindko, Pushto, Mirpuri as well as Arabic. Some of these languages are only spoken, others are written from right to left. Many students are only literate in English and have little experience of English in their home environment. When the students arrive in Year 7, most are competent and confident communicators (BICS), but are at different stages of developing CALP. Many students have acquired BICS as far as Step 4 or 5 in Speaking and Listening on NASSEA's EAL Assessment Guidance (NASSEA, 2001), but they only achieved N or B in the KS2 SATs. They may not even have been entered in the SATs because their reading and writing skills were below the level of the tests.

Baseline Reading Tests

Until 2011, the school used the NFER Nelson Group Reading Test II (Form C or D) for baseline assessments because they were standardised and provided reading ages (RAs) for all students in KS3 at the beginning of the academic year. The tests consisted of 45 sentences which students completed by selecting a word from a choice of five. The advantage was that it was relatively quick because all students were tested together and it was intended to test understanding. In principle, if the same test was given at the end of the year, progress during the year could be assessed. However, I observed that there was often a discrepancy between student RAs and their SATs results; many students who had achieved Level 4 in the KS2 English SATs had RAs at least two years behind their chronological age (CA). This risk of underachievement could apply even to students who achieved a good Level 5. Also, students showed varying amounts of progress in the end of year tests. Indeed, some students had lower scores at the end of the year than at the beginning (and from one September to another), which could suggest that they did not fully understand the sentences and were guessing at an answer. Many recent arrivals could achieve only a few correct answers and a low RA, even though they might seem to have good oral skills. There was a danger that this could be misinterpreted as that they had special educational needs (SEN) and lead to being wrongly placed in the lowest set, with lower expectations and perpetual underachievement. At the end of the year, EAL students may still have a low RA even though they may have made significant progress in other curriculum areas and there should be no cause for concern – for example, a student with only two years of English language experience achieved Level 5 in science at the end of Year 7 but her RA in September Year 8 (6.05) was over a year lower than in Year 7 (7.06).

When analysing 40 tests one year, I found only five words which were almost always correct. Problems were caused by, for example:

- lack of general, specialist or cultural knowledge (words such as: bolt, gale, saddle, theatre, tulip);
- idiomatic language ('raced' in a non-literal context);
- homophones (knot/not);

→

- prepositions ('to' instead of 'from');
- wrong word association (for example 'chemist' confused with 'clinic' for buying toothpaste and 'tiles' being associated with floors rather than 'roofs');
- unusual/old-fashioned polysyllabic words (fruit being sold from a 'barrow'; confusion of department/apartment, praise/price/prize).

I therefore concluded that, although the NFER tests were standardised, they were only appropriate for testing monolingual English speakers because most sentences assumed prior knowledge of English culture.

Development of alternative reading tests

In an attempt to eliminate cultural bias, I developed an Alternative Reading Test for the end of Year 7 and 8. Although this was not standardised, it was probably fairer than the NFER test (see pp. 150–157) because it was based directly on what had been taught in the curriculum of Year 7 and 8. Subject colleagues were asked to provide six key words from their scheme of work (ranging from basic to advanced), which all students had experienced at some stage in the year. I produced a test in a similar format to the NFER test by fitting the words into sentences and giving multiple choices for the answers (see Alternative Year 7 Reading Test at the end of this chapter). The 'Collins KS3 Word Bank Dictionary' was used to create some sentences if the key word was listed. Word choices were made in such a way to ensure that the students had to use a wide range of knowledge about words in order to select the correct answer, e.g.:

- homophones (write, white, right, light);
- similar sounding words (pleasure, leisure, treasure, measure);
- words from the same context (pilgrim, journey, pilot);
- words with similar combinations of letters (digits, fidgets, gadgets);
- same beginnings (obligation, obedient, obstruction, objective).

The test was challenging for most students and seemed to be useful for identifying students with high scores who:

- were gifted;
- could remember what they have learnt across the curriculum, throughout the year.

Those achieving lower scores included pupils who:

- had learning difficulties;
- had poor attendance, lack of motivation and/or poor behaviour;
- were new to English and making good progress; their errors highlighted areas still needing further support in their English-language acquisition;
- were new to English and making less progress than expected, suggesting that more formative assessments should be made to determine the most appropriate type of support.

Moreover, the tests could also identify the words and concepts across the curriculum which were causing most difficulty. Mainstream colleagues were informed of the results so that appropriate adjustments could be made in succeeding years.

→

The NFER New Group Reading Tests

The NFER Group Reading Tests (GRT) were discontinued in 2011 so since then, the school has used the NFER New GRT (3A or 3B) for baseline testing. Out of 52 questions, only 20 are sentence completion like the old one. The rest are in four passage comprehensions, which are designed to test the KS3 English Assessment Focuses (AFs) (which can now be accessed on TES Connect: http://www.tes.co.uk/teaching-resource/APP-in-English-Learning-Objectives-and-amp-AFs-6062016/).

I marked all the Year 7 to Year 9 papers and analysed the results of the two top set English groups in Year 7 and 8. I found that in both groups two of the students only got 50% of the answers correct, although some in Year 8 got over 90% of the marks and in Year 7 over 80%. Many students throughout KS3 had RAs which were well below their chronological ages. Another interesting result was that the Year 7 student who had the highest KS2 English SATs result (Level 5c) achieved the lowest RA (9:03) and one of the brightest Year 8 only got 52% correct answers – with a RA two years below her previous year's! However, there were some students who achieved better than expected scores. Overall some achieved RAs two or three years above their CA and some two or three years below … or more.

In the sentence completion section, I found similar cultural and linguistic issues as in the old NFER GRTs. The most surprising error was in the very first question, which said 'A calf is a baby ___' (cow). 'Calf' is both an unknown word and difficult to pronounce because of the silent letter – many students (even in the top Year 9 set) said it was a baby horse, cat, dog. This problem clearly reflected that both cultural and linguistic concepts were creating difficulties. Some errors arose because students had previously misheard words in other contexts e.g. there was confusion between 'shattered'/'sheeted' and 'sheltered'; inscription/description, illuminated/lubricated. Several of the sentences contained old-fashioned words, for example 'drudgery' in one and 'after it was picked, the fruit was packed in punnets' (the other choices were: decanters/pallets/compost/trowels).

In the passage completion section there were texts relating to *Tightrope Walkers, Youth Challenge, Wind in the Willows* and *The Eiffel Tower*. The results showed some interesting points:

- The writer's use of language was the weakest assessment focus (AF5). For example, one question asked, 'What is the effect of calling the tightrope a "silver thread"?' Many students could recognise 'silver thread' as a metaphor and gave that as the answer but they could not explain what the effect was, for example, showing that the narrator thinks it is thin.
- Most students had the greatest difficulty with the pre-1914 text *Wind in the Willows*, which had more old-fashioned language, whereas all students achieved better results for the *Youth Challenge* section which contained more familiar vocabulary and context.
- Problems in retrieving specific information highlight the need for the teaching of skimming and scanning skills. Weak inference and deduction skills indicate that students are unable to see deeper meanings or wider and more general implications.

These results are shared with all colleagues so that strategies to compensate can be incorporated into lesson plans. The needs of individual students are also shared in order to ensure that able EAL students are not assumed to have special educational needs just because they have a low reading age. For example, in her initial assessments, one new arrival of Libyan

$\rightarrow$

heritage was able to write copious amounts of Arabic in mature language which showed correct use of connectives, punctuation, verb tenses, punctuation as well as feelings and opinions. Although she produced less English writing on the same subjects, it was also correctly formed with some knowledge of sentence structure and grammar. However, her RA was seven years and six months and her spelling age was seven years and three months. If only the reading and spelling tests had been considered, there might have been a danger of the student being placed in the bottom set because it was thought she had speech, language and communication difficulties (SPLD), which is clearly not the case.

3.2 Observing as a tool for assessment

In section 2.2 p. 129, I mentioned the importance of observation for understanding the behaviour and learning of multilingual and EAL learners. It is particularly important to take as many factors into account as you can in your professional judgements, to ensure that you decide on the right provision to help pupils make progress. This is often the case when you are trying to assess the knowledge and understanding of multilingual and EAL learners. If a child is at an early stage of acquiring English and so has a limited capacity to produce spoken English, they may show their understanding of an instruction, an idea or a concept non-verbally. For example, watching carefully how young children place magnetic letters while trying to spell a word or how they physically write on a whiteboard can reveal a lot about what they understand about letter sounds and symbols. In the same way, watching how they use their fingers or concrete resources when counting in maths can tell you a lot about their understanding of numbers and number bonds, which they may not be able to put into English words. More broadly, watching how a child interacts with other pupils, in the playground and in other settings besides the classroom at different points in time, can show you a lot about their overall language development, self-confidence and identity as a learner.

In many ways, observing is a key professional skill for all teachers, and you will quickly find that you are constantly making a mental note of things you observe or notice about a child. Get into the habit of writing down things that strike you as significant. In many Early Years classrooms, this is part of the routine and there are notebooks to hand so that staff can do this, and then collect up comments about individual pupils in a portfolio. This practice is not so common once pupils move through primary and into secondary schools. But it is something you could introduce in your class. As well as this kind of spontaneous observing and recording, it is useful to arrange more focused observations from time to time in order to collect evidence about a particular child's progress, or evaluate a specific approach or strategy in your teaching.

Remember that in observing, as in any form of research, you must always act ethically and be sure to take account at all times of any ethical issues connected with the activity and the pupils involved. This is particularly important when you are a trainee, as you are working always under the guidance of others, who will take ultimate responsibility for your actions. Here are a few ethical points to consider when carrying out observations.

- Always seek 'informed consent' before beginning an observation by making sure that pupils know you are observing them – teachers have responsibilities for protecting their pupils.
- Be aware of legal considerations and child protection issues.
- Make sure that confidentiality is maintained.
- Interpret and analyse – don't judge!
- Think about how you will use your findings – why are you carrying out the observation?
- What do you do if you observe something inappropriate or dangerous – to intervene or not to intervene?

The last point has clear links to safeguarding, and it is a good idea to check with your class teacher beforehand if there might be any sensitive issues related to a child you plan to observe. If anything did emerge during the course of the observation, for example, inappropriate behaviour or comments that come up in conversation, your role as a trainee teacher is to pass them on immediately to your class teacher and then withdraw from the situation. Any resulting action may need to be kept confidential and, as someone who is in the school for a limited period, you must not be involved.

Activity 6.4
Observing

During your next school placement, if possible, arrange to spend 20–30 minutes observing a multilingual or EAL learner in their classroom, in order to gain a sense of how they behave and participate in the classroom. Have a brief conversation with the child before you begin, so that they are aware of what you are doing. Here are a few 'dos and don'ts' to think about in setting up your observation.

1. Do remember to record contextual features – layout of classroom, organisation, lesson topic, resources used, etc.
2. Do set up a specific focus for your observation, e.g. a particular child, teacher's use of questions as a teaching strategy, etc.
3. Don't judge – only write down what you see and hear.
4. Don't observe for long periods of time – usually ten minutes at a time is enough, then break for a minute or so, and then continue.
5. Do recognise your own biases and viewpoints – no observation is neutral.

The interview data reported in this case study is taken from a larger dataset of 53 audio-recorded interviews collected as part of the EAL Science Project (a collaborative project between the University of Sheffield and Sheffield City Council, 2013–2015) in five primary schools in Sheffield, South Yorkshire. This case study presents data from the same school as in Chapter 3, but the participants in this study are from Years 3–6.

3.3 Pupils' and teachers' views

Talking about teaching and learning science in the EAL context: interviewing teachers and learners in primary classrooms – case study by Oksana Afitska

The interviews related to the participants' experiences of teaching and learning science in the EAL context. One of the major issues repeatedly mentioned by the teachers was that the learners found it difficult to remember and retain new scientific vocabulary. This situation, of course, is also true of English 'monolingual' pupils who struggle to retain new vocabulary. Therefore this teacher's observation was not just about a 'problem' for EAL learners. The teachers emphasised that it was the remembering and recalling of scientific terms specifically that caused the learners most difficulties, rather than the understanding of their properties and functions, suggesting that – subject-wise – EAL learners can do just as well as their English native-speaking peers. Excerpts below exemplify these two points:

Remembering and retaining vocabulary and conceptual vs. linguistic problems	
Y3/T: it is the remembering of terminology, key terms, key words [...] getting the pupils to remember the names of the organs [...] because quite a lot of it is quite complicated, it is not simple stuff [...] it is the recall of it, a lot of pupils struggle to retain this information Y3/T: Straight away you know it is language that they are struggling with [...] 'Name me a part of a body which you use to swallow food?' and they will say: 'It is here (the teacher points to his neck) and it is called the food tube and it begins like with 'o' (meaning oesophagus) [...] they understand the concept but it is the actual terminology; if you said to them: 'What's this called?' they'd say: 'It's a food tube', 'What is it used for?' 'It takes your food down into your stomach' they'll tell you that but if you ask 'What's the name for it?' pupils will struggle with language they won't – they'll say: 'I can't remember' [...] you'll know it is not the principle that they are struggling with, it is terminology, the actual words, the language that they struggle with.	Y4/T: Probably understanding and using vocabulary ... they have to understand the meaning ... if they discuss they need to get specific language that they'll need to use so it's more like language than concepts, to be honest ... for instance if we are doing solids and liquids and gases they'll be able to tell you what's the solid what's the liquid but scientific language they will struggle with – 'particles' and 'melting', 'evaporation' they will struggle with that kind of language but they will be able to understand the concept of it Y6/T: it is remembering ... they find it [difficult] ... being able to recap it ... there will be only few that will be able to recall that information Y6/T: maybe not the concept but the words associated with that concept (that the learners tend to forget) ... because as soon as I prompt it they are able to recall it (specific scientific vocabulary)

→

It must be noted here however, that even though the mainstream class teachers in this specific school, except for the Year 5 teacher, tended to rank the learners' poor ability to remember and recall scientific vocabulary as one of the major difficulties in their science classrooms, the project questionnaire and test data suggest that the learners also had difficulties in understanding scientific concepts, functions, processes and principles. Among other problems identified by the teachers were:

- an inadequate stock of resources designed specifically for teaching learners with EAL;
- the amount of time that it takes to develop or adapt resources to suit the needs of the learners;
- lack of time to support learners more extensively, for example, assisting them with specific aspects of the subject before or after the lessons;
- limited opportunities to provide detailed feedback on homework and to follow up on it;
- insufficient use of parental resources;
- problems related to making use of home, i.e. first, language for learning.

The excerpts below exemplify these points.

EAL resources	
Y3: [...] and think right that's appropriate I'll teach that, that's not really appropriate and then you start putting together your resources and you think right my top pupils I want them to do this and in order for them to do that I need to make this resource for them, you think about differentiation and most of the time you have to spend time making the resources Interviewer: where do they come from? Y3: sometimes if you can't find them you just have to make them ... that's what takes most of the time, the planning part is not hard once you have an idea [...] you can have eight lessons planned in half a day but to prepare (materials) it could take you hours, it can take you several hours to prepare the flipchart you know, to search for any videos, any activities to do with your lesson Y5: I make them (pictures and diagrams) Interviewer: How long does it take you to prepare resources? Y5: A long time (laughs) that's what I do, I do not know – a few hours for each hour lesson	Y4: we have got equipment at school and vocab sheets and the rest I have to make ... sometimes I literally make them out sometimes I adapt things from the internet depending on what the needs of my class are [...] Interviewer: how long does it take you to develop one lesson? Y4: quite a while really because even within that class the differentiation is quite big so to differentiate the activities takes quite a while, and to make flip charts with lots of visuals – Interviewer: couple of hours? Y4: yeah yeah yeah probably about two hours, yeah Y6: I just search the web to find good pupils' explanation of something that I can then extend with them [...] I find different areas that I think will be suitable [...] you got to adapt it (the existing resource) to how it suits your class [...] it can take a good couple of hours if not more
Out-of-class support	
Y4: no, probably not, she (the teaching assistant) generally would support (pupils) during the lesson...	Y3: Maybe before the lesson and after the lesson would be good but again it is just finding the time...

→

Use of parental resources	
Y4: key is also to get parents on board having translated into home language that they (pupils) could take home to discuss with their parents because often they do not relate what they do in the school to (what) they do at home, for instance, you know melting chocolate and ice into water … whereas if they have this conversation at home that could assist … just the vocabulary workbook they could work through […] or maybe every term having parents in for half an hour saying that's what we will be doing in science Interviewer: do you think the parents will be coming? Y4: I think some would again it's about those parents who would not come in but I think if we encourage that or we spent half an hour of every first science lesson of the term with parents in school with their pupils learning about it together I think it will be quite useful	Y3: [The teacher proposes that the parents are given a 'Key facts' book and suggests how parents can make use of it] in the next six or seven weeks we will be covering these terms and (then the parents are invited to) explain (these terms to) them (pupils) in their first language and (to) give plenty of pictures rather than just one word, (to) put them into sentences trying to explain it to your pupils – 'opaque' means this and then you (i.e. the researchers who are developing materials for parents) get nice sentences written in their (the parents' and the pupils') first language so when parents see it, they say: 'Yes I know what it means' and then they can tell a child: 'You read in English and I will try and explain to you what it means in the first language'

Feedback on homework
Y3: mark it […] very brief feedback very, very brief feedback […] just the amount we got to mark on our day to day basis […] mark spelling mistakes underline grammar mistakes, punctuation mistakes … (these) will be noted, trying to encourage pupils to go back but it is just finding time … tight timetable, finding the time to let pupils to go back and correct those mistakes Interviewer: you do not follow up on homework in class? Y3: No

Use of first language for learning purposes – the teachers' perspective
Y4: …the trouble with this is that sometimes you do not know how secure they are with their home language the concepts in home language often cause more confusion than help…

Learner interview data suggest that the learners are just as aware as their teachers of the 'knowledge-confusion' phenomenon described above. This phenomenon may happen when the subject-specific content that was initially taught via the medium of a second language (i.e. the English language) is explained or clarified to the child via the medium of his/her first language (i.e. the home language), where neither of the languages is familiar enough to the child, as suggested in the following excerpts.

Use of first language for learning purposes – the learners' perspective	
Y4/P1: I speak English because sometimes I forget to speak Hungarian because it is confusing	Interviewer: You said you do homework in English, why?

→

Interviewer: what exactly is confusing?	Y4/P2: because sometimes it is confusing in Urdu because then you have to use scientific words
P1: first I speak in Slovakian at home in Slovakia and then I came here and I started learn English so I forgot some of the Slovakian words and Hungarian words so sometimes it is complicated	Y5/P1: I normally like to speak Punjabi but I get like mixed up with the words, not all of it a little bit of it
Interviewer: so is it everyday words that you have forgotten in Hungarian or is it science words that you have forgotten?	Interviewer: Do you know how scientific words are said in your home language?
P1: yeah, science words	P1: no, I do not

It must be noted here that even though the learners have reported avoiding using their first language for learning purposes both in the classroom and at home, the data suggests that they continue using it comfortably for non-schooling purposes, for example on the playground.

Use of first language for non-learning purposes episode
Interviewer: Do you use your first language in pair and group work?
Y6/P1&P2: not that much, no
Interviewer: On the playground?
Y6/P1&P2: yeah!

We also do not know what effect it might have if home languages were used more systematically in the classroom to introduce, discuss and develop understanding of key scientific concepts and for pupils to discuss ideas with each other, reporting back to the teacher in English.

Having identified the areas where the problems for EAL learners tended to occur most frequently in their science lessons, the teachers commented on the techniques and strategies that they used to overcome, or at least minimise, these problems as much as they could. One specific technique that was used across the entire school was reciprocal reading. The teachers made the following comments on this technique:

Reciprocal reading
Y4: we tend to do it as a whole class, like reciprocal reading, like I'll set them off and we will make a prediction about what we think it might be and then they read through individually and ask any words that they do not know; we put all these words on a board and I will explain [...] then I'll read it out loud and stop when somebody puts their hand up ... and we will get a bank of those words and they will have to go into their (pupils') science books
Y6: I think I have learnt over years that you slow down and you do reciprocal reading [...], so you get the pupils to read or you read them the text and ask the pupils to ask about the words that they do not understand in science text, and you ask pupils: 'Are there any words that you do not understand?' and kind of go through the meaning of those words.
(For the reciprocal reading technique see: http://www.educationscotland.gov.uk/Images/ ReciprocalReadingGuide_tcm4-812956.pdf)

Reciprocal reading supports the comprehension of new words, and the teachers also used other techniques for this purpose. Some made extensive use of visuals, such as labelled pictures and diagrams; others (specifically, the Year 4 teacher whose lesson is reported in the case study in Chapter 5) went even further and reported spending an entire lesson every time a new topic was to be introduced, familiarising learners with the core vocabulary needed for that specific topic.

Using visuals	Pre-teaching vocabulary for new topic
Y3: some of the terminology is not easy we try and look at pictures and images to support them […] you will have a picture of intestines and the word written next to it Y4: … for EAL learners who struggle with vocab I'll have pictures to go with (the words), things like that	Y4: Prior to topic I tend to do a lesson solely on vocabulary that we are going to use during a topic and I will give them a sheet with pictures of vocabulary so that they will practise the word, beginning with just recognising the word and after I'll set them off using the dictionary to find out the meaning so we do quite an introduction before starting a new topic

In relation to developing the learners' speaking skills in the target language, the teachers reported using speaking frames and sentences starters (see Chapter 5 case study for more examples). Moreover, the Year 3 teacher also reported using phonics to help learners read difficult words and the 'say/cover' technique to help them pronounce, spell and remember the words. All teachers used group work or partner work to give learners opportunities hear good models of target language from their linguistically more advanced peers as well as opportunities to practise the target language in a safe environment.

Using phonics and 'say/cover' technique	Using group-work for language support
Y3: we try to bring phonics into it we try and break up the words Y3: it is about saying it: I say it – you say it, you say it – I say it, cover it up, you know, strategies like that	Y4: if it is a language-enriched environment I will put the good speakers with bottom ones to help them with language which comes up Y5: If they struggle with English they are put with someone who can speak English and can model it

The learners also reported taking an active part in their learning by putting their hands up and asking questions when they had difficulties understanding scientific concepts or words:

Learner participation and active learning	
Y5/P1: you put your hand up	Y6/P2: we put our hand up and ask our teacher
Y5/P2: then you ask Miss to clarify it for us	Interviewer: is it that you do not understand the terms the language –
Interviewer: do you always understand when she clarifies it to you?	Y6/P2: the language, yeah
Y5/P1&P2: yeah	

The data in this case study presents the views of only a few teachers and learners from one specific school. While it cannot be generalised, it does raise some important issues that may be relevant to EAL learners in other contexts.

Learner voice – case study by Pete Ruse and Linda Sandler

At one secondary school, the EAL Department conduct annually a series of exit interviews with Year 11 pupils who have arrived at the school as early stage EAL learners. The outcomes of these interviews are collated and used for a variety of purposes – training, informing governors of the department's work (a highly significant purpose as it is not always obvious), and feedback for the department and pupils. Over the years, this exercise has informed developments in practice, such as deploying dedicated teaching assistant support for international new arrivals (INAs) and prompting staff generally to smile at pupils and be welcoming. This year the interviews were video recorded. The pupils were asked about their experiences when they first came to the school. Here are the responses of four pupils:

Dj: I was scared. Didn't know how to speak (English). Sometimes girls you didn't speak their language they talking to your name and you didn't understand what they saying. Every day I cry when I went home 'cos I doesn't know how to speak English. Grades affected because of not know how to speak English. (Previous grades were) not so bad.

(In maths lessons) I didn't know the numbers. I was embarrassed … I am good in maths but first time I didn't understand him to tell me the numbers. I just have in my brain … I can't say it. It's too difficult. It was so hard.

A: I was afraid to say something – it came out wrong so I didn't say anything.

I thought I knew English. I could understand what people said (in Africa). What didn't help was English accent because I was used to American accent in Africa.

D: (In English lessons) … I was not able to speak properly. I was nervous inside and can't fully (get) out the words.

The school like so hard 'cos I didn't understand the English. And then to make a new friend. For to understand what the teacher is saying in the class.

M: I was the only one who could speak my language. Like D has friends who can speak Portuguese and I am on my own. Even if I went to google translate it would not let me because my language (Ndebele) is not there.

The (English) accent was bit hard for me.

And about their previous experiences of education:

Dj: My worst subject was English in Africa. I doesn't like English. In my school in Portugal every time I get lowest grade in English and I cry a lot in my class. And then my mum say – you going to England to study the English.

When I'm coming here I didn't want to come in England but I didn't have any choice.

I think to myself I want to learn English and then I can do what I want to do.

→

This school very different from Portugal. How to learn and how to teach is very different.

The thing I think is if at first I understand the English is when I gonna be a good student here, get good grade, because the [indistinct] in Portugal is hard … Harder than here … because … if they give you a test, every two weeks, you do your tests, you didn't get to do your plan like you do here, to do your plan or something [she is talking about revising]. You need just to do it in your hair [pointing to head].

M: (School here) is different. This school is big. And, like, our lessons that were different. Like, when I'm going to English it's just down there, but to go to English in my class (in Zimbabwe) I have to walk a long distance.

D: This school is big, like, in Portugal school is middle size. More pupil in the school.

And about what helped them:

D: The first people see, the first Portuguese people see was A, in science, then I said to her 'do you speak English, ah, do you speak Portuguese?' Then says 'yes' then I was happy … Cos he can help me as well …

[EAL lunchtime] homework club help me with homework … good friends, they help me as well, with the homework.

[outside lessons] Got friends quickly. They say: 'what's your name?' and I say: 'D', then they say: 'what lesson you got next?' and I say: 'science or maths'. You [EAL teacher] help me. EAL teachers help me … help me to get good grade … yes, to understand. You give me dictionary to see what it means. That's help me.

Dj: [meeting others with the same L1] Yes, really helpful to show me my class …. So hard to talking with girl who talking English.

You [EAL teacher] help me, miss.

M: I come [to EAL lunchtime club] for help, like read book … Like watched TV and my dad helped me with the accent because he's been in this country a long time.

A: I had some students help me … Teachers … people from reception helped me.

And plans for the future:

M: I want to be a nurse. I applied in college for Health and Social Care. I have done my interviews and I'm waiting for my grades. I have to have good grades to go there.

Dj: My intention is to be a doctor. But now I think I'm not gonna do it this year. You need good grades in English. You need to get Cs and 5 GCSE to get in college or sixth form. It's 'A' level but I'm not worry about this. I'm doing retailing.

When I was in Portugal I get good grades in my own GCSEs. I just have less level in English. All my grades was good. I chose to be a doctor but now I think I'm not gonna do it because I don't have a good level for my GCSE. Now I'm doing retailing. [Happy?] Yes, I'm happy for that.

A: I will be study travel and tourism in college because I'm studying French and I want to, like, work in a sort of a hotel that I can translate French into English or any other language that I can learn.

→

D: I wanna be a football player. I got grades to do football in college … football academy. For football academy you need to get D so I think I'm gonna get D in some things.

And advice for school (with respect to early stage EAL learners):

Dj: More time in lessons to do their work.
A: To be nice to them and smile and just try to help them as much as they can.

One recurring positive feature of exit interviews is the EAL lunchtime homework club, where pupils develop cross-year and cross-language friendships based on their common experiences as international new arrivals. It is a forum that allows them to support each other and draw on each other's experience. Here, they are in a space that values their use of their first languages (L1s) and this has allowed EAL practitioners to encourage learners to use their L1s in classrooms to learn, to make notes in L1, for example.

This year's exercise has prompted thinking among staff about how to better support the transition from school process, including college applications and interviews. It has prompted thinking about how to make space for learners to talk about their aspirations earlier in their school careers so they can become clearer about where they want to go and how they might get there. Clear, strong goals are motivating and can guide learners through what can be a daunting process of simultaneously acquiring English and engaging with subject content and skills. One development already planned is to establish a series of themed EAL homework club lunchtimes around different topics and issues. Life goals might be one, interview practice another. What came across really strongly, though, is how significant a life event it is for these learners to come to another country with another language environment. We can forget how scary that can be and it is a good thing that as education practitioners we are reminded of it.

3.4 Consulting with parents

Tony's story above (see the vignette in section 2.2, p. 130) reveals a great deal about the importance of finding out about a child's home and community experiences of learning and of literacy, a point that has been emphasised many times throughout this book. In terms of assessment, it can help you interpret what the child does in school in much more holistic ways and lead to much better informed decisions about what to provide for the child.

As part of the assessment cycle, teachers also have the responsibility of reporting pupils' achievements to their parents, and providing an opportunity for them to discuss their child's progress. As a trainee, you may be involved in this, and you need to gain some experience in this area. An important issue in relation to multilingual and EAL learners is the need to make sure that the arrangements for reporting and consulting meet the parents' needs, which may differ according to their language and cultural backgrounds. In some families, it is not the parents who take the responsibility for communicating with the school about the child's education: it may be an uncle or aunt, or even an older sibling. There may be the need for an interpreter, which might be someone working in the school or someone from the community.

Learning Outcomes Review

The four learning outcomes for this chapter are about developing your understanding of the different purposes and types of assessment as a whole, as well as specific issues related to EAL and multilingual learners. The chapter also introduces you to some practical ways in which you can use assessment processes to support and promote learning for your multilingual and EAL learners. Thinking about school-based experiences you have had in general and with EAL and multilingual learners in particular, reflect on the learning outcomes using the questions below.

Self-assessment questions

1. What are the key differences between assessment *for* learning and assessment *of* learning? What are the general issues related to each in assessing the achievements and attainment of EAL and multilingual learners?
2. Why do you think it is so important that learning needs are not confused with language needs for multilingual and EAL learners?
3. Why are assessment for learning strategies, such as profiling and sampling, particularly important for multilingual and EAL learners? What specific issues have you faced (or might you face) in sampling the work of a child who is relatively new to English?
4. What factors may make consulting with parents of multilingual and EAL learners about their pupils' achievements and attainment different from consulting with the parents of 'monolingual' pupils, and how is it the same?

Further Reading

Briggs, M. (2011) Assessment. In: Hansen, A. (ed.) *Primary Professional Studies* (pp. 184–203). Exeter: Learning Matters.
This chapter provides a full overview of assessment and introduction to assessment for learning and assessment of learning in primary classrooms.

Hall, D., Griffiths, D., Haslam, L. and Wilkin, Y. (2001) *Assessing the Needs of Multilingual Pupils: Living in Two Languages*, 2nd edn. London: David Fulton.
This short book provides very clear guidance on assessing multilingual and EAL pupils, avoiding the pitfalls of conflating EAL with SEN.

National Association for Language Development in the Curriculum (NALDIC) (2009): Introduction to NALDIC formative assessment descriptors: an introduction to NALDIC's EAL assessment descriptors.
Assessment descriptors KSl: formative EAL assessment for KSl EAL learners.
Assessment descriptors KS2: formative EAL assessment for KSl EAL learners.
http://www.naldic.org.uk/eal-initial-teacher-education/ite-programmes/assessment-for-learning (accessed 28 October 2014).

These three documents, which can all be downloaded from the NALDIC website, provide a comprehensive model for assessing pupils, taking account of the languages they use outside school. They are useful for pupils in secondary school, especially new arrivals, as well as primary pupils.

References

Department for Education (DfE) (2011a) *Independent Review of Key Stage 2 Testing, Assessment and Accountability: Final Report* (The Bew Review). London: DfE. https://www.gov.uk/government/collections/key-stage-2-ks2-testing-review (accessed 28 October 2014).

Department for Education (DfE) (2011b) *Assessing Pupils' Progress (APP) Overview*. London: DfE. http://webarchive.nationalarchives.gov.uk/20130401151715/http://www.education.gov.uk/publications/eOrderingDownload/Assessing_pupils_progress.pdf (accessed 28 October 2014).

Edwards, V. (1995) *Writing in Multilingual Classrooms*. Reading: Reading and Language Information Centre, University of Reading.

Gravelle, M. (ed.) (2000) *Planning for Multilingual Learners: An Inclusive Curriculum*. Stoke-on-Trent: Trentham Books.

Gregory, E. (2008) *Learning to Read in a New Language: Making Sense of Words and Worlds*. London: Sage.

Hall, D., Griffiths, D., Haslam, L. and Wilkin, Y. (2001) *Assessing the Needs of Multilingual Pupils: Living in Two Languages*, 2nd edn. London: David Fulton.

The Northern Association of Support Services for Equality and Achievement (NASSEA) (2001) *EAL Assessment System*. Dukinfield: NASSEA. http://www.wigan.gov.uk/Docs/PDF/Council/Schools-Portal/n/nassea20booklet.pdf (accessed 19 November 2014).

Quality and Curriculum Authority (QCA) (2000) *A Language in Common: Assessing English as an Additional Language*. Sudbury: QCA Publications. http://www.naldic.org.uk/Resources/NALDIC/Teaching%20and%20Learning/1847210732.pdf (accessed 28 October 2014).

Safford, K. (2003) *Teachers and Pupils in the Big Picture: Seeing Real Pupils in Routinised Assessment*. Reading: NALDIC. http://www.naldic.org.uk/eal-publications-resources/Shop/shop-products/op17 (accessed 28 October 2014).

Alternative Year 7 Reading Test

End of Year Reading Test – Year 7

Name:_____   Form:_____   Date:_____

Raw Score:_____   Percentage:_____   RA _____   CA_____

Read each sentence carefully. Look at the list of words. Choose <u>one</u> word from the list which completes each sentence best. Underline the word.

1. The school rounders _____ won the game.

   term

   team

   time

   tear

2. At the theatre they saw a _____.

   plea

   pray

   poem

   play

3. He changed the _____ to make the text look clearer.

   font

   fund

   front

   formula

4. We belong to the _____ race.

   boat

   sports

   human

   humour

5. The _____ of cricket are complicated.

   runs

   rules

   role

   routine

6. The players ran onto the _____.

field
file
fiend
fierce

7. A _____ angle is 90 degrees.

write
white
right
light

8. She read the _____ carefully before beginning her project.

brief
birth
breathe
breadth

9. The number 1492 contains four _____.

fidgets
digits
gadgets
minutes

10. They gave a _____ account of the war.

battle
based
biased
beside

11. She crossed the _____ on a camel.

desert
develop
design
deserve

12. She _____ so well that we won the match.

blow
below
bowled
boiled

13. Is this _____ of information fact or opinion?

    source

    sauce

    sores

    scarce

14. We tried to _____ what the story was about.

    point

    portrait

    phrase

    predict

15. They were better at _____ than bowling.

    knitting

    writer

    painter

    batting

16. You can relax in your _____ time.

    pleasure

    leisure

    treasure

    measure

17. Muslims fast in _____.

    religion

    rebellion

    Ramadan

    remember

18. The _____ went to Makkah for the Hajj.

    journey

    pilot

    personal

    pilgrim

19. She studied a _____ language at school.

    foreign

    French

    forget

    forward

20. The paper came out of the _____ with the words on it.

    product
    private
    printer
    pointer

21. The south of France has a warm _____.

    climax
    climber
    migrate
    climate

22. The _____ displayed what she had typed.

    mouse
    monitor
    motor
    module

23. _____ can be odd or even.

    Names
    Letters
    Cucumbers
    Numbers

24. The Norman _____ was in 1066.

    connect
    conquest
    conscience
    construct

25. Who _____ the best package?

    deserving
    described
    desire
    designed

26. There was new _____ on her computer.

    software
    sometimes
    solution
    source

27. She knew where all the letters were on the _____.

   knowledge
   kilometre
   kitchen
   keyboard

28. I used a _____ to write my History homework.

   computer
   connection
   consequence
   component

29. There is no _____ to support this idea.

   escape
   estimate
   evidence
   evaluation

30. A faithful Muslim is _____ to the will of Allah.

   obligation
   obedient
   obstruction
   objectives

31. _____ Geography is the study of mountains and rivers.

   Physical
   Psychology
   Philosophy
   Photocopy

32. Look at the records on the school's _____.

   library
   classrooms
   database
   lessons

33. They _____ the results of the experiment.

   apparatus
   anniversary
   approximately
   analysed

34. Three quarters is a _____.

fraction
fiction
fashion
friction

35. There was an attractive leaflet to _____ people to come.

person
parade
persuade
permission

36. Who did you vote for in the ____?

education
edition
electricity
election

37. They measured the _____ of the field.

perimeter
centimetre
percentage
kilometre

38. The magician is a clever _____.

charity
chapter
challenge
character

39. Bradford has a large Asian _____.

commandment
committee
communication
community

40. Britain is a _____ where people elect their government.

democracy
demonstration
dictionary
dependency

41. There are several _____ in an experiment.

   vegetables
   valuables
   variables
   varieties

42. After the experiment her _____ was that water boils at 100°C.

   condition
   competition
   concentration
   conclusion

43. This _____ began in Roman times.

   settlement
   sentence
   statement
   section

44. Myths and fables are _____ stories.

   triangular
   typical
   traditional
   thesaurus

45. Looking after the environment is good _____.

   commandment
   civilization
   circumstances
   citizenship

46. The _____ of the project was set out clearly.

   significant
   specification
   spectacular
   secretary

47. _____ is measured with a rain gauge.

   Precipitation
   Punctuation
   Prediction
   Preparation

48. Her _____ told the truth about her life.

   anthology
   alliteration
   autobiography
   antonym

Mark Scheme

1. team	25. designed
2. play	26. software
3. font	27. keyboard
4. human	28. computer
5. rules	29. evidence
6. field	30. obedient
7. right	31. Physical
8. brief	32. database
9. digits	33. analysed
10. biased	34. fraction
11. desert	35. persuade
12. bowled	36. election
13. source	37. perimeter
14. predict	38. character
15. batting	39. community
16. leisure	40. democracy
17. Ramadan	41. variables
18. pilgrim	42. conclusion
19. foreign	43. settlement
20. printer	44. traditional
21. climate	45. citizenship
22. monitor	46. specification
23. numbers	47. precipitation
24. conquest	48. autobiography

7 Promoting independence: using home languages and cultures in learning

Learning Outcomes

This chapter will help you to achieve the following learning outcomes:

- develop awareness of the importance of promoting independent learning in your pupils;
- gain knowledge of practical classroom strategies that promote independence in learning, using pupils' linguistic and cultural resources;
- gain understanding of some strategies through which families and communities can become involved in their children's learning;
- gain some practical ideas for using multilingual and EAL learners' linguistic and cultural 'funds of knowledge' to promote learning across the curriculum, including working with multilingual colleagues.

Introduction

This chapter provides practical examples of strategies and resources to promote multilingual and EAL pupils' independent learning across the curriculum, grounded in the theories about language, multilingualism and learning discussed in Chapters 2 and 3, in particular the concepts of 'funds of knowledge' and of talk for learning. In Chapter 3 'funds of knowledge' was introduced as a theoretical concept to explain the importance of understanding your pupils' home and family learning and experiences for their success in school. The most important funds of knowledge for EAL learners is, of course, the languages they speak and write in other contexts besides mainstream school. With this in mind, in section 2 there is a discussion of the community-based learning contexts that many multilingual pupils attend.

The use of home languages in mainstream classrooms is still a controversial area, particularly for secondary schools, many of which have 'English only' policies in their classrooms. There is no recognition or support for the use of different languages in learning in current official policy. But, as I have argued at several points in this book, there is a great deal of research that supports the idea as an important one for promoting positive attitudes towards education among multilingual pupils. And more than this, research (such as Cummins' work, described in Chapter 3) has for many years shown the cognitive benefits for learning when pupils are allowed to access their full language repertoires in classroom activities. This is discussed further in section 3.1 and a case study by Charlotte Wood gives an example of using language repertoires as funds of knowledge in science to positive effect. The second case study in this section, by Shila Begum, describes learning to count in home and family contexts.

All of the approaches, strategies and activities outlined in this chapter are particularly valuable for multilingual and EAL learners, as they ensure that their learning is always grounded in meaningful contexts and experiences. At the same time, they are equally valuable, sometimes in different ways, for all pupils in mainstream schools. Throughout the chapter, there are discussion points and activities to help you think about the ideas you are reading about, and there are some suggestions for further reading at the end of the chapter.

These are the main sections and subsections of the chapter:

1. **Promoting independent learning**
    1.1 Principles for independent learning

    1.2 Practical strategies to promote independent learning

2. **Involving families and communities in learning**
    2.1 The work of supplementary/complementary schools

    2.2 Bringing home languages and cultures into school

    2.3 Dual language books

3. **Working with multilingual colleagues**
    3.1 Using personal funds of knowledge

    Spanish in science – case study by Charlotte Wood

    Learning place value in Bangla – case study by Shila Begum

1. Promoting independent learning

1.1 Principles for independent learning

The theories introduced in Chapter 2 (pp. 41–44) help us to recognise the active and dynamic nature of learning. Learners are not merely 'empty vessels' waiting passively to be filled with knowledge, they are active agents in the processes of interaction through which learning happens and new knowledge is constructed. This view of learning, particularly in relation to language learning, is supported by such theoretical ideas as Vygotsky's ZPD (pp. 41–42) and Cummins' linguistic interdependence hypothesis (pp. 62–66). Unfortunately, one major and potentially very dangerous effect of developments in initial teacher training and CPD over recent years is that we now tend to see teaching and learning as two separate things. Instead of promoting understanding of the subtle relationships between the two, much initial training is about teaching methods, strategies and activities, which is only one part of the picture. CPD has largely come to be seen as packages of 'training' to be delivered in pre-digested chunks to waiting audiences of teachers, often by commercial companies. It could be argued that there is an unrealistic aim embedded in many government initiatives, that of finding the infallible, 'perfect' methods of teaching that will always work with all pupils and have guaranteed success. Such methods do not exist. The onus on targets and results feeds into this, putting pressure on teachers and schools to predict with certainty what their pupils will attain. This is particularly so in secondary schools, but primary schools are equally held hostage to their targets.

Once they get to know their pupils, teachers may be able to predict outcomes to a certain extent, but they cannot possibly be expected to predict with 100% accuracy what results they will attain, nor even what their pupils will learn from the activities they provide. The negative implications of the 'universal model' of assessment for EAL learners are spelt out in Chapter 3 (section 2.1, pp. 57–60). There are many examples in this book which show how pupils interpret what teachers ask them to do in creative and sometimes idiosyncratic ways, often coming up with new and inventive interpretations. Teaching and learning is always a dialogue, and the practical implications of this are explored in the next section. One of the essential skills of an effective teacher is the ability to construct the kinds of 'safe spaces' which offer the best opportunities possible for their pupils to learn through using their personal knowledge and experience to achieve deep understanding of the new content being presented (see Chapter 2, section 1.2, pp. 30–33). In this way, teaching is more productive, learning is stronger and – perhaps even more importantly – pupils are developing the skills which help them to become confident, independent learners.

In *The Developing Language Learner* (2009) Allwright and Hanks argue eloquently that learners should be regarded as 'key developing practitioners' (p. 2), in just the same way as teachers are regarded as practitioners whose skills and understanding continually develop (hence the existence of books such as this). They go on to introduce 'five propositions about learners' (pp. 4–7), which are worth repeating here as they sum up what I think are essential elements in being and becoming independent learners. Here, re-worded slightly, are Allwright and Hanks' propositions:

- Learners are unique individuals who learn and develop best in their own ways.
- Learners are social beings who learn and develop best in a mutually supportive environment.
- Learners are capable of taking learning seriously – they are motivated to learn.
- Learners are capable of independent decision-making.
- Learners are capable of developing as practitioners of learning – in other words, they can learn how to become independent learners.

Allwright and Hanks' writing is based on their research and practice around the world with language learners of different ages, beginning in Brazil in the 1990s. Their conclusions are relevant for both primary and secondary pupils in England. They link with ideas that have been around in the education system in England for many years, such as the need for high expectations, both by teachers and by the demands of the system itself and of the importance of recognising learners' identities. They also link with various theoretical ideas I have introduced in this book, such as the ways that language, culture and identity are connected in learning (see Chapter 2, section 1.2, pp. 30–33), and also with Sonia Nieto's vital point that everyone is capable of learning, but we learn best in our own individual ways. The risks of categorising EAL learners as needing to be taught alongside SEN pupils (see Chapter 3, section 2.1, p. 57) or in so-called 'low ability' sets are many. In the next section, I explore a range of strategies to promote independent learning, based on another important way of thinking about teaching and learning which benefits from 'the power of talk' – **dialogic teaching**.

Activity 7.1
Understanding independent learning

Read through the following two teaching and learning episodes and think about them in relation to the two questions below. Discuss them with colleagues or fellow students, if you have the opportunity. The pupils in both episodes are in Year 6.

- Which of the two episodes gives a better example of independent learning? Explain your reasons for your choice – what specific aspects of the activities will promote independence?
- How might you develop the activities in the other episode, to promote more opportunities for independence?

Episode 1

In the last lesson in a set of literacy lessons on narrative poetry, the teacher's aim is for his pupils to provide some evidence of their responses to a long narrative poem they have been working on. After a whole-class introduction where he uses questioning to make sure the pupils can recall the story and understand the messages underpinning the poem, he organises them into groups according to their ability in reading. He gives each child a photocopy of the poem and each group a different set of questions to discuss, written on a big card. He informs them that he expects each pupil to write their own responses to the questions by the end of the lesson. There is a teaching assistant on hand to help those pupils who find writing difficult. The pupils set off on their task: there is little talk between them in the groups as they mostly concentrate on producing their written responses. Towards the end of the lesson, they are largely working in silence.

Episode 2

In a history lesson, the teacher's aim is for her pupils to understand the experiences of children being evacuated during the Second World War. They already have quite a lot of subject knowledge about the war, including the reasons for the evacuations, how they were organised, how many children were involved and so on. There is a collection of reference books available in the classroom, as well as computers with relevant websites accessible. After a short whole-class introduction to review their prior knowledge about the Second World War through question and answer, the teacher asks her pupils to organise themselves into small groups and then sets them the task of writing a letter from a child evacuee to their parents at home the day after they have been evacuated. Each group is to work together to produce one letter, to be read out to the rest of the class at the end of the lesson. They are allowed to refer to any of the books and websites as they wish. The lesson becomes a bit noisy at times, but by the end, each group has more or less finished the task.

1.2 Practical strategies to promote independent learning

The notion of 'safe spaces' for learning, raised in the previous section and in other parts of the book, has practical implications for teachers working in multilingual classrooms. It links with Wolfe and Alexander's (2008) concept of 'dialogic teaching'. In this section, I explain briefly what these two ideas mean for teaching, and why they are important in developing independence in learning, particularly for EAL pupils. Activity 7.2 provides some practical examples of how you can use these ideas to develop activities that promote independent learning across the curriculum. They are the kinds of activities that can be adapted to different ages and subject areas. The idea of 'safe spaces' comes from cultural studies. It is not really about physical spaces, though these, of course, are important. It is about the kinds of relationships that need to develop between teachers and pupils in order to promote mutual respect, trust and the willingness to take risks, by both parties. A major factor in this in multilingual classrooms is in the use of home languages. I have argued strongly that languages are resources for learning and of the rich potential of multilingualism. But teachers take a big risk when they allow their pupils to use languages that they do not understand in their classrooms: perhaps they will say rude words or abuse the trust invested in them in other ways. Also, how on earth do you assess something that you do not understand yourself? In using their own languages, pupils also take a risk: perhaps they will be laughed at, or they may not be very confident speakers of their home language, as is the case with many second or third generation multilingual pupils. But, in the right kind of 'safe space', allowing pupils to use their full language repertoires can open out opportunities for learning, leading to meaningful interactions which promote critical thinking and deep understanding of the issues being discussed.

In the same way, the kinds of dialogic talk advocated by Wolfe and Alexander can lead to interactions that both support pupils' understandings of the concepts they are being taught and help them to develop the cognitive skills they need to succeed as learners, in a wide range of ways. But there is no package of 'dialogic activities' that teachers can take off the shelf and simply deliver to their pupils. Developing a dialogic approach is more about the ways that things are done, the relationships that are constructed and the attitudes and values behind the activities. Wolfe and Alexander suggest five 'teaching principles' that help teachers to think about how to plan activities that are genuinely dialogic. They say that teaching is more likely to be dialogic if it is:

- **Collective**: participants work together.
- **Reciprocal**: participants listen to each other and consider alternative viewpoints.
- **Supportive**: participants express their ideas freely without fear of embarrassment and help each other to common understandings.
- **Cumulative**: participants build on each others' answers to develop coherent lines of thinking and understanding.
- **Purposeful**: the classroom talk is open and dialogic, but also planned and structured with specific learning objectives in view.

They also provide a useful checklist of the kinds of 'things' (i.e. functions – see Chapter 2, section 1.4 p. 41) that pupils need to be able to do with language, and which promote independent learning and real understanding. These functions become more complex as you go down the list:

- Narrate
- Explain
- Analyse
- Speculate
- Imagine
- Explore
- Evaluate
- Discuss
- Argue
- Justify

These checklists are very useful for your planning. They have many parallels with Cummins' Quadrant (see Chapter 4, section 1.2, pp. 78–81). You could incorporate the 'function words' into your learning objectives in subjects across the curriculum to remind you of the kinds of language your pupils need to use in the activity, and of what they are learning to do with language.

Activity 7.2
Activities to promote independent learning

Here are some examples of activities designed to promote independent learning through dialogic talk. Think about which functions of language and kinds of talk and thinking they entail and help to develop, using Wolfe and Alexander's list above. They all entail more than one kind of talk, and are the kinds of activities that can be used with pupils of different ages. Do the following for each activity:

- Decide which language functions (using the list above) each activity would help to develop.
- Write two learning objectives, using relevant function words, for each activity.

1. In science, before beginning their first lesson on a new topic related to living things, pupils in **Year 5 or 6** are given five minutes to write down as much as they can about what they already know. They are told that the writing is just for them; the teacher will not look at it. They can write in any language they wish. After the five minutes, they have two minutes to share and compare their ideas with their talk partner (see p. 87). After this, the class comes back together for a brief plenary before they start the lesson.

(Continued)

(Continued)

2. In history, as part of their study of World War 1, pupils in **Year 7 or 8**, who have been studying the topic over several lessons, are told that they are to have a visiting speaker who they will be able to interview on the causes of the war. Then they are organised into groups of four and given ten minutes to come up with five questions to ask the visitor. Following this, the pupils are organised into pairs to practise asking and answering questions. While this is going on, the teacher collates all the questions and the activity finishes with the class deciding which are the best questions to ask the visitor.

3. In maths, pupils in **Year 1 or 2** have been learning their times tables up to 6x. As a consolidation activity, they are organised into mixed ability groups and each group is given a set of cut-up tables sums on small cards (see Figure 7.1). In their groups, they have to organise the cards correctly (there may be some incorrect answers). Following this, the group is given a set of blank cards and asked to write any missing correct answers, then come up with questions of their own, which they write on the cards, to ask another group.

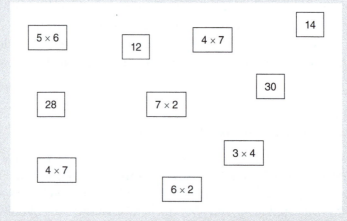

Figure 7.1 Activity 3: Times tables check – cards

4. In geography, **Year 3 or 4** pupils are beginning a new topic on the location of different countries in the world, as well as the ideas of latitude, longitude, the tropics and so on. The teacher works from a blank map of the world on the smart board, and asks pupils to come up in turn to point out countries they know or have visited, countries their families came from, countries where they have relatives and so on. After this, the teacher marks in the equator and the Tropics of Cancer and Capricorn, and sets the pupils a task for the next lesson, which is to find out what they can about the words 'latitude' and 'longitude'.

5. In literature, **Year 11** pupils are working in groups to revise their knowledge of *Romeo and Juliet* in preparation for a written assignment. Each group is working on a different scene and has a chart to fill in where they need to write details of

characters, main events and closing actions, as in Figure 7.2. The pupils have copies of the play. When they finish their charts, two pupils from each group move to another group, who give them a quiz on their scene.

Act:	Scene:	
Characters	Main events	Closing actions

Figure 7.2 Activity 5: Romeo and Juliet scene summary chart

6. In maths in **Year 9 or 10** (though this could happen in most classrooms and in other subject areas), two pupils who have recently arrived from Poland are told in Polish what the new topic of study is going to be and are given the opportunity to write down what they already know about it, and then explain (all in Polish) how they studied the topic previously in Poland.

7. In design and technology, **Year 8** pupils are evaluating the plans they have made for designing a garden for people with sight impairments, following a set of specifications. Working in pairs using different-coloured highlighters, they are checking each other's plans against the specifications. Some pairs of pupils share the same home language. The teacher has asked them to devise their own way of coding the plans to show which specifications they meet and which they do not and has said that they can use their home languages if they wish. After completing the task, they have to report back in a whole-class plenary.

8. In French, which is the MFL that all the class are studying in **Year 5**, multilingual pupils are invited to share the ways they say things related to the topic they are studying in their own languages. The teacher builds up a comparison chart on the whiteboard and then invites everyone in the class to point out any similarities or differences between the words.

2. Involving families and communities in learning

2.1 The work of supplementary/complementary schools

Many EAL pupils go in the evenings or at weekends to community-based schools to learn to speak, read and write their community languages and to learn about their home cultures. Such schools have existed in England for as long as different languages have been part of our society. Most commonly called **supplementary schools** in the past, they are now often known as **complementary schools**, which acknowledges the ways in which they can complement learning in mainstream schools, and contribute to educational success. In most major cities in England, there are many such schools – sometimes up to 50 or 60 – meeting in mainstream school premises, people's homes, community centres or places of worship. Some have been functioning for over 50 years: in Bradford, for example, there is a Polish Saturday school which has been running since the 1960s, attended by children from all over West Yorkshire. Complementary schools have a variety of aims and purposes, depending on the hopes and aspirations of the communities that establish and nurture them: maintaining heritage languages and cultures is a very important aim, but there are others. Making up for the problems faced by pupils in mainstream schools can be a big motivating factor – such is the case for schools set up by African-Caribbean parents in the 1970s, who felt that institutional racism in the education system was affecting the chances of their children.

Complementary schools take a big role in the teaching of modern languages that are not available in mainstream schools. Indeed, mainstream schools can benefit from this in that pupils taught in complementary school can then take the GCSE or A level exam in the language they have been taught, thus boosting the school's results. Many different languages are taken at GCSE in this way. Polish is an interesting example in this respect – it is now fifth highest on the list of languages taken at GCSE, with a high level of success, but all the teaching takes place outside of mainstream settings.

Until very recently, complementary/supplementary schools were a hidden aspect of education in England, hardly known about and largely ignored. The Swann Report (DES, 1985) can take some responsibility for this, with its strong recommendation that, on the grounds of 'equal opportunities', the teaching of community languages should have no place in mainstream education and should entirely be the concern of the communities themselves. But in recent years, research is beginning to open out the wide range of ways in which complementary schools operate (e.g. Conteh *et al.*, 2007) and to reveal the advantages of communication between complementary and mainstream schools, to the benefit of the pupils who attend them, their teachers and their families.

Activity 7.3
Finding out about community-based learning

- Look on the website of the National Resource Centre for Supplementary Education (http://www.supplementaryeducation.org.uk) to find out about the supplementary/community schools movement and whether there are any such schools in the area you live or study.
- Talk to the pupils that you teach to find out whether they take part in any out-of-hours learning and if so, what form it takes. If you can, try to arrange a visit to

a supplementary/complementary school and observe one or two lessons. Even if you cannot understand the languages being taught, you can get a sense of the approaches taken by the teachers, and the responses of the children.
- Think about the ways they are similar to or different from the approaches taken in other schools that you know.

2.2 Bringing home languages and cultures into school

The first point to emphasise in this section is that, while it is certainly very helpful if you can speak even a little of the home languages of the pupils you teach, it is not really a disadvantage if you can't. It is much more important that you have a positive attitude towards the language diversity of your pupils, and that you understand something of the ways that languages work and of how knowledge of other languages influences the learning of English. The theories discussed in Chapters 2 and 3 should give you some starting points in this. This said, if you can say a few words in some of the languages spoken by the pupils in your class, it will promote a positive and welcoming classroom ethos – even if you just say 'hello' in a child's language, it will make their face light up and make them feel included in the class. The 'monolingual' pupils in your class also benefit from such a welcoming approach to other languages. Awareness of the language diversity of their communities is a very valuable way to break down barriers and promote social cohesion.

Language and cultural diversity can become a feature of your classroom through interactive displays, through the stories you choose to read and study with your pupils, the choices of content you make in different areas of the curriculum, and in many other ways. Time can be found in PHSE to allow the pupils to bring in news and information about family and community events and about family in other parts of the world. The school and classroom can visibly reflect the diversity and global connections of the community in which it is situated. One school I worked in had clocks in the reception area and in the classrooms, set to the times of the countries of origin of the pupils' families. If pupils go on visits to extended family in their countries of origin, this can be turned into a positive aspect of their education by asking them to find out information to tell the class on their return and to bring back artefacts, if possible. Once back at school, they can be encouraged to bring in photos and to talk about where they went and what they did. Having a map available of the country visited can be very helpful, so that routes can be traced and places identified. If proficiency in English is an issue, a family member could be invited in to the class to support the child in talking about their visit, or questions could be written down and taken home for parents to answer. This can lead to fascinating discussions, such as the one described in Conteh (2003: 42–4) about an unusual medical treatment witnessed by a Year 3 child on a visit to Pakistan. Zofia Donnelly's case study (see Chapter 3, section 1.2, pp. 52–54) illustrates the way that much richer discussion can be generated by allowing pupils to talk about their family experiences in their home languages.

Simple routines, such as doing the register in different languages, can promote awareness of language diversity; the pupils can respond to their names with a greeting in any language they know. If a child brings a new language to the class, they can be asked to teach their classmates the greetings. This can be reinforced with a poster showing '*How many ways can we say hello?*' which is regularly reviewed and updated. I once visited a Year 3 class where a boy, keen to find a new greeting to add to the poster, met me at the door and asked, 'Miss, can you speak any languages?' As well as greetings, other simple language features can be brought into the class as part of whole-class routines and in sharing times, possibly during PHSE. Primary pupils find counting in different languages fun and interesting. Start off by introducing a way of counting up to five in another language and then find out what languages the pupils themselves can count in. This can be surprising, as they may have been taught to count in their home languages by their grandparents or other family members. This project can grow and become an ongoing subject of interest, involving parents, research on the internet and a working wall display. In secondary classrooms, activities like this can take on a more research-focused approach, where pupils are set off to find specific information on the internet or from others in the school, and then develop into quizzes, powerpoint presentations and so on.

Another excellent activity, which links to literacy, geography and RE, is finding out about the pupils' names and their origins. This can be done with pupils of any age. The following vignette illustrates an activity with Year 1 children.

Vignette 1

Name tree

Lisa, a trainee on her final placement in a Year 1 class in a multilingual school, decided to make a 'name tree' as part of her literacy work. She began by making a large cut-out tree shape (without leaves) for the classroom wall. Then she introduced the activity by showing the pupils a photo of her own daughter and telling them what her name meant and why she was given it. After this, she gave each child a letter and a leaf cut out of green paper to take to their parents. The letter, which was available in different languages, gave brief information about the project and asked the parents to help their child to write their name on one side of the leaf, in their own language as well as English if possible, and a sentence about what the name meant and why they were given it on the other. The parents were enthusiastic about the project, and the leaves soon began returning to the classroom, along with positive comments from parents, who noticed the name tree sprouting leaves (Figure 7.3). Lisa organised her literacy lessons to allow each child to stand up, show their leaf, give a brief explanation of their name and then attach it to the name tree. The teacher, TA and other adults in the class added their own names. When all the names were on the tree, Lisa invited the parents to come and see the completed name tree. She also prepared a presentation with the pupils about the project for a whole-school activity.

Figure 7.3 A name tree on display in a classroom

Using family and community funds of knowledge in your teaching makes the learning engaging and meaningful for all your pupils, not just those who are multilingual or EAL learners. It can be done across the curriculum, not just in literacy. There are some excellent examples of topic work which allow pupils to explore their own communities' histories while achieving learning objectives for geography, history, RE, science, ICT, literacy and other subjects on the Multilingual Learning section of the Goldsmith's Department of Educational Studies website (http://www.gold.ac.uk/clcl/multilingual-learning/).

Vignette 2

The Rag Trade

The Rag Trade project, details of which can be found on the Goldmsith's website, is a particularly powerful example of bringing home languages and cultures into school. It was carried out with Year 5 and 6 pupils in Tower Hamlets in East London, and linked both with the community's history and the current situation in Bangladesh, where most of the pupils' families had relatives.

(Continued)

(Continued)

The work began with finding out about the tailoring industry in the East End of London, which was in decline as a result of being increasingly outsourced to Bangladesh, exploiting cheap child labour. Factories in London, which in the past had employed many of the pupils' grandparents, were closing down. In one activity, the pupils in London thought of questions to ask the child workers in Bangladesh. They decided to translate the questions into Bengali so the children could understand them. This is what they came up with.

Questions to send to children in Bangladesh

- Do they make clothes for themselves? (*Ora ki nijeder jonno kapor banai?*)
- Do they get enough money? (*Ora ki poriman poisha pai?*)
- If they don't get their work done do they get beaten? (*Ora jokhon kaj shesh korte pare na oderke ki mare?*)
- How do the pupils know how to make the clothes? (*Bachara ki bhabe kapor shilai korte jane?*)
- Why are the pupils doing the work when there are so many adults to do it? (*Boro manush thakte bachara keno kaz kore hoi?*)
- Where do the pupils live? (*Ei bachara kothai thake?*)
- How do the pupils feel about working? (*Bachader kemon lage kaz korte?*)
- What happens to the people when they get hurt while they are working? (*Kaz korar shomai betha pele manushra ki kore?*)
- How many minutes break do they get? (*Ora koto shomoi'er jonno birotipai?*)
- Is this happening now? (*Egolo ki ekhon hoche?*)
- How can we help them? (*Amra oderke ki bhabe shahajjo korte pari?*)

These questions constitute a powerful, authentic written text. They were sent to Bangladesh and the responses built into further topic activities. They demonstrate not just the pupils' understanding of the topic they were studying, but their strong emotional engagement and empathy with the people whose lives they were studying. Such work offers rich opportunities for pupils from all cultural and language backgrounds to be experts in particular aspects of knowledge and learning.

Activity 7.4
Reflection on funds of knowledge for learning

In a small group, reflect on one of the case studies you have just read, either about the name tree or about the Rag Trade. The following questions can help you think about and discuss it.

1. What do you think made it effective as an opportunity for promoting independent learning?

2. What literacy learning objectives do you think the pupils achieved in the activity?
3. What language functions from Wolfe and Alexander's list do you think pupils would use in the activity?
4. What are the implications for planning activities such as these as part of your teaching (look back at the principles for planning in Chapter 4)?
5. Think of similar activities you could do in your class, using your pupils' funds of knowledge as a resource for their learning. If you can, plan and carry out a simple activity for your class to promote awareness of language diversity.
   If you are on placement, consult your class teacher about what might be a good starting-point.

Activity 7.5
Diversity across the curriculum

Choose a topic from the history, geography, RE or science curriculum, and think of ways in which you could develop activities which key into pupils' funds of knowledge, starting either with a significant object, picture or a local issue. Look back at the principles for planning in Chapter 4 and devise two or three activities, which could be the starting-point for teaching the topic.

You could do this activity with a small group of colleagues: each take a particular curriculum area and discuss the outcomes.

2.3 Dual language books

Dual language books are a powerful resource for learning in many ways. The University of East London website (UEL, 2014) is the best source of information and ideas, along with Raymonde Sneddon's book (2009, see Further Reading at the end of the chapter). Dual language books are usually stories published in two languages, and there are also a few information texts. Both languages can be shown on one page or the two languages can face each other on alternate pages. Books published in the UK generally have English as one of the languages and many publishers produce series of dual language books where the same story is written in different languages, all along with English. Sets of these can be very useful in promoting language diversity. Pupils who are not speakers or readers of the languages concerned but who can read English can read and compare the texts of the story in the different languages.

The importance of helping pupils to develop a positive identity as learners was discussed in Chapter 2, and dual language books can be a very effective means to do this. The story of Mushtaq (Chapter 3, p. 64) illustrates this clearly. Dual language books made by the pupils themselves were a powerful way for him to use his knowledge of literacy in Bengali as a means to becoming a reader of English. Cummins and Early's book *Identity Texts* (2011) discusses the importance of dual language books, reporting projects done round the world where they have proved to be 'an effective and inspirational way of engaging learners in multilingual schools'.

Research Focus: Dual language texts

For pupils who can read their home language, dual language texts can provide a means of learning English, as well as developing metalinguistic awareness, which is an important capacity for understanding and analysing academic language. Dual language books can be useful for pupils who can speak but not read their home language. Discussing the pictures can help them follow the story and develop their understanding of the structure, character, setting and so on. The Dual Language Action Research Project, reported on the UEL website, describes research into using dual language books with pupils new to English and provides many practical ideas for ways of using dual language books to promote literacy as well as raising pupils' self-esteem and identity as learners.

Activity 7.6
Dual language texts

Find out what you can about dual language texts – Mantra lingua is one of the main publishers and they have an extensive website. If you are able to, get hold of some dual language texts representing the languages of the pupils you are teaching and share them with a small group of pupils.

3. Working with multilingual colleagues

There are many ways of using home languages and cultural experiences to help open out pupils' conceptual understanding in subjects across the curriculum. In a school with a positive, welcoming ethos, knowledge of languages is seen as something to be celebrated and – more importantly perhaps – to be shared as a resource to use in strategies that promote pupils' learning. Multilingual colleagues have an important role to play in this. Multilingual teachers are still very much in the minority in mainstream schools in England. Their importance is not just in supporting the learning of their pupils, but also in raising all pupils' awareness of the importance of multilingualism in our society and as a role model of the positive benefits of multilingualism.

It is more common to have multilingual teaching assistants or support assistants who work alongside the teacher and support individual or small groups of pupils. Their presence can benefit the whole class. Varian-Roper (in Gravelle, 2000: 73–4) has some excellent examples of the ways that multilingual assistants can link content teaching and language teaching in maths and also provide a bridge for parents. Zofia Donnelly's case study in Chapter 3 (pp. 52–57) shows how a visiting teacher can both support and open out the learning and the teacher–pupil relationships in a multilingual setting. Here are some suggestions of ways of working with multilingual colleagues.

- Tell a story together in two languages.

- Jointly assess pupils in different areas of the curriculum in order to evaluate their conceptual understanding as well as their language.

- Jointly plan an activity where you identify the language demands and think of ways that the concepts could be introduced multilingually.

- Ask your multilingual assistant to prepare materials to be sent home, which explain some of the things you have done in school, and also how parents can support their pupils at home.

The following vignette illustrates good collaboration between multilingual colleagues. A trainee used his own basic knowledge of French to help a child new to English to engage actively in a science task. With the support of the school's PMFL teacher, who was a French specialist, he was able to support the child in showing how much he understood about the concepts being developed in the lesson.

Vignette

Working with multilingual colleagues

Ben undertook his first block placement on his PGCE course in a Year 3 class in a large school where most of the pupils were second or third-generation Pakistani heritage. There was one 'new to English' child in the class, also of Pakistani heritage, but recently arrived from France where members of his extended family lived. Ben discovered that the child was fluent in French as well as Urdu. The class were doing a science topic where they were exploring the qualities of different materials, and Ben had prepared a recording sheet for the pupils to write down their findings about different objects in the classroom. With the help of the teacher responsible for PMFL, Ben wrote a French translation of the questions and statements above the English version on the sheet for the new pupil. The child was then able to carry out the investigation himself and write the names of the objects and some descriptive words in French on the sheet. In this way, Ben could appreciate his pupil's understanding of the science concepts in the activity, at the same time as providing a link for him to learning the words in English. Figure 7.4 shows the sheet which the child produced, with the teacher's writing above each question and the child's answers in the relevant spaces.

(Continued)

(Continued)

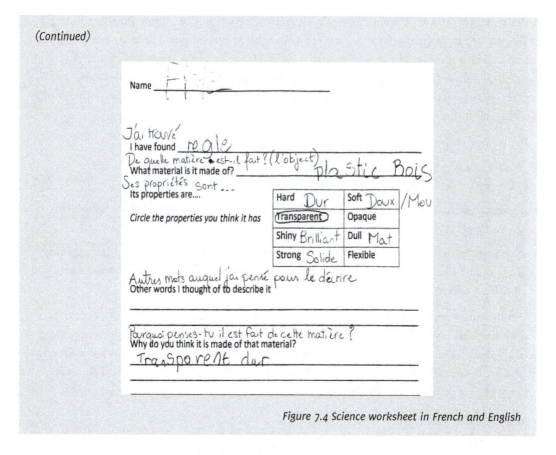

Figure 7.4 Science worksheet in French and English

3.1 Using personal funds of knowledge

The two case studies in this section consider personal funds of knowledge in different ways. First Charlotte Wood, a secondary science teacher, discusses how she used her knowledge of Spanish in order to help a newly arrived pupil feel included and begin to learn the subject content of the lessons. Then, Shila Begum, an Early Years teacher, describes how she learned place value in Bangla and what it showed her about the importance of valuing children's knowledge of counting in their home languages.

Spanish in science – case study by Charlotte Wood

During my PGCE in secondary science, through classroom observations, attending EAL sessions at university and attending NALDIC meetings, I developed an understanding of EAL and how as a teacher I can adapt my lessons and resources to help EAL learners. Throughout my first placement I had the privilege of working alongside a Spanish EAL student. Although the school had a high percentage of EAL students (68.5%), my pupil was the only Spanish speaker and was finding it hard to be incorporated into mainstream lessons. As a result, her English was

→

progressing slowly. Washbourne (2011) suggests that speaking to an EAL learner in their first language can help develop fluency in English and build upon what is already known in the learner's first language. As a Spanish speaker, I could speak to the learner in her home language and prepare suitable bilingual resources to support her in her learning. She was in a low ability GCSE biology group, target grades being Es and Ds, whom I taught twice a week. During these lessons a teaching assistant was present to assist a child with SEN and not the EAL students. From here on, I shall discuss the methods I used to try and get an L1 learner to learn in an L2 environment.

Creating a safe environment

My initial focus was to make the student feel welcome in the classroom, as learning can best take place if the learner is in a 'safe space'. I made sure I knew the correct pronunciation of her name, smiling as she entered the classroom and having a small conversation with her in Spanish: '¡Hola! ¿Como estás?' – 'Hello, how are you?' and asking about her day. Instantly I started to build a positive relationship with the student, and broke down any initial communication barriers that she may have thought were there. Once I had created a safe environment for the student to work in I was able to try out a variety of techniques to see which was the most effective in supporting her learning.

Storch and Wigglesworth (2012) have noted that the use of the learners' L1 is a controversial issue in an L2 classroom. However, Schweers Jr. (1999) comments that L1 can be used to give complex instructions to students with a basic level of English, and also to check comprehension. Whilst teaching the Spanish student I found it useful to explain a task to her in her first language. This would allow her to understand the activity and what I wanted her to achieve. For example, as part of the lesson on decay I had asked the students to design a compost bin, which met four criteria: it would attract decomposers, have insulation from the cold, be able to circulate air and allow some water to enter to provide moisture. I told the student in Spanish to imagine that she lived in the countryside near Barcelona and wanted to recycle waste food to be more environmentally friendly. I then went on to tell her that she had to include all four criteria to produce the best compost bin. As a result of being able to associate the task with her life back in Barcelona, she designed a compost bin with all the required criteria.

Use of key words and questioning

Teachers ask thousands of questions every week. When teaching EAL students, teachers have to tailor their questions to take account of their needs. Having seen that the use of key words was valuable in the development of the student's English skills, I provided her at the beginning of each lesson a key word sheet including Spanish translations. Instead of asking her to find the words in the dictionary, I asked her to learn these words for the next lesson, when I checked to see if she could remember them. This was a quick activity whilst other students were completing a different starter activity, recapping what we had learnt in the previous lesson. It also allowed me to prepare questions. Despite the point that closed questions are not very helpful in many situations, they can be very helpful in some instances.

$\rightarrow$

I found that by asking the student a closed question which required her to answer with a key word which she had learnt, she was able to answer quickly. I made sure I didn't ask her to describe or explain a concept without building up steps to get to the answer. This allowed the learner to build understanding gradually and so scaffold her understanding of the science concepts. For example, during a lesson on the carbon cycle I would ask questions such as 'Which process produces carbon dioxide; respiration or photosynthesis?', 'What do plants do to get rid of carbon dioxide?'.

As part of a revision exercise I gave the class a range of exam questions on a learning mat. The students had to move around the classroom to help each other complete the learning mats and answer all the questions. I differentiated this resource for my EAL learner by providing her with a learning mat that contained accessible questions, usually only requiring recall of knowledge, or one-word answers, such as, 'Name three food groups.' Although this wasn't initially stretching the student to answer the more complex questions, her level of English at the time of the activity didn't allow for her to answer questions such as, 'Explain why these food groups are important.'

Matching activities – using first language

In science many words have a Latin origin. As a result, by using key words in a card sort activity, the student was able to build upon her own prior science learning from Spain to gain an understanding of the topic being covered. For example in a lesson on photosynthesis I made it clear that the word in Spanish was 'fotosíntesis' and so very similar to the English version. She was instantly able to associate what we were learning with her prior experience, giving a foundation for new learning to occur. The concept of visual learning was used in a card sort activity. The students had to match pictures to key words and definitions. This helped the Spanish student by activating her prior knowledge of the key words, associating them to images and definitions, thus expanding her subject knowledge and also improving her English skills.

Conclusion

At times I found it difficult to make sure that all the resources for the EAL learner were accessible. However as weeks progressed, I discovered what styles of learning suited her, allowing for me to focus further on resources linked to those styles. In particular, the use of visual aids was of great importance when supporting her, and she was able to associate these with her prior subject knowledge allowing for progress to be made. Finally, the most productive resource for me was the use of my Spanish speaking skills to make the student feel welcome and create the safe environment within which successful learning could be achieved. It also allowed me to make resources containing written Spanish to allow the student to access the work that the students were covering during the lessons. Given that not every EAL student speaks Spanish, I still want to continue my development of generic skills for teaching EAL learners, as I feel in a modern society we need to make it our aim as teachers to allow for them to receive a well-balanced education.

Learning place value in Bangla – case study by Shila Begum

As a small child growing up in a remote village in Bangladesh I would often hear family members counting out money when they bought something from the local market or from the traders that came directly into the village. I would hear people counting their cows, chickens and ducks and I was aware of a game called five pebbles. My first vague awareness of numbers was when I went with my uncle to pick up my older sister and cousins from school. I remember walking to the school, often barefoot, and from quite a distance hearing the rhythmic chanting of numbers. I couldn't help but tap my hands and feet to the rhythm of the rhyme and soon looked forward to hearing it each day. However as a young child I didn't ask any questions about the rhyme or express the enjoyment I felt by listening to it.

In 1986 I left Bangladesh and came to England aged five and a half and soon my knowledge and understanding of numbers in English flourished. I was taught how to count and write the numerals as well as perform different number operations. At around the age of seven, my parents sent me to Bangla classes at the local mosque. There I heard the same familiar rhythmic chanting of numbers. Once again I felt an irresistible urge to tap my hands and feet to the rhythm of the rhyme, just like I did all those years ago back in Bangladesh.

This time I was much more curious and very eager to discover what this incredible rhyme was so I hurried home to confront my older sister. My sister was surprised by my inquisitive questioning and informed me it was a special number rhyme in Bangla to help children to learn the numbers from 0 to 100. I asked my sister if she would teach me the rhyme and started to learn the rhyme from her. Both my parents and sister were delighted about my sudden desire to learn the Bangla numbers and were equally surprised at how quickly I picked it up. They were also fascinated when I tapped my hands and feet along with the rhyme, though my sister explained that if I had behaved like that in a school in Bangladesh I would have been punished.

The place value rhyme is very simple and not only does it enable children to learn the numbers 0 to 100 but also teaches about place value and the multiples of ten to a hundred. The example below demonstrates how the rhyme goes.

0	1	2	3	4	5	6	7	8	9
One	___	zero	10						
One	ten	one	11						
One	ten	two	12						
One	ten	three	13						
One	ten	four	14						
One	ten	five	15						
One	ten	six	16						

→

One	ten	seven	17
One	ten	eight	18
One	ten	nine	19
Two	tens	are	20
Three	tens	are	30
Four	tens	are	40
Five	tens	are	50 ... and so on.

I decided to try out this number rhyme at the Saturday class I work at with multilingual children aged 5 to 11. I wanted to see if the rhyme had any impact on the children. They received it very well and soon responded to the rhythm and beat similarly to how I responded when I was a child. Some children commented on how they thought it sounded like a rap and you could dance to it. Even though the rhyme was initially done in Bangla with a group who were mainly Punjabi speakers, the children became familiar with the pattern and were soon able to predict the next equivalent number in English, for example after the number 29 one child remarked '3 tens are 30 Miss, it is like the times tables'. The children were fascinated and amazed at how they could apply their knowledge and understanding of numbers to a rhyme in a different language. I encouraged the children to listen to the rhythm and demonstrated how they could tap on their hands and soon children began to tap along with the rhyme. Isa commented, 'It makes you want to dance Miss'. Later we came up with an English and Punjabi equivalent to the rhyme, which demonstrated to the children the universal nature of numbers. We accompanied the activity with visual number cards to reinforce understanding of place value and numbers further.

Learning Outcomes Review

The four learning outcomes for this chapter are all to do with linking the theories you read about in Chapters 2 and 3 to your thinking about the kinds of strategies and resources that will promote learning for your EAL and multilingual learners. You may be able to take some of the specific ideas described in the chapter into your own planning, but it is more likely that you will use your professional judgement to adapt them to your own classroom setting and the pupils you are teaching.

Self-assessment questions

1. As well as the examples discussed in this chapter, what other kinds of 'funds of knowledge' do you think could be used in your teaching across the curriculum?

2. (*If you are not multilingual yourself*) What issues do you think you might face in working with multilingual colleagues to promote pupils' learning? Think of some examples of ways in which you could work with a multilingual colleague, using your different expertise positively.

3. (*If you are multilingual yourself*) What issues do you think you might face in using your multilingual expertise to promote pupils' learning? Think of some examples of ways in which you could work with the pupils and with your colleagues using your multilingual skills to promote learning.

Suggested answers for Activity 7.2

These are just some ideas – there are many other possibilities.

Activity	Function words	Learning objectives
1	narrate discuss	to put simple information into words to compare simple ideas
2	analyse justify	to form a range of questions correctly to justify choices of questions for interview on a specific topic
3	explain analyse	to recall simple information to discuss possible questions and answers in a game
4	narrate imagine	to narrate personal information to explore locations of countries in the world
5	discuss explore	to analyse key information to justify answers to questions
6	narrate explain	to recall prior knowledge to explain a particular maths topic
7	evaluate justify	to compare different ways of checking information to justify choices in information retrieval
8	speculate evaluate	to compare words in different languages to identify similarities and differences in languages

---

Further Reading

Conteh, J. (ed.) (2006) *Promoting Learning for Multilingual Pupils 3–11: Opening Doors to Success*. **London: Paul Chapman Publishing.**

This book contains chapters written by teachers about projects they planned and carried out to promote listening and speaking with their multilingual and EAL learners. The examples show how they build a multilingual approach to become an integrated part of their ongoing planning and teaching, not as an add-on. In this way, they open out the learning and promote independence in their pupils.

Sneddon, R. (2009) *Multilingual Books – Biliterate Pupils: Learning to Read Through Dual Language Books*. Stoke-on-Trent: Trentham Books.
Developed from action research work by primary teachers, this book features case studies of multilingual pupils aged from six to ten, and the ways in which dual language books support their learning. It illustrates how young pupils can work simultaneously in two languages to read unfamiliar texts, and to analyse the differences between their languages. It offers ideas for teaching pupils languages as well as developing their multilingualism.

References

Allwright, D. and Hanks, J. (2009) *The Developing Language Learner: An Introduction to Exploratory Practice*. London: Palgrave Macmillan.

Conteh, J. (2003) *Succeeding in Diversity: Culture, Language and Learning in Primary Classrooms*. Stoke-on-Trent: Trentham Books.

Conteh, J., Martin, P. and Robertson, L. (eds) (2007) *Multilingual Learning Stories in Schools and Communities in Britain*. Stoke-on-Trent: Trentham Books

Cummins, J. and Early, M. (eds) (2011) *Identity Texts: The Collaborative Creation of Power in Multilingual Schools*. Stoke-on-Trent: Trentham Books.

Department of Education and Science (DES) (1985) *Education for All – The Report of the Committee of Inquiry into the Education of Children from Ethnic Minority Groups* (The Swann Report). London, HMSO.

Gravelle, M. (2000) *Planning for Multilingual Learners: An Inclusive Curriculum*. Stoke-on-Trent: Trentham Books.

Schweers Jr, C.W. (1999) Using L1 in the L2 classroom. *English Teaching Forum*. 37(2): 6–9.

Sneddon, R. (2009) *Multilingual Books – Biliterate Pupils: Learning to Read Through Dual Language Books*. Stoke-on-Trent: Trentham Books.

Storch, N. and Wigglesworth, G. (2012) Is there a role for the use of the L1 in an L2 setting? *TESOL Quarterly*, 37(4): 760–70.

University of East London (UEL) (2014) Multiliteracy in Action: Using and Researching Dual Language Books for Children. http://www.uel.ac.uk/duallanguagebooks/index.htm (accessed 19 November 2014).

Washbourne, A. (2011) *The EAL Pocketbook*, 3rd edn. Hampshire: Teachers' Pocketbooks.

Wolfe, S. and Alexander, R.J. (2008) Argumentation and Dialogic Teaching: Alternative Pedagogies for a Changing World. http://www.beyondcurrenthorizons.org.uk/argumentation-and-dialogic-teaching-alternative-pedagogies-for-a-changing-world/ (accessed 19 September 2014).

8 Conclusions: synthesising learning and moving on

Your initial training can only give you an introduction to the professional attributes, knowledge and skills you need in order to understand multilingual and EAL learners' needs and make provision for their successful learning in your classroom. This is the same for any aspect of becoming a teacher. In this final chapter, at the start of your career as a teacher, you are invited to reflect on what you have learnt so far. Through considering the knowledge you have gained from reading this book, as well as other experiences you may have had on your course of training, you will synthesise your understanding of EAL as a key attribute of some of your pupils' experiences, and the implications of this for what is coming to be described as EAL pedagogy. Following this, you are invited to think about how you might move on in the development of your professional expertise in this important and growing aspect of the teacher's role, in both primary and secondary contexts. At the end of the chapter, there are suggestions for further reading. Do not forget, also, about the further reading suggestions at the end of each chapter in the rest of the book.

As you have no doubt become aware through your experience in school and through your reading, the whole field of EAL teaching and learning is a growing one that has relevance for all teachers. Over recent years, it is increasingly becoming recognised that there is a body of both theoretical and practical knowledge that all teachers need in order to develop language based and culturally informed pedagogies that will benefit all pupils, not just EAL learners. One of the aims of this book is to provide you with the principles that underpin such pedagogies, which see language diversity as a resource, rather than a problem, in classrooms. Through the more theoretical chapters in Part 1 as well as the more practical ones in Part 2 with their case studies from practising teachers in specific classrooms, we have tried to show how theory and practice need to work together in developing principled responses to meet the needs of multilingual and EAL learners. We have shown how you can play to your learners' strengths, recognising what they bring to their learning, rather than applying ready-made, commercially published 'packages' of teaching strategies and activities. The understanding that your learners are active, creative individuals is crucial in developing an EAL pedagogy, as is recognising the professional agency that you have as a teacher, along with those of other professionals you will be working with.

It is becoming increasingly clear that such approaches to teaching and learning are good for all pupils, not just those categorised as EAL. A well-structured, theory-informed and thoughtful EAL pedagogy will not only promote success for multilingual and EAL learners, it will also contribute to more positive attitudes generally towards language and cultural diversity and thus to greater awareness and opportunities for learning for all pupils. Both researchers and practitioners are coming to recognise the value of the 'multilingual turn' in languages education and its benefits for society generally, both inside and outside of language classrooms. Recognising multilingualism in this way brings many positive benefits for social cohesion and justice in the wider community. These are exciting times, with rich possibilities for newly qualified teachers who have the interest in and the commitment to the positive, inclusive values that promoting EAL in this way offers. Becoming specialist teachers and future leaders in this field offers many professional rewards, as well as fulfilling vital roles in our future education system.

1. Myths revisited

In Chapter 1, I introduced four 'myths' about language teaching and learning. I suggested that they needed to be challenged, as they represent commonsense, intuitive, but often unhelpful notions that are not supported by research about language and learning in relation to multilingual and EAL learners. In order to help you synthesise your knowledge and understanding about EAL, this section provides a brief reflection on each of the myths, showing how what you have learnt in this book reveals their shortcomings and suggests positive ways of moving forward.

1.1 Languages should be kept separate in the classroom, or learners will become confused (sometimes called 'language interference')

In the first part of the book, there are many ideas that call the 'language interference' myth into question. In Chapter 2, links are made between language and identity, an idea which has relevance for all pupils. A child whose accent or dialect is ignored or treated as a form of 'bad' English in the classroom is just as likely to feel excluded as a bilingual or multilingual child who is made to feel that it is unacceptable to speak any other language than English. Language, identity and learning are intimately connected, as the theories introduced in Chapter 2 show. In Chapter 3, the examples of 'translanguaging', such as Sameena's counting in two languages (p. 50), as well as Cummins' theoretical idea of the CUP (p. 62), and the definition of bilingualism as 'living in two languages' (p. 17) all show in different ways how it is wrong to construct languages as separate phenomena that must be kept apart. Similarly, the principle about linking home and school learning is illustrated by many different practical examples in the second part of the book, especially in Chapter 7, which shows how the theoretical concept of 'funds of knowledge' plays out in practice. Dual language books, cross-curricular work with artefacts, a worksheet in science with additional French words that 'opened up' the science concepts for a newly arrived child – these are all examples of practical ways to link home languages and cultures to school learning in order to promote your pupils' conceptual learning and language development multilingually.

1.2 Pupils will 'pick English up' naturally in the classroom; they do not need to be explicitly taught (sometimes called 'immersion')

The vignettes of different 'EAL learners' presented in Chapter 1 show a range of ways in which pupils clearly do not simply 'pick up' English in the classroom, and somehow become successful learners without any conscious understanding and planning on the part of the teacher. 'Immersion', if it is not properly understood and managed, can very quickly become 'submersion'. For social and cultural reasons through no fault of himself or his family, Joseph, in section 2.3 (p. 18), was struggling to do as well as he clearly had the capacity to do. If his teachers had been able to find out more about his home background and country of origin, this might have helped them to think about how to support him in more informed and appropriate ways. Safina, in section 2.1 (p. 16), was doing very well in speaking and listening, but had found the written demands of the Year 6 SATs difficult. The evidence is that she will find it harder and harder to cope with the academic language demands of the subjects she is learning as she progresses through secondary school. The contrasts between Stefan's and Jan's progress as new arrivals in section 2.2 (p. 17) clearly indicate that it was not simply a matter of 'picking up' English for them.

Many of the theoretical questions raised by these examples are addressed in Chapter 3 with Cummins' model of BICS and CALP, which explains some of the complexities of the development of academic language, essential for success in the ways demanded by the school. Then, the approach to planning for both language and conceptual progression provided in Chapter 4 offers principled and practical ways to ensure that pupils are provided with carefully structured activities to support both their language and conceptual development across the curriculum. Chapter 5 gives many suggestions for providing a language-rich classroom environment and linking language, literacy and content in your teaching. Chapter 6 provides advice on assessing conceptual learning for pupils whose English development is at an early stage, as well as a way of understanding multilingual pupils' development as distinctive from those who are not learning multilingually.

1.3 Language diversity is a 'problem', and it is better if pupils speak English all the time in classrooms

In Chapter 1, it is established that language and cultural diversity have long been a feature of everyday life in Britain, and the clear signs are that they will always remain so. The children of Safina, Stefan, Jan, Joseph, Hamida and Radia, should they choose to remain in Britain, will be citizens of an increasingly multilingual and multicultural society. In Chapter 2, I argued that we all experience language diversity in our daily lives, even if we think of ourselves as being monolingual users of English only. Following this, in Chapter 3, I present the idea of bilingualism or multilingualism as a continuum or spectrum. Some of us may place ourselves towards the 'monolingual' end of the continuum in our experiences and knowledge of language diversity, and others may see themselves positioned more towards the more expert, multilingual end, with high levels of competence in listening, speaking, reading and writing in different languages. Language diversity is a theme in all the chapters in Part 2 and it takes centre stage in Chapter 7. Here, there are many practical ideas for making language diversity a positive feature and resource in your classroom, no matter what languages are spoken by the pupils you teach, nor their ages. Even simple activities like doing the register in different languages can promote a positive ethos in a very accessible way and open doors to learning about different languages for your pupils, as well as reinforcing the links between identity and learning for those whose languages are represented.

1.4 It is impossible, or very difficult, to learn a new language beyond a young age (sometimes called 'the critical period')

The vignettes in Chapter 1 show multilingual learners of different ages mostly becoming competent and confident speakers, readers and writers of English. The important point to draw from this is that they do so in a variety of ways, and so need different kinds of teaching and support. The example of Stefan and Jan (pp. 17–18), both from the same language background and in the same school in England for the same length of time, illustrates very clearly that there is no universal, standardised way to becoming a competent user of English. The learner's age is only one factor that must be taken into account, as are the languages they already know in both spoken and written modes. Mushtaq, whose story appears in Chapter 3, arrived in England at the age of nine. His experience of learning to read was a positive one that encourages us to have confidence in our pupils as independent learners, according to the principles discussed in Chapter 7, section 1 (p. 159). Mushtaq understood how to manage his own learning and quickly became a competent reader and writer of English, once his skills and capacity in his first language of Bengali were recognised.

All these examples illustrate how the idea of the 'critical period' in the sense of there being an age beyond which it is always very difficult to learn a new language is a myth. However, it is also clear that the distinctiveness of pupils' 'EAL development' at different ages must be understood. The descriptors developed by NALDIC (see the details in Further Reading in Chapter 6), as well as the *Language in Common* steps, both offer excellent starting-points for assessing individual pupils' progress as bilingual language users. They are also helpful in developing your own understanding of the distinctiveness of multilingual and EAL learners' development and progress.

2. Moving forward – some suggestions for further reading and professional development

A major concern of this book has been to help you to understand the importance of theory for your classroom practice and for your professional understanding and development as a teacher, no matter what your subject area or age range. Of course, theory by itself is of no value in teaching, but neither are packages of strategies or lists of practical suggestions with no theoretical rigour behind them, and no clear statement of the principles from which they have been developed. If you depend on these in your teaching, you will quickly run out of ideas and be at the mercy of ready-made plans with no real understanding of how and why they have been constructed in the way they have.

This book gives you a theoretical explanation for all the practical advice it provides, as well as the practical implications of the theories. This is intentional – the hope is that you will be able to go on to develop your own theory-informed and principled ways to plan, teach and assess the learning of the pupils you teach, especially those who are multilingual. As you move through your induction year as an NQT, you could suggest to your school mentor that you use some of the activities in this book to help develop your professional expertise in the field of EAL.

The further reading suggested at the end of each chapter gives you some starting-points for your own independent CPD. The list given below, mostly taken from the references for each chapter, will help you to move further in your understanding of how to integrate theory and practice in your teaching to promote the learning and achievement of multilingual and EAL learners. Books speak to readers in different ways – these are mostly titles which have inspired me in my teaching and to which I have returned many times, with some new ones added in. I hope some of them will speak to you and become your favourites, as well as offering you useful guidance for your teaching and forming the basis of further study. As time goes on, you may be offered the opportunity or feel the need to pursue higher qualifications, and the study of EAL has rich potential. Use the NALDIC website (www.naldic.org.uk) – and join the association – to keep up to date with developments in the field of EAL, including opportunities for further study and professional development.

3. Suggestions for further reading

Cummins, J. (2001) *Negotiating Identities: Education for Empowerment in a Diverse Society*, 2nd edn. Ontario, CA: California Association for Bilingual Education.
This book gives a thorough explanation of the three key Cummins' theories which are introduced in this book – CUP, linguistic interdependence, BICS and CALP, showing how his ideas have developed over the years. Other important ideas are also discussed and the educational implications are fully explained.

Cummins, J. and Early, M. (eds) (2011) *Identity Texts: The Collaborative Creation of Power in Multilingual Schools*. Stoke-on-Trent: Trentham Books.
This book provides a collection of case studies and examples of 'identity texts', which are texts created by multilingual learners in a wide range of educational settings round the world. They illustrate how such work can contribute to a pedagogy that plays to the strengths of pupils from diverse language and cultural backgrounds.

Datta, M. (2007) *Bilinguality and Biliteracy: Principles and Practice*, 2nd edn. London: Continuum.
This book shows how multilingual children can benefit academically from opportunities to develop their biliterate skills. With case studies and examples of children's work, it shows how children's bilinguality provides opportunities for the development of literacy throughout the curriculum.

García, O. (2009) *Bilingual Education in the 21st Century: A Global Perspective*. Chichester: Wiley-Blackwell.

This inspiring book provides an overview of bilingual education theories and practices throughout the world. It questions assumptions regarding bilingual education, and proposes a new theoretical framework for the teaching and assessment of bilingual learners. It explains why bilingual education is good for all children and adults throughout the world, and gives examples of successful bilingual programmes.

Gonzalez, N., Moll, L. and Amanti, C. (eds) (2005) *Funds of Knowledge: Theorizing Practices in Households, Communities and Classrooms.* **New York: Routledge.**
The concept of 'funds of knowledge' is based on the premise that all people have valuable knowledge formed from their life experiences. This book gives readers the basic methodology of funds of knowledge research and explores its applications for classroom practice. It argues that instruction must be linked to students' lives, and that effective pedagogy should be linked to local histories and community contexts.

Gregory, E. (2008) *Learning to Read in a New Language: Making Sense of Words and Worlds.* **London: Sage.**
This book introduces an 'Inside-Out' (starting from experience) and 'Outside-In' (starting from literature) approach to teaching children to read. It draws on examples of children from different countries engaged in learning to read nursery rhymes and songs, storybooks, letters, the Bible, and the Qur'an, in languages they do not speak fluently. It argues that there is no universal method to teach children to read, but rather a shared aim which they all aspire to: making sense of a new world through new words.

Kenner, C. and Ruby, M. (2012) *Interconnecting Worlds: Teaching Partnerships for Bilingual Learning.* **Stoke-on-Trent: Trentham.**
Working together with multilingual pupils and their teachers from both mainstream and complementary schools in London, Kenner and Ruby developed some powerful strategies, which played to the children's strengths and used all their language resources for learning, and they write about them in inspiring ways in this book.

Nieto, S. (1999) *The Light in their Eyes: Creating Multicultural Learning Communities.* **New York: Teachers College Press.**
Another inspiring book, which focuses on the significant role of teachers in transforming students' lives. It considers recent theories, policies and practices about the variability in student learning and culturally responsive pedagogy and examines the importance of student and teacher voice in research and practice.

Wells, G. and Chang-Wells, G.L. (1992) *Constructing Knowledge Together: Classrooms as Centers of Inquiry and Literacy.* **Portsmouth, NH: Heinemann.**
The book focuses on literacy, providing case studies together with discussions of literary and sociocultural theories of learning and teaching. The examples of theory integrated with practice offer a framework for teachers to develop their own approaches to promoting literacy for their pupils.

Appendix 1: Model answers to the self-assessment questions

The learning outcome questions at the end of each chapter are, on the whole, very open, and there are no fixed answers for many of them. They are intended to help you reflect on the issues raised in the chapters, and develop your own professional understanding of them. The points given below help you to do this by suggesting possible factors you might consider.

Chapter 1 Introducing multilingual and EAL learners

1. This question is designed to get you to think about your own identity, and what matters to you as an individual, as this can sometimes become problematic when you are working with children from different language and cultural backgrounds. Traditionally, identity has been defined by broad, general factors such as gender, social background or ethnic group. But it may also be about features that are more personal to you, such as where you come from, your religion, your family circumstances, the music you like, the football team you support and so on. Think about times when you might have felt annoyed, upset or threatened because of something that was important personally to you.

2. This question is designed to get you to think about specific out-of-school factors that may impinge on children's learning and influence their achievements and attainment. These may relate to issues connected with the family's home circumstances, or there could be things which, if you knew about them, would be important in helping to promote their learning and academic success, e.g. literacy skills in another language.

3. This question is designed to get you to reflect on the choices teachers can make in dealing with individual children. There are no fixed answers, and in many circumstances no 'right' ways to behave as a teacher. But what you have read in this book may have helped you to consider some principled ways of understanding children's progress more widely than simply through what is happening in the classroom. For example, Joseph's teacher(s) might have tried to find out more about Sierra Leone than the fact that there was a war and some awful things happened.

4. Again, no fixed answers here, but try writing your vignette based on the models given in the chapter. When you have done so, you could share it with colleagues or classmates to widen your awareness of bilingual and EAL learners.

5. Many Gipsy and Roma pupils coming from Eastern Europe have suffered racism over many years in their countries of origin, and can thus be very reluctant to send their children to school. Aspirations are low, and some parents fear 'losing' their children if they apply for university or courses away from home. There have been negative reports in the media about Gipsy and Roma

families arriving in some towns in England, and also programmes about marriage customs that, it can be argued, present negative images of traditional cultural practices.

Chapter 2 All about language and learning

1. The main implications of sociocultural theories and the ZPD are about the kinds of activities that will offer the greatest opportunities for learning. These clearly need to focus on speaking and listening, and involve children in using talk in a wide range of ways, with plenty of time devoted to small-group discussion-type activities. The progression in cognitive demand also needs to be considered, so medium-term planning is important in order to ensure that the learning objectives become increasingly demanding. At the same time, contextual support needs to be maintained.

2. The main differences are to do with what the grammars encompass and what their purposes are. Most conventional grammars consider words and perhaps sentences. They deal with semantics (meanings), **morphology** (grammar within words – the morphemes with which words are made up) and syntax (the order of words in sentences). Functional grammars, on the other hand, consider whole texts and the ways that words and sentences are used in their construction, according to the purposes and audiences of the text and the content it is intended to communicate. Functional grammars are more about understanding languages in use as part of culture and society and conventional grammars are more about describing languages as systems without reference to their social and cultural contexts.

3. Sociocultural theories argue that interaction, through talk as well as other means, is at the centre of the learning process. They emphasise the importance of making oral language a central aspect of all the learning that pupils are expected to do in their classrooms, no matter what the subject or conceptual learning involved.

4. For the reasons given above, i.e. that it is through engaging in activities that focus on oral language that children will learn most effectively. This is a key conclusion of the *National Curriculum Review* (DfE, 2011), which contains many useful references to support the development of your understanding in this area.

5. This is an open question – you may be able to ask your pupils.

Chapter 3 What does it mean to be multilingual?

1. This question obviously needs to be answered through reflecting on your own views and opinions. It would be useful, perhaps, if you reflected on what you thought about bilingualism and multilingualism before reading the chapter and what you thought about it afterwards. The conventional view is that bilingualism is about having full competence in two or more languages, whereas the ideas expressed in the chapter are intended to help you to see it as a much more fluid, diffuse concept, including social and cultural aspects as well as language.

2. Again, the answer to this question depends very much on your own personal and educational experiences. Perhaps you could also make it the topic of a group discussion as part of developing your professional understanding about the role of language diversity and bilingualism in children's learning.

3. The answer to this question would include ideas such as using a wider range of ways of assessing learning than the usual writing-focused tasks, possibly using practical activities and perhaps visual means. There is also the possibility of assessing children's conceptual understanding of the particular subject content in their home languages.

Chapter 4 Planning across the curriculum for multilingual and EAL learners

As a means of reviewing the learning outcomes of this chapter, a planning checklist is included at the end of the chapter (p. 97) which you could use to evaluate your planning for teaching and subject across the curriculum on your next placement.

Chapter 5 Strategies and resources for learning across the curriculum

1. Drawing out the language demands is important because it will help you in your planning to ensure that you develop clear progression in increasing the language demands of the activities and also become aware of the kinds of academic language you are introducing to your pupils. It will also help you to understand better the ways in which you can introduce the concepts of the subject to your pupils.

2. Reading for pleasure is crucial as without it, pupils will not sustain their efforts in reading and go on to become independent readers. It is vital for pupils at all stages of learning to read. Pupils also need to learn to read critically so that they can understand and be aware of the possible ways that facts can be used to persuade and influence opinions, and the ways that biases can be developed. They also need to be able to read in order to infer meanings and the viewpoints of the writer.

3. Language awareness activities are a positive resource in all schools, and particularly in schools with low numbers of multilingual pupils as they may not have the awareness and experience of language diversity that pupils living in more linguistically and culturally diverse areas may have – this can be a disadvantage as they grow up. In these settings, the first strategy would be to find out what language diversity is present in the local community and then perhaps arrange visits for the children to relevant places and/or visitors to come into school. The same principle of building on personal and community resources applies.

Chapter 6 Assessing multilingual and EAL learners across the curriculum

1. The purpose of assessment *for* learning, sometimes known as formative assessment, is to find out what your learners can do and what they find difficult, in order to plan how to help them make further progress. Assessment *of* learning is the same as summative assessment, and its main purpose is to identify what point children have reached on an externally decided, standardised scale of attainment in order to assign levels or other external criteria. In assessing the achievements and attainment of EAL and bilingual learners, the distinctive nature of their language development and learning always has to be borne in mind.

2. The main reason is that if we do confuse *learning needs* and *language needs* for bilingual and EAL learners, we will not be able to make the appropriate provision to help them make progress and succeed.

3. AfL processes are very valuable for multilingual and EAL learners as they offer a range of ways to find out about their learning more holistically. Using custom-made tools such as the NALDIC EAL descriptors or the *Language in Common* steps will enable you to reach a deep understanding of a child's strengths and needs, and what to do to help them make progress. The issues faced in sampling the work of a child who is relatively new to English are, of course, to do with communication. The child may not understand what is expected of her or him, there may be cultural issues in the task that you are not aware of and finally the child may understand the concept under consideration, but not have enough English to express or explain it in a way that is comprehensible to you.

4. The main point here is to recognise that parents from different cultural backgrounds may express their concerns and interest in their children's progress in different ways. Sometimes, Asian-heritage parents can appear passive as they do not question their child's teacher or engage in discussion. This may be because they see the teacher as the authority figure, and their role is to support what the teacher says, rather than agree or disagree with it.

Chapter 7 Promoting independence: using home languages and cultures in learning

These are open questions, and the answers will largely depend on your own experiences and opinions. The suggestions given are indicative.

1. Besides knowledge of other languages and cultural backgrounds, the kinds of things that may occur to you here could be practical skills such as cooking, sewing, carpentry, etc., artistic and musical expertise, personal knowledge related to family and community, and so on.

2. Points here might include anxiety about trying to speak languages you do not feel very confident with, not understanding completely what is going on, losing control of the lesson and so on. You could discuss this with a multilingual colleague and perhaps come up with ideas about how you might work together.

3. Points here might include anxiety about being considered an 'expert' in a particular language, about performing in that language, which you have never done before, about understanding how to assess what pupils say or write, and so on. You could discuss this with a colleague who is not multilingual, and perhaps come up with ideas about how you might work together.

Appendix 2: Glossary

Academic language Academic language is the kind of language that is used in textbooks, in tests and in formal classroom discourse. Learners need to understand and be able to use it themselves in speaking and writing in order to carry out cognitively complex activities and to achieve success academically.

Accent Accent refers to the ways people pronounce the languages they speak. Accents can be specific to a country, a region, a town or city, a social group or an individual. Speakers of English have many different accents according to their social and cultural backgrounds and where they come from.

Achievement An assessment of achievement reveals the knowledge, skills, understandings and capabilities of a learner, as well as the progress they are making compared with learners of similar age and capability.

Additive bilingualism Additive bilingualism is where the acquisition of a new language does not replace the first language; instead the first language is promoted and developed. It is linked to high self-esteem, and improved cognitive flexibility.

Attainment Attainment is a measure of how well a learner is performing in a particular subject, linked to an external set of criteria, such as the National Curriculum Attainment Targets, assessed through the SATs (see below).

Authentic language In contrast with the language used in many school textbooks, curriculum programmes and teaching resources, authentic language is the kind of language that people use in their everyday lives to do the things they want to do.

BICS (basic interpersonal communication skills) Cummins made a distinction between two kinds of language knowledge and proficiency (see **CALP** below). BICS refers to the conversational fluency that most learners of a new language can develop relatively quickly in everyday, face-to-face social interactions.

Bilingual A word with many definitions, in this book it refers to anyone who has access to and uses more than one language in their everyday life, no matter what their level of proficiency.

CALP (cognitive academic language proficiency) CALP is the second type of language knowledge and skill that Cummins identified in his research (see **BICS** above). CALP is associated with academic learning and is the language of cognitive processes such as analysing, synthesising, arguing and persuading.

Clause A grammatical notion, a clause is the smallest grammatical unit that can express a complete proposition. A typical clause consists of a subject and a predicate, where the predicate is typically a verb phrase – the subject is sometimes not stated.

Codeswitching Codeswitching refers to a speaker's use of more than one language in one utterance or conversation. It is a natural and normal aspect of the speech of many bilingual people.

Cognitive language Cognitive language is the kind of language required to engage in cognitively challenging activities, e.g. Latinate words, complex grammatical structures and long, tightly-structured texts. It is linked to academic language (see above).

Complementary/supplementary schools These are schools outside of the mainstream system, usually funded and run by different linguistic and cultural communities outside of school hours, sometimes in the premises of mainstream schools but often in other community premises. Their purpose is most often to maintain and develop knowledge of heritage languages and cultures. Many pupils who study their home languages in such schools go on to do GCSEs and A levels in those languages.

Context of use Part of the functional grammar approach, the context of use of a text is the set of social and cultural factors which surround it and contribute to its construction, i.e. why, when, how and where it was produced (the purposes), who it was produced for (the audience) and what it is about (the content).

CUP (common underlying proficiency) CUP relates to Cummins' theories of bilingualism and is a term to describe the ways in which our processing of language is supported by all the languages we know. Rather than possibly 'interfering' with each other, it is clear from many different kinds of research that knowledge of different languages feeds into a common 'reservoir' of knowledge, understanding and capacity to express meaning.

DARTS (directed activities related to texts) DARTs are activities that encourage the learner to analyse how a text is constructed and how its meanings are expressed at word, sentence and text level. There are two types: 'disruption' activities where the learner is expected to alter the text in some way, e.g. changing the tenses, and 're-construction' activities, where the text needs to be re-assembled or completed in some way, such as a cloze activity.

Dialect Dialects are the varieties of a language in terms of grammar and vocabulary. English has many different dialects, both regional within Britain and international across the globe.

Dialogic teaching This term was introduced by Robin Alexander, who has written extensively about it. He is referring not just to a teaching strategy or technique, but to a whole approach to teaching which values the knowledge and viewpoints of the learner and so seeks to develop ways in which they can be voiced and integrated into the construction of knowledge in the classroom.

EAL (English as an additional language) EAL is a term used to refer to those children in the education system who speak, and possibly read and write, other languages besides English. The term EAL is now increasingly used to identify a distinctive 'field' of language teaching and learning.

EFL (English as a foreign language) EFL refers to the branch of English language teaching and learning concerned with teaching people from other countries who plan to live, work or travel in England (see TEFL below).

ELT (English language teaching) A broad term used to cover the range of fields of English language teaching and learning.

Field of knowledge A field of knowledge has parallels with an academic discipline or curriculum subject, but is perhaps less formally defined, and could have more limited scope, i.e. within a wider subject or branch of academia.

Formative assessment The kind of assessment that seeks to understand how much learners know about a particular topic or concept, and what problems they may have, in order to plan future teaching to meet their needs. It is now sometimes called Assessment for Learning.

Functional approach (to language, including grammar and literacy) The functional approach to language is one which considers whole texts (either spoken or written, see below) in their contexts of use (see above) and the choices the speaker or writer has made in constructing them. The main implications of this are the need to teach grammar and literacy in context, rather than in discrete exercises.

Funds of knowledge 'Funds of knowledge' refers to the learning, often social and cultural and sometimes academic, which a child engages in within their home and community contexts, and which forms the prior experience they bring to school.

Genre Genres are different text types, defined by the purposes and audiences for which they are intended and the kinds of language and structural elements with which they have been constructed.

Grammar Grammars are systematic ways of describing languages. There are many different kinds of grammars, which each pay attention to different aspects and elements of language.

Halal Anything which is halal is acceptable within Islamic rules and standards. Something which does not meet these standards is defined as *haram*.

Heritage languages In England, the term 'heritage languages' normally refers to the languages of the individual's country of origin, spoken by people who have migrated to England, or whose ancestors did so.

Hot seating Hot seating is a technique used in drama and role play where a participant is asked to sit on a chair in the role of a character, e.g. from a story or from a historical period, and answer questions put to them by the audience in that role. It is a valuable teaching strategy in different subjects across the curriculum.

Identity The word 'identity' is used in many different ways to describe an individual's sense of who they are, where they belong and how they would define themselves.

Jigsawing Jigsawing is a technique used in discussion-based activities where participants each have partial information about the topic under consideration and they have to collaborate in different ways in order to disclose the full information.

KWL (know, want to find out, learn) grid A KWL grid can be used in various ways, to help in planning a project or introducing a new topic in teaching.

KWHL (know, want to find out, how to find out, learn) grid An extension of KWL and a useful device in lesson or activity planning.

Language awareness This is defined as explicit knowledge about language, and conscious perception of its importance in language learning, language teaching and language use.

Language diversity This term refers to the range of languages, besides English, that are used by people in Britain on a daily basis.

Linguistic interdependence Another of Cummins' theories, linguistic independence refers to the idea that knowledge and understanding of one language links to and supports the development of knowledge and understanding in another.

Metalanguage This is the language that we need in order to be able to talk about, investigate and analyse language.

Metalinguistic awareness Metalinguistic awareness is the deeper understanding of how languages work as systems and the capacity to explain them, gained from studying and analysing languages, and comparing different languages.

Monolingualising Monolingualising is a term introduced by some researchers to describe the way that the curriculum can impose a message that English is the only language that matters, and that other languages are much less important.

Morphology This is the grammar of words: the ways in which words are formed and change. The idea is that all words have 'root morphemes', onto which further morphemes can be added according to their grammatical functions in sentences and texts.

Multilingual/multilingualism With the recognition that societies are becoming increasingly multilingual, the term is being used more and more to capture the sense that we need to understand more about how people live in settings where different languages are increasingly used alongside each other, and the implications for education.

Multiliterate The capacity to read and/or write more than one language, at any level.

Multi-modal Texts which are multi-modal are constructed with a mix of forms, usually including aural and visual elements, and also conventional text forms.

National Association for Language Development in the Curriculum (NALDIC)
NALDIC is the national subject association for English as an additional language (EAL). It was founded in 1992 and is recognised today as the foremost organisation promoting effective teaching and learning for bilingual and EAL children in schools in the UK.

Nominalisation A dominant feature of academic writing, nominalisation is the process of turning verbs into nouns, so that the text is no longer describing actions, but more focused on objects or concepts, so the tone of the writing becomes more abstract and formal.

Pedagogy The processes of teaching, which are informed by professional knowledge, skills and understanding, mediated by the judgements made by the individual teacher.

Received pronunciation (RP) RP is the prestigious form of pronunciation of English that is associated with high status and educational success. Traditionally, it is the way of speaking that had to be adopted by members of society who wished to be received in court.

Register The variety of a language used for a particular purpose or in a particular social setting, defined by the context, the purpose, and the speaker or writer.

Repertoire Repertoire refers to the whole range of knowledge about languages an individual possesses, in terms of listening, speaking, reading and writing. It can change many times over an individual's life course, according to a wide range of social, cultural, academic and personal factors.

SATs (standardised assessment tasks) SATs are the tasks in English and maths, commissioned by the government, to identify and record the attainment of children at the age of 7 (Key Stage 1) and 11 (Key Stage 2).

Scaffolding Scaffolding is an idea (sometimes called a 'theory of instruction') that goes along with the notion of the ZPD (see below). It refers to an approach to planning activities in order to offer learners opportunities to acquire new knowledge securely while at the same time developing as independent learners.

SLA (second language acquisition) SLA is the process of developing the skills and knowledge to communicate in an additional language, as distinct from the knowledge that might be learnt through direct teaching.

Semantics Semantics is the part of language knowledge and study to do with meaning in words, sentences and whole texts.

Sentence There are as many definitions of the sentence as there are books about grammar. Essentially, a sentence is a complete and coherent unit that makes sense on its own.

Standard English Standard English is the high-status form of English grammar and vocabulary associated with educational and economic success, spoken by people in England.

For many people, it is one of several kinds of English they have in their repertoires. People speak standard English with a wide range of regional and social accents.

Summative assessment This is formal, normative assessment which seeks to identify an individual's attainment judged according to fixed measures or standards.

Superdiverse Superdiverse is a term from sociology to describe contemporary societies where migration over many years has led to complex communities whose members possess an increasingly wide range of language, cultural, social and economic backgrounds.

TEFL (teaching English as a foreign language) TEFL is a pedagogy for teaching English to people who wish to live in, work in or visit Britain and other English-speaking countries. It is often carried out before the learners travel, and can also take place in short courses in the English-speaking host country.

Texts Texts can be either spoken or written. They are complete, communicative events transacted through language that has been selected to take account of the speaker(s)' or writer(s)' purposes, meanings and audiences.

Transitional bilingualism Transitional bilingualism is a contrasting term to additive bilingualism (see above). It describes the situation where an individual, in acquiring a new language, loses their capacity to use existing languages in their repertoires. It is associated with low levels of academic attainment and success.

Translanguaging Translanguaging is a recently developed term used to describe the ways that multilinguals make choices from their language repertoires to express their meanings and perform their identities in the ways most appropriate to them. Unlike the term 'codeswitching' (see above), it helps us to consider languages as fluid and seamless, rather than as separate and isolated systems.

Word class All words belong to lexical categories called word classes (which are sometimes called parts of speech) according to the part they play in a sentence. Words can belong to different classes according to the jobs they are doing in the text.

ZPD (zone of proximal development) The idea of the ZPD comes from Vygotsky's theories about learning as a sociocultural process, in which the interactions between learners and their teachers are an important element. The ZPD is Vygotsky's term to describe the 'gap' between what the learner knows and what they do not yet know, which can be bridged with the support of a more knowledgeable other.

Appendix 3: Principles for planning for multilingual learners

These six key principles for planning lessons and activities for multilingual learners have been developed from the ideas discussed in Chapters 1 to 3. In Chapters 4 to 7, I use these principles to present practical examples of activities and strategies to promote multilingual children's learning in speaking and listening, reading and writing across the curriculum.

1. Developing a positive ethos that reflects language and cultural diversity at whole-school level supports home–school links, and encourages families and schools to work in partnership.

2. In the classroom, providing opportunities for multilingual pupils to use their first languages in everyday activities opens out potential for learning and affirms their identities.

3. Pupils need every possible opportunity to explore ideas and concepts orally in all subjects across the curriculum.

4. Before beginning extended writing activities, pupils need plenty of chances for collaborative discussion and practical experience.

5. Promoting awareness of language systems and structures by allowing multilingual pupils to analyse and compare the different ways of saying things in the languages they know helps develop their CALP and also promotes language awareness among their monolingual classmates.

6. Providing extensive opportunities for hands-on experience enhances language learning and learning more generally.

Index

Added to a page number 'f' denotes a figure and 'g' denotes glossary.

ability groups 86, 87, 92
abstract nouns 65
academic language 62, 65, 102–3, 172, 192g
    see also CALP
accents 31, 192g
achievement 192g
    assessing see assessment
    raising 24–5
    see also underachievement
active learning 42, 110, 144
additive bilingualism 35, 58, 192g
advanced bilingual learners 15, 16–17
Afitska, O. 103–10, 140–7
Africa: Altered States, Ordinary Miracles 39
Aitsiselmi, F. 50
Alexander, R.J. 77, 162
Allwright, D. 59, 160
Alternative Reading Test 136, 150–7
appropriacy 32, 36
Arbeia 13
ascription 23
aspirations, raising 24–5
Assessing Pupil Progress (APP) 132
assessment 125–48, 190
    conflicting policy paradigms 59
    potential barriers to 58
    principles 126–8
    standardized 128–30
    universal model 59, 160
    see also formative assessment; self-assessment;
        summative assessment
Assessment Focuses (APP) 134, 137
assessment for learning 84
    consulting with parents 147
    observation as a tool for 138–9
    profiling and sampling 131–8
    pupils' and teachers' views 140–7
    purpose 190
asylum-seekers 15, 18–19
attainment 192g
    assessing see assessment
attendance 23–4
attitudes 12, 33, 51, 182
authentic language 37, 39, 192g
authentic texts 38–9, 102, 170

Bangladeshi pupils 16
baseline reading tests 135–6
Begum, S. 177–8
belonging 12, 33, 35, 44

Bengali 16, 66
Bew Review (2011) 128
BICS (basic interpersonal communication skills) 65–6, 77,
    129, 183, 192g
big books 39
bilingualism 17, 58, 188, 192g
Bradford research, language use 50, 51
Bronfenbrenner, U. 57
Bruner, J. 42
buddies 92–3
Bullock Report (1975) 57

CALP (cognitive academic language proficiency) 43, 65–6,
    70, 77, 129, 183, 192g
Chang-Wells, G. 42–3, 79
child wellbeing 57
circular migration 13
classroom organization 84–92
clauses 192g
co-construction 41, 43
codeswitching 49, 193g
cognitive challenge 88, 92, 129
cognitive demand 77, 78, 79f, 80f, 188
cognitive development 42
cognitive language 65, 193g
collaborative talk 42–3, 84–92
colleagues, working with 110–14, 172–8
communities, involvement in learning 165–71
community learning contexts 66–7
community-based learning 166–7
community-based schools 31
complementary learning community 57
complementary schools 31, 50, 66, 165–7, 193g
comprehending texts 40
conceptual development 77, 78, 183
conceptual knowledge 61
conceptual problems 140
Conradi, A. 120–3
Constructing Knowledge Together 42
Conteh, J. 33, 43, 55–6, 79, 167
content knowledge 76
content learning, linking language learning and
    100–14
context see cultural contexts
context-embedded activities 42, 66, 77, 79, 97
contexts of use 37, 38–9, 193g
contextual support 77, 78, 79f, 80f, 127, 188
continuing professional development (CPD) 159
counting, in different languages 168
critical approach, need for 61

critical period 25, 184
cross-curricular
    assessment 134–8
    learning 31, 56, 99–124, 182, 189
    planning 74–84
cultural backgrounds 12, 19, 40, 59, 127, 131, 147, 185,
    187, 190, 191
cultural contexts 42, 52, 127, 188
cultural diversity 14, 70, 167, 182, 183
cultural knowledge 10–11
culture(s)
    bringing into schools 167–71
    language and identity 33–5, 51
    and learning 42, 129
    understanding and celebrating 21–2, 58
Cummins, J. 45, 51, 58, 59, 62–5, 159, 172
Cummins' quadrant 77–81, 163
CUP (common underlying proficiency) 45, 62–5, 77,
    182, 193g
Curriculum 2000 58
curriculum planning 73–97
Czech Republic 13, 17, 21, 23, 24

DARTs 103, 193g
decoding 40, 41
deficit model 2
Department for Education 10
The Developing Language Learner 160
dialects 31, 182, 193g
dialogic talk 161, 163
dialogic teaching 162, 193g
difference, defining 10–15
differentiation, in planning 93–6
discrimination 23
displays 101
diversity
    understanding 20
    see also cultural diversity; language diversity; superdiversity
Donelly, Z. 52–7, 167, 173
Dowden, R. 39
Dual Language Action Research Project 172
dual language books 35, 171–2
Dutcher, N. 48

EAL
    defined 193g
    linking/confusing SEN and 58, 59, 129, 130
EAL and multilingual learners 9–25
    assessing see assessment
    census data 10
    deficit model 2
    defined 15–25
    envy of linguistic skills 54
    finding out about the languages of 50–1, 65
    knowledge and experience of 10–11, 17, 31, 33, 61, 75,
        92, 128
    literacy pedagogy 40

EAL and multilingual learners *cont.*
    need to encounter authentic language 37
    planning for *see* planning
    principles for working with 1–2
    recognition/valuing of home languages 33, 35
    simultaneous worlds of 40
    see also language learning; multilingualism
Early, M. 172
Eastern Europe 13, 17, 21, 22, 23, 24
ecological theory 57
Education Act (1981) 129
Edwards, V. 132
EFL (English as a Foreign Language) 25, 194g
Ellis, D. 39
ELT (English language teaching) 62, 194g
England
    debate about teaching reading 40
    superdiversity in 13–15
English (language) 13, 31, 34, 48, 58
equal access 59
ethics 138–9
ethnic minorities 50
ethnic minority pupils 10, 52
ethnicity 10, 11f, 12
European Union 13
Excell, D. 125, 134–8
exit interviews 145–7
expert guidance 80
Expert Panel Review of the National Curriculum (DfE) 43
externalisation 41

fair test(s) 43, 59, 128
familiar stories, using 117–20
families
    importance in learning 56
    involving in learning 165–71
    mediation in learning 67
    working with 24
    see also parents
feedback (homework) 142
fiction text 39
field of knowledge 194g
'filling a grid' activity 83–4
first languages 54, 55–6, 58, 62, 70, 142–3,
    147, 176
'five propositions about learning' 160
5Ws 31, 33, 35, 44, 102
fluency 175
formative assessment 90, 107, 127, 194g
    see also Assessment for Learning
Framework for Languages (KS2) 61–2
Framework for Teaching (DfEE) 58
friendship groups 87
function words 163
functional approach 32–3
    curriculum planning 75
    defined 194g

functional approach *cont.*
  to literacy 39–41
  teaching languages 35–9
functional grammars 188
funds of knowledge 44–5, 54, 169, 182
  defined 44, 194g
  importance of recognising culture 21
  out-of-school experiences and 35, 56, 67
  using personal 174–8

García, O. 39, 49, 51, 54
genres 39, 194g
Gibbons, P. 79
Gonzalez, N. 44, 54
grammar(s) 35, 36, 37, 39, 188, 194g
graphic organisers 103
Gravelle, M. 74, 127
Gregory, E. 40, 41, 129
group reading tests (NFER) 135–6, 137–8
groups/grouping 18, 84–92, 97, 144
Gussin Paley, V. 12
Gypsy pupils *see* Roma and Gypsy pupils

halal 14, 194g
Hall, D. 17, 51, 80, 131
hands-on experience 70, 77, 100
Hanks, J. 59, 160
haram 194
heritage languages 16, 31, 50, 66, 166, 194g
higher level teaching assistants (HLTAs) 81
historical influences 42
Holdaway, D. 39
holistic approach, child wellbeing 57
home, learning at 67
home countries 22–3
home languages
  bringing into schools 167–71
  learners' eagerness to use 52
  policy contradiction 58
  recognising and valuing 33, 35
  use of 97, 158, 162
homework clubs 147
homework feedback 142
hot seating 86, 194g
Hughes, T. 36–7

'iceberg' diagram 63
identity
  academic success 44
  attitudes 12
  culture, language and 33–5, 51
  defined 194g
  as learners 35, 84, 138, 171
  personal and professional 12, 13, 187
  Roma and ascription of 23
  value and respect for 45
  see also language identity

Identity Texts 172
immersion 25, 183
inclusion 58
independence (literacy) 102–3
independent learning 191
  practical strategies to promote 162–5
  principles for 159–1
informed consent 139
initial teacher training 159
internalisation 41, 42
interviews, with multilingual children 50–1
The Iron Man 36–7
isolated learners 15, 19–20

jigsawing 86, 87, 195g
joint planning 81–4

Kenner, C. 54, 56
key developing practitioners 160
key words 175–6
knowledge
  see also field of knowledge; funds of knowledge;
    language knowledge; prior knowledge; subject
    knowledge
knowledge about language (KAL) 61, 62
knowledge-confusion phenomenon 142
Korzun, A. 93–6
KS2 Framework for Languages 61–2
KWHL 76, 195g
KWL 76, 195g

language(s)
  counting in different 168
  culture and identity 33–5, 51
  defined 30–3
  function words 163
  interviews 50–1
  knowledge about 61, 62
    see also language knowledge
  negative messages about 51
  repertoires 31, 32, 41, 50, 63, 196g
  school census data 10
  teaching
    myths and misconceptions 25, 51, 62–3, 182–4
    see also functional approach; language-based pedagogy
  see also cognitive language; heritage languages; home
    languages; modern languages
language awareness 70, 120–3, 189, 195g
language buddies 92
language demands 75, 76, 77, 79, 88, 97, 100–10, 111,
  183, 189
language development 77, 78, 84, 129, 138, 183
language diversity 14–15, 30, 31, 58
  defined 195g
  as a feature of the classroom 167
  NCC guidance 58
  pedagogy and positive attitudes to 182–3

language diversity *cont.*
  as a positive feature of school life 120–3
  as a problem 25, 183–4
  promoting awareness of 168, 171
  recognising and valuing 34, 39
  as a resource 2, 58
A Language for Life (Bullock report) 57
language identity 49
A Language in Common (QCA) 125, 127,
    184, 190
language interference 25, 50, 51, 63, 182
language knowledge 10–11, 12, 31, 76, 192
language learning
  cross-curricular 31, 56, 99–124, 189
  importance of talk for 42–3
  linking content learning and 100–14
  misjudging conversations 54–5
  multilingualism 48–9
  myths and misconceptions 25, 51, 62–3,
    182–4
  sociocultural theories 30–1, 41–2
  strategies and resources 99–124, 189
  use of first languages 54, 55–6, 58, 62, 142–3
  using stories for 117–20
  see also EAL and multilingual learners
Language learning strategies (LLS) 61, 62
language needs 58, 59, 66, 129, 190
language support, groupwork 144
language-rich environments 101, 102
'learn to talk' 43
learner participation 144
learning
  attitudes to 33
  barriers to 58, 126
  see also active learning; independent learning; out-of-school
    learning
learning buddies 93
learning environment 54
learning needs 58, 59, 66, 129, 190
learning opportunities 61
lesson planning 70, 77
linguistic interdependence 62–5, 159, 195g
linguistic problems 140
linguistic skills, envy of 54
listening triads 88
literacies 40
literacy 43
  cross-curricular teaching 102
  functional approach to 39–41
  learning and story 80, 114–20
  linguistic interdependence 63–4
  see also National Literacy Strategy; reading; writing
Literacy Hour 39
literacy practices 40
'living in two languages' 17, 51, 59
lunchtime homework clubs 147

Mandarin 48
Many Pathways to Literacy 40
matching activities 176
maximum identity investment 44
meanings, of words 34, 100, 101, 102
medium-term planning 77, 188
mentors 92–3
meta-stance 84
metalanguage 195g
metalinguistic awareness 195g
metaphor 65
middle-ability groups 92
minority groups 12
mixed-ability groups 87
modern languages 166
Moll, L. 44
monolingual people 48, 49
monolingual pupils 49, 51, 57–8, 92, 120, 129, 140, 167
monolingualising curriculum 57, 195g
monolingualising society 54
morphemes 188
morphology 188, 195g
mother tongue 48, 54–6
multi-modal communication 30
multi-modal texts 39, 196g
multiculturalism 13
multilingual colleagues 172–8
multilingual labels 35
multilingual society 31
multilingualism 13, 17, 47–67, 188–9
  defined 195g
  in education
    Cummins' theories 62–6
    learner's experience 52–7
    policy constructions 57–62
  global context 48–9
  learning outside school 66–7
  merging of SEN and 59
  working definition 51
  see also EAL and multilingual learners
multiliteracy 16, 195g

NALDIC 80, 184, 196g
names, finding out about 168
'naming the parts' model 60–1
national assessment procedures 128–9
national census, ethnicity 10, 11f
National Curriculum 40, 57–62
National Curriculum Review (2011) 188
National Literacy Strategy 39, 58
new arrivals, including 92–3
new arrivals excellence programme 19
new to English pupils 15, 17–18, 74
NFER reading tests 135–6, 137–8
Nieto, S. 41–2, 52, 160
nominalisation 196g

non-fiction texts 39, 102
non-verbal communication 138

observation 138–9
'odd one out' activity 101–2
O'Grady, A. 115–17
oral language *see* talk
out-of-class support 141
out-of-school experiences 35, 56, 67
out-of-school factors 187
out-of-school learning 56–7, 66–7

'pair to four' groups 87
Pakistani-heritage 14, 16, 17, 22, 34, 50, 104
parental resources 142
parents
    consulting with 147
    relationships with 19
partnership teaching 110, 111–14
Parvana's Journey 39
passive voice 65
pedagogy
    defined 196g
    for EAL and multilingual learners 40, 57, 181–2
    funds of knowledge concept 45
    literacy 39, 40
    see also language-based pedagogy
peer mentors 92
peer-led learning 104
personal funds of knowledge, using 174–8
personal identity 12
personification 39, 54, 65
phonics 39, 40, 41, 144
planning 73–97
    checklist 97
    for collaborative talk 84–92
    Cummins' quadrant 77–81
    developing plans 74–7
    differentiation in 93–6
    importance of joint 81–4
    including new arrivals in lessons 92–3
Poland 13, 17
policy construction 57–62
Polish 17, 31, 66, 166
politeness 38
political influences 42
Porritt, C. 88–92
positive ethos 70
power 40
pre-teaching vocabulary 144
primary modern foreign languages (PMFL) 61
Principles for Planning for Multilingual Learners 100
prior experiences 3, 19, 42, 76, 176
prior knowledge 82, 92, 97, 117, 128, 136
professional development 184–5
    see also continuing professional development

professional identity 12
professional standards 1
profiling 131–8
progression in learning 77, 78–9
Punjabi 16–17, 22, 33, 34, 50

questioning 175–6

Rag Trade project 169–70
re-construction activities 193
reading
    debates about teaching 40
    for pleasure 114–17, 189
    see also reciprocal reading; shared reading
reading tests 135–8, 150–7
received pronunciation (RP) 20, 196g
reciprocal reading 143–4
reference texts 102
reflection 80
refugees 15, 18–19
register 196g
relationships 12, 19
repertoires (language) 31, 32, 41, 50, 63, 196g
'repetitive' responses 106
resources 141, 142
Roma and Gypsy pupils 21–5, 187–8
Roman Empire 13
Rose Review (2006) 40
Ruse, P. 81–4, 111–14, 145–7

safe spaces 34, 45, 54, 108, 160, 162, 175
safeguarding 139
Safford, K. 58, 59, 128
same-language groups 18
sampling 131–8
Sandler, L. 81–4, 145–7
SATs (Standardised Assessment Tasks) 16, 17, 18, 126, 128, 196–7g
say/cover technique 144
scaffolding 42, 77, 196g
school buddies 92–3
school census, language data 10
self-assessment 84
self-confidence 35, 138
self-worth 54
semantic strength 101
semantics 188, 196g
SEN (special educational needs) 18, 58, 59, 129
sentences 196g
shared reading 39
shared understanding 80
'simple view' of reading 40
'simultaneous worlds' of language 40
SLA (second language acquisition) 62, 196g
Slovakia 13, 17, 21
Sneddon, R. 171
social mediation 41, 42

sociocultural theories 30–1, 41–2, 188
sojourners 15, 20–1
specialist teachers 110, 182
spoken text 38
standard English 31, 196–7g
Storch, N. 175
stories/story-telling 17, 35, 117–20
story-based activities 80
subject knowledge 61, 176
summative assessment 110, 127, 190, 197g
superdiverse 197g
superdiversity 13–15
supplementary schools 31, 66, 165–7, 193g
support assistants (multilingual) 172–3
Swann Report (1985) 166
Sylheti 16
syncretic, literacy learning as 40

talk
  importance for learning 42–3, 79
  planning for collaborative 84–92
  see also dialogic talk
'talk to learn' 43
talking partners 87
Talking Partners Programme 88–92
teacher-guided reporting 79
teacher-led approach 181
teachers
  choices in dealing with children 187
  ethnicity and language 12
  finding out about pupils' languages 50–1, 65
  professional standards 1
  skills of effective 160
  skills for specialist 110
  understanding of pupils' knowledge 127
teaching assistants (multilingual) 81, 172–3
technical language 38–9
TEFL (Teaching English as a Foreign Language)
    25, 197g
text frames 103
text reconstruction 103
texts
  appropriacy 36–7
  challenging 82

texts cont.
  contexts of use 37
  defined 197g
  functions of 38–9
  for learning 75–6
  teaching non-fiction 102
  see also authentic texts; multi-modal texts;
      reference texts
theory 29
theory of instruction 42
thinking skills 43
'three modes of interaction' 79–80
topic work 102, 169
traditional stories 117–20
transitional bilingualism 58, 197g
translanguaging 49–50, 51, 54, 182, 197g

underachievement 52, 135
universal model, assessment 59, 160
University of East London website 171
Urdu 16, 22, 51, 66, 135

Varian-Roper, Z. 127, 173
Vince, G. 9, 21–5
visual learning 176
visuals, using 144
vocabulary 140, 144
Vygotsky, L. 30, 41, 159

Washbourne, A. 103, 175
'washing lines' activity 101
Wells, G. 42–3, 79
white majority pupils 11
white majority teachers 12
White Teacher 12
whole-class groups 87
Wigglesworth, G. 175
Wolfe, S. 77, 162
Wood, C. 174–6
word activities 101–2
word class 197g
words (English) 34, 100, 101, 102
written texts 38–9

zone of proximal development 41, 188, 197g